Disappearances and Police Killings in Contemporary Brazil

The book offers an interdisciplinary qualitative study of the history of policing in Brazil and its colonial underpinnings, providing theoretical accounts of the relationship between biopolitics, space, and race, and post-colonial/ decolonial work on the state, violence, and the production of disposable political subjects.

Focused empirically on contemporary (1985–2015) police killings and disappearances in favelas, particularly in Rio de Janeiro, the books argues that the invisibility of this phenomenon is the product of a colonial mindset – one that has persisted throughout Brazil's experience of both dictatorship and re-democratisation and is traceable to the legacies of the Portuguese empire and the plantation system implemented. Analysing the development of the police as a colonial mechanism of social control, Villenave shows how the war on drugs reproduces similar colonial logic and renders some, overwhelmingly black, lives disposable and thus vulnerable to unchecked police brutality and death.

The book will be of interest to students and scholars of international politics and also contributes to critical security studies, postcolonial and decolonial thought, global politics, the politics of Latin America, and political geography.

Sabrina Villenave is affiliated at the University of Manchester, at the Department of Politics. Her research interest focuses on critical security studies and its late critique on race and racialisation. She is interested in postcolonial and decolonial critiques of international relations, and in the legacies of African slave trade organised by the Portuguese empire. Currently she is working with the themes of 'War on Drugs' in Brazil as a legitimiser of police violence against favela dwellers, under the frame of exceptionality, security apparatus and the de-politicisation of disappearances after the dictatorship in the country under the theoretical frame of necropolitics.

Interventions

The Series provides a forum for innovative and interdisciplinary work that engages with alternative critical, post-structural, feminist, postcolonial, psychoanalytic and cultural approaches to international relations and global politics. In our first five years, we have published 60 volumes.

We aim to advance understanding of the key areas in which scholars working within broad critical post-structural traditions have chosen to make their interventions, and to present innovative analyses of important topics. Titles in the series engage with critical thinkers in philosophy, sociology, politics and other disciplines and provide situated historical, empirical and textual studies in international politics.

We are very happy to discuss your ideas at any stage of the project: just contact us for advice or proposal guidelines. Proposals should be submitted directly to the Series Editors:

- Jenny Edkins (jennyedkins@hotmail.com) and
- Nick Vaughan-Williams (N.Vaughan-Williams@Warwick.ac.uk).

'As Michel Foucault has famously stated, "knowledge is not made for understanding; it is made for cutting". In this spirit The Edkins–Vaughan-Williams Interventions series solicits cutting edge, critical works that challenge mainstream understandings in international relations. It is the best place to contribute post disciplinary works that think rather than merely recognize and affirm the world recycled in IR's traditional geopolitical imaginary.'

Michael J. Shapiro, University of Hawai'i at Manoa, USA

Edited by Jenny Edkins, Aberystwyth University and Nick Vaughan-Williams, University of Warwick

Disappearances and Police Killings in Contemporary Brazil
The Politics of Life and Death
Sabrina Villenave

Information Classification: General
For more information about this series, please visit: https://www.routledge.com/series/INT

Disappearances and Police Killings in Contemporary Brazil
The Politics of Life and Death

Sabrina Villenave

LONDON AND NEW YORK

First published 2022
by Routledge
2 Park Square, Milton Park, Abingdon, Oxon OX14 4RN

and by Routledge
605 Third Avenue, New York, NY 10158

Routledge is an imprint of the Taylor & Francis Group, an informa business

© 2022 Sabrina Villenave

The right of Sabrina Villenave to be identified as author of this work has been asserted in accordance with sections 77 and 78 of the Copyright, Designs and Patents Act 1988.

All rights reserved. No part of this book may be reprinted or reproduced or utilised in any form or by any electronic, mechanical, or other means, now known or hereafter invented, including photocopying and recording, or in any information storage or retrieval system, without permission in writing from the publishers.

Trademark notice: Product or corporate names may be trademarks or registered trademarks, and are used only for identification and explanation without intent to infringe.

British Library Cataloguing-in-Publication Data
A catalogue record for this book is available from the British Library

Library of Congress Cataloging-in-Publication Data
A catalog record has been requested for this book

ISBN: 978-0-367-46983-2 (hbk)
ISBN: 978-1-032-18717-4 (pbk)
ISBN: 978-1-003-03251-9 (ebk)

DOI: 10.4324/9781003032519

Typeset in Times New Roman
by SPi Technologies India Pvt Ltd (Straive)

To my ancestors.
They started a life journey and marked out the path I now walk.

Contents

List of Acronyms   x
Preface   xii
Acknowledgements   xv
Note on translation   xvii

Introduction: between a pacification that disappears and policing that kills   1
  Book rationale 3
  Conceptual framework 7
  Challenges in dealing with the (in)visible 11
    Contemporary cases 13
    A book on disappearances in contemporary Brazil: what was possible to investigate? 17
  Structure of the book 21
  Notes 24

1 Between a revealed past and a treacherous present   25
  Introduction 25
  Disappearances during the dictatorship in Latin America: Argentina as the archetypical case 26
  Political disappearance: a 'travelling' concept 29
  Contemporary cases of disappearances which follow different political contexts 31
  Disappearances: an elusive practice 32
  Between the 'wrong' victim and the 'wrong' perpetrator 35
    The 'wrong' victim 35
    The 'wrong' perpetrator 39
  Messy data for a messy reality 41
  Disappearances: between life and death 46
  Conclusion: expanding the conceptualisation of enforced disappearances 49
  Notes 50

viii Contents

2 Between nation-building and modernity   52
  Introduction 52
  *Nation-state: a project between coloniality and
    modernity 55*
  Between the logic of exception and metaphors of war 59
    *Logics of exceptionality in the context of the 'war on
      terror' 60*
    *Logics of exceptionality in the context of the 'war on
      drugs' 62*
  Police as apparatus 66
  Governing death and racial capitalism 68
  Racial and colonial capitalism 70
  From biopolitics to necroeconomics 72
  Life as excess: securitisation as excess regulation 74
  *Conclusion: situating Brazil within the conversation between
    Foucault, Agamben and Mbembe 76*
  Notes 77

**3 The police apparatus: between highly noticeable killings and
   unnoticed disappearances**   79
  Introduction 79
  Roots of an institutionalised police 81
    From colony to empire (1500–1888) 81
    *The First Republic (1889–1936): police action in semi-
      urban areas 83*
  *The Vargas Era and 'The New State': organising a nation-
    state through authoritarian rule 86*
  The military dictatorship (1964–1985) 90
    *The armed forces and the police: the security apparatus
      against leftist groups: torture, killings, and 'political
      disappearances' 92*
  Re-democratisation in Brazil: new actors and a dispositif *in
    the governmentality of death 95*
    Autos de resistência 96
    *Militia groups and death squads: summary executions,
      mass slaughter, and disappearances 99*
  Conclusion: governing death 101
  Notes 103

4 Black bodies: the meat of lowest value in the market   104
Introduction 104
Race in Brazil 106
   A hierarchic system based on race 108
   Contextualizing slavery in Latin America 112
Making Brazil a 'racial democracy' as part of the nation-building process 119
   Rendering race invisible by whitening the population 121
Dictatorship and the violence against indigenous communities 124
Conclusion: making difference invisible 127
Notes 129

5 Hidden in plain sight: liminal spatiality in Brazil   130
Introduction 130
Conceptualisation of camp in Agamben's work: development and critiques 131
Modern camps, abject spaces 135
The conquest of Brazil: a mindset predicated on the notion of territory and population 138
   From a place to tame to a camp to kill: urban peripheries as abject space following a colonial rationale 140
   Rio de Janeiro's favelas as abject space 141
   São Paulo's peripheries as abject space 145
The colonial logic of death in favelas and peripheries 148
   The skull's revenge: at the threshold of bare life 148
   Patricia and Juan: at the threshold of the camp 150
Conclusion: on abjection and the logic of coloniality 153
Notes 154

Concluding thoughts   156
Where does it leave us? Possibilities for further research 159
Notes 161

Bibliography   162
Index   179

Acronyms

AI	Amnesty International
AI-1	Institutional Act Number One (*Ato Institucional Numero 1*)
AI-5	Institutional Act Number Five (*Ato Institucional Numero 5*)
ARENA	National Renewal Alliance
BOPE	Special Police Operations Battalion (*Batalhão de Operações Policiais Especiais*)
CEV-Rio	Truth Commission of the state of Rio de Janeiro (*Comissão Estadual da Verdade do Rio de Janeiro*)
CCTV	Closed-circuit television or video surveillance
CV-SP	Truth Commission of São Paulo (*Comissão da Verdade do Estado de* São Paulo)
DINA	National Intelligence Directorate (*Dirección de Inteligencia Nacional*)
DOI-CODI	Department of Information Operations and the Centre for Internal Defence Operations
DOPS	Central Police for Social and Political Control (*Departamento de Ordem Política e Social*)
FUNAI	The National Indian Foundation (*Fundação Nacional do Índio*)
HRW	The Human Rights Watch
IBGE	The Brazilian Institute of Geography and Statistics (*Instituto Brasileiro de Geografia e Estatisticas*)
Ipea	Institute for Applied Economic Research (*Instituto de Pesquisa Economica Aplicadas*)
ISP/SSP-RJ	Public Security Institute at Rio de Janeiro (*Instituto de Segurança Pública do Estado do Rio de Janeiro*)
LAV UERJ	Violence Analysis Lab at the University of the State of Rio de Janeiro (*Laboratório de Análises da Violência*)
LASA	Latin American Studies Association
MDB	Brazilian Democratic Movement
Necvu-UFRJ	Citizenship, Conflict and Urban Violence at the Federal University of Rio de Janeiro (*Núcleo de Estudos da Cidadania, Conflito e Violência Urbana*)

NEV-USP	Violence Studies Research Centre at the University of São Paulo (*Nucleo de Estudos da Violência*)
NGO	Non-Governmental Organization
NSDD	National Security Directive Administration
NTC	National Truth Commission (*CNV Comissão Nacional da Verdade*)
NTCR	National Truth Commission Report
OAS	Organization of American States
PCC	The First Command of the Capital (*Primeiro Comando da Capital*)
PC do B	Brazilian Communist Party (*Partido Comunista do Brasil*)
PL	Proposed bill (*Projeto de Lei*)
PNAD	The Brazilian National Household Sample Survey (*Pesquisa Nacional por Amostra de Domicílios*)
UNWGEID	Working Group on Enforced or Involuntary Disappearances of the United Nations
UPP	Pacifying Police Unit (*Unidade de Policia Pacificadora*)
SENAD	National Secretary for Drug's Policies (*Secretaria Nacional de Políticas sobre Drogas – Ministério da Justiça*)
SIVAM	Amazon Surveillance System (*Sistema de Vigilância da Amazonia*)
SIM	Mortality Informational System (*Sistema de Informação de Mortalidade*)
US	United States of America
USAID	United States Agency for International Development

Preface

I was born during the dictatorship in Brazil. It is hard to believe that, under such terror, life could have continued 'as normal', with small daily rituals, like buying bread from the closest *padoca* on the corner, going to work and getting on with our lives, while others were being tortured in the *porões da ditadura*. Under these circumstances, one of the bravest things a family could do was to allow life to follow its natural course and celebrate the arrival of a newborn. My family was not directly involved in the political struggle or any of the resistance movements, and their recollections from those years sound oddly uneventful. Except, that is, for the time my father was approached by the Military Police while not carrying his identity card. Identity became very important during those years. It is still very much the norm that you do not leave the house without your identity card. I remember when my father told me about that day. There was a mix of regret and shame at not having done something he was supposed to, something that would have saved him so much trouble. But there was also a tinge of bitterness. My grandfather, who would have been required to go to the police station to secure my father's release, never arrived, leaving my father to spend the night in jail. I cannot fully comprehend my grandfather's reasons for doing this, but having been an undocumented migrant at the time sounds like a reasonable explanation. My mother, on the other hand, had grown up with my grandmother working as a housemaid for a high-ranking Naval commander whose home life appeared beyond reproach, but who faced criticism for defending the torture of political dissidents. Even today, when there is such a concerted effort to rewrite and deny Brazil's dictatorial past, my mum is emphatic in her assertion that it *did* happen: people did disappear, while others walked the streets in fear.

About 30 years after the end of the dictatorship in Brazil, the country saw the beginning of another wave of conservatism. With similar rhetoric, it is hard to avoid seeing many parallels to the processes, attitudes, and political forces of the time that preceded the dictatorship. Many are now looking into the reasons behind the rise of far-right movements in Brazil, trying to locate a point of origin to the latest wave (see for example, Rosana Pinheiro-Machado). At the time when I was conducting my fieldwork research, Dilma Rousseff was undergoing impeachment proceedings. As I discuss later in the Introduction, with all that was going on, and the accusations of a new coup being underway, many of those I interviewed – past victims of the dictatorship – were shaken by the current political climate.

Some of the most vivid memories from my fieldwork research involved taking part in the many events organised around the memorialisation of the past, an initiative often put forward during investigations carried out by local truth commissions. I remember one evening in particular: the theatre is crowded, and many have been unable to find a seat. Their faces are lit up in anticipation of what is about to take place. These meetings are at the core of the resistance movement, a place to gather, where past members meet the younger generation. A venue and time to reflect on the current state of national politics. Someone takes the mic and a list of names is read out. The names belong to those who have been victims of state violence, usually people "disappeared" by the dictatorial regime. The crowd shouts "Present!" after each name. The excitement in the air grows with each affirmation. It is as if these people have suddenly become corporeal, a fleshly presence in opposition to their enforced absence. The collective shouts make present those whose fates have not officially been recognised as linked to torture and resistance. A few years late, the names of Marielle Franco – a city councillor of the Municipal Chamber of Rio de Janeiro – and her driver, Anderson Gomes, would also be read out at these meetings.

Much of the research presented in this book has been inspired by the national effort – especially during the Workers' Party's time in power – to break with the pact of silence and ensure that the lives and strength of so many can be known and celebrated. Brazil's former president, Dilma Rousseff, is a past victim of torture under the military dictatorship and was the country's first female president. After many years of democracy, the pact of silence surrounding the dictatorship was finally broken with the establishment of the National Truth Commission in 2011. Many would say that Dilma paid a high price for this. The National Commission's efforts paved the way for more than a hundred similar initiatives across the country. Many cities created their own commissions with differing focuses. Organisations such as the *Comissão Camponesa da Verdade* investigated violence against rural workers, while a truth commission was also set up by the Metalworkers Union to investigate crimes against unionised workers. Many of these initiatives fed information back to the National Commission. Unfortunately, many of the Commission's results and potential developments were obstructed by the impeachment of Dilma Rousseff in 2016 and the rise of the far-right in Brazil.

Among all the stories yet to be told, there is a segment of the population that is not recognised in public discourse as being part of the national struggle for the defence of democracy. Inhabitants of the favelas, a mostly racialised population that endures great economic hardship, have had their participation in the resistance silenced to the point where it is almost impossible to uncover. Today, these people are usually remembered as victims of paramilitary extermination groups, and therefore in no way related to the period of the dictatorship. The frequency with which people are still killed and disappeared by extermination groups means that their lives, and deaths, are continually depoliticised.

Against the odds, many initiatives have attempted to break this silence. Among them, the Rio de Janeiro Truth Commission has investigated how inhabitants of the favelas were particularly affected by the regime, uncovering some among this population who were actively opposed to the dictatorship. And the São Paulo City Hall, while taking part in an investigation into clandestine graves at the Perus Cemetery, also issued a call for those who believed their family members to have been executed by the regime to present themselves. Unfortunately, only a few people answered this call. The purpose of this book is to contribute to uncovering a little part of the story lived by these unknowns. A population silenced for so many years that their story under the military regime has almost disappeared completely.

Acknowledgements

Numerous individuals and institutions have supported the writing of this book. The first full draft was written as a PhD student at the University of Manchester, a very special place to me. I am grateful to Maja Zehfuss and Andreja Zevnik who I was lucky to have as supervisors. My admiration for them has only grown. Maja would often ask me to explain my views, and I learned the value of being precise in my writing and coherent in my actions, to the best of my abilities, as well as the ethical attitude behind this stance. Andreja always pushed me to think beyond the example, to link my ideas to a broader scene that could be connected to the examples of so many others. Thank you both for your continuous support and encouragement. For the invaluable help and support I would also like to thank Interventions series editors Jenny Edkins and Nick Vaughan-Williams, and from the Routledge team, specially Claire Maloney and Robbert Sorsby. Thank you to my friends and colleagues in Social Sciences at the University of Manchester for your support and engagement, and to those at the Global Politics Cluster, who have always provided intellectual stimulation during the various stages of this research. To those I met at the Gregynog Lab, for giving me an unexpected sense of community – you guys are inspiring; thank you! To Erica Simone Almeida Resende for believing in the first ideas of this research and to rescue me from my moments of anxiety. To Flavia Guerra and Tatiana Teixeira for their support and motivation.

I would like to also thank all of the organisations that facilitated my fieldwork research, and the people I have had the honour of meeting, both in Brazil and elsewhere. I hope to help achieve some justice on this issue that speaks to the hearts of so many. I am grateful to the FGV – Fundação Getulio Vargas – in Rio de Janeiro and São Paulo for organising my placements in both cities. Special thanks go to Letícia Carvalho de M. Ferreira and Fabio Alves de Araujo for all their encouragement in researching contemporary disappearances.

Late additions to the manuscript were partly read by Andreea, Erna, and Jenna; thank you for your comments and feedback. You have provided more than welcome and friendly support during my lonely pandemic days.

I would like to also express my gratitude to those who are a source of joy and friendship, Ana Lucia, Daniela, Raquel, Maria Leonor, Marie Christine,

Mataji, and Kala. To my family, who supported my sense of wanderlust even if missing me: Julia, Erinalda, Didier, and Leonardo.

The doctoral thesis on which this book is based was made possible by a scholarship from the International Cooperation Programme CAPES/COFECUB at the University of Manchester and was financed by CAPES – the Brazilian Federal Agency for Support and Evaluation of Graduate Education within the Ministry of Education of Brazil.

Note on translations

All translations from Portuguese texts, articles, and interviews are by the author, and any errors in translation are solely her responsibility.

Introduction

Between a pacification that disappears and policing that kills

It was mid-July 2013 when the bricklayer Amarildo Dias de Souza, a resident in the favela of Rocinha in Rio de Janeiro, the largest favela in Brazil, disappeared after being taken by the police for questioning. According to *O Globo* and *Rede Globo*, the newspaper and TV channel owned by Grupo Globo, Brazil's largest media group, Amarildo's family reported him missing after he had not been seen for two days. The story was covered in print publications and on prime-time national news over the course of weeks. From a helicopter, a TV broadcast reported the interruption of traffic flow on the main throughway that connects the area of Lagoa to Barra da Tijuca in Rio caused by protests by favela residents, who were demanding an enquiry into the disappearance of Amarildo. The case was featured in the national and international news and provoked social mobilisation, investigations, and prosecutions. Police officers from the Pacifying Police Unit (UPP) located at Rocinha, were accused of being responsible for Amarildo's disappearance.

Shortly afterwards, Amarildo's relatives met with the state governor, Sergio Cabral, and the case started to be investigated by the 15th District Police Unit. Rodrigo Pimentel, a former police officer who works as a criminology expert on the local news, announced that the public CCTV equipment in front of the Pacification Unit had been damaged on the day that Amarildo disappeared. The Homicide Unit took over the case two weeks after Amarildo went missing. Eight police officers who were on duty on the day that Amarildo disappeared were summoned to testify. Investigators also analysed the CCTV images from the UPP and the GPS equipment from the police vehicles. In the first week of August, Jornal Nacional evening news broadcast the images from the CCTV located opposite UPP at Rocinha. The images showed Amarildo getting into a police vehicle to be taken to another police unit, from where he should have been subsequently released. The Homicide Unit then considered two hypotheses: either Amarildo was killed by drug dealers, or he was killed by the police.

Two months later, a police report was forwarded to the Public Prosecution Agency of Rio de Janeiro. The report indicated that ten police officers, all serving at the UPP Rocinha, took part, or were aware of, the death as a result of torture perpetrated against Amarildo, followed by the concealment of his body. The Public Ministry accepted the submission made by the Civil Police,

DOI: 10.4324/9781003032519-1

which is responsible for criminal investigations in the country and ordered the arrest of the police officers. Another 15 police officers from the same unit were also under investigation. Amarildo's body was never found.

In 2008, the announcement of Rio de Janeiro as the host city of the World Cup in 2014 and the Olympic Games in 2016 started a process of military interventions. The pacification of Rio's favelas aimed to make the city safe for the tourists that would flow into the city during the games. For the first time in decades, disrupting a tradition of non-intervention, the federal state announced funds for Public Security. In the same year of 2008, before any policy or investments in Public Security had time to show any of the promised results, the number of homicides in Rio de Janeiro started to drop. It could have been a reason for celebration if the figures of missing persons have not been increasing. In 2013, the disappearance of Amarildo de Sousa brought back public attention to 'political disappearances' – well-known from the dictatorship in the country.

Amarildo's disappearance in July 2013 coincided with the eruption of demonstrations across the country known as the 2013 Protests, or the 2013 World Cup Riots, which captured the attention of the international media. Brazil's largest protests in two decades started because of a rise in public transport fares (Amar 2013; *The Guardian* 2013a, 2013b, 2013c). Earlier protests had been handled with brutality by the police, which led to an escalation of civil unrest and spread to include an extensive list of grievances and demands, including corruption, poor public services, and the high cost of stadiums being built for the 2013 FIFA Confederations Cup and the 2014 World Cup (Amar 2013; *The Guardian* 2013a, 2013b, 2013c).

The massive public protests that erupted in June 2013 brought together a broad, and often contradictory, spectrum of collective actors, from trade union groups to right-wing nationalists. Amar (2013) observed that protesters, and the vast public who supported these demonstrations, were shocked by the level of police brutality, which included the action of the Special Police Operations Battalion (BOPE) shock troops and the use of a deadly level of tear gas and armoured vehicles, not to mention the scenes that circulated on social media (*The Guardian* 2013c) of police officers beating unarmed protesters. Amar (2013) highlighted that the 'displacement' of BOPE and military police invasion tactics indexed 'an extension of racial militarisation from *morro*, to *asfalto*' (308), that means, from the hilltop favela slums into the paved streets of public squares and middle-class downtown commercial areas. This 'displacement' also contributed to greater awareness, sparking debates on police violence outside academic circles.

Amarildo's case found an echo in the demonstrations, intensifying debates about two important aspects of public security. For the first time after the dictatorship, a missing person's case questioned the boundary between disappearance and extrajudicial killing (Araujo 2014). On the one hand, it sparked protests against the 'pacification'[1] programme to 'clean up' favelas before the World Cup and the 2016 Olympic Games – a major stake in the efforts by Rio's administration to improve public security prior to those events (*New York Times*

2011; Amar 2013; Costa Vargas 2013; Oosterbaan and van Wijk 2015). On the other hand, there were questions with regard to the possibility that extrajudicial killings were taking place covered up by 'resistance killings' (Araujo 2014).[2]

An important aspect of police killings is its racial component. In the report 'You Killed My Son: Homicides by Military Police in the City of Rio de Janeiro' published by Amnesty International (2015) pointed out that out of every five victims of homicide resulting from police intervention in the city of Rio de Janeiro – the so-called resistance killings – four are black males. As will be discussed in this book, resistance killings are deeply associated with the 'war on drugs'. The 'war on drugs', on the other hand, follows a rationale based on two main aspects: firstly, the idea that a certain population – notably black males – are considered dangerous; secondly, that certain areas – notably favelas – are home for drug cartels.

Book Rationale

Murder committed by police officers on duty, known as resistance killings (*autos de resistência* in Portuguese) in the sanitised language of law enforcement, are included in the Criminal Code as a lawful homicide. This act was first signed by the Security Secretary of Rio de Janeiro during the dictatorship in the country and later became an article in the National Criminal Code. According to the act, there is no crime if the agent acted out of need, self-defence, in strict compliance with a statutory duty, or in the exercise of law (Misse et al. 2013). Misse et al. (2013) highlighted that different categories granted to these crimes influences how those cases are conducted in the criminal justice system without contestation of the police officers' version presented. Misse et al. (2013) compare this situation with the example of the United States. In the U.S., the killings committed by police officers on duty follow the same investigation path as any other homicide and are not classed under a different category. Although the outcomes of these investigations perhaps suggest that they are treated differently, nevertheless, the problem is that the resistance killings have been distorted by the police who can make crime scenes appear confrontational.

Police officers took Amarildo from one of the main UPP units in Rio de Janeiro. The occupation of Rocinha was broadcast live and showcased as an invasion that was carried out 'without one single shot' (*El Pais* 2011; *New York Times* 2011; Veja 2011). In the eyes of the media, the operation at Rocinha reassured the international public that Rio de Janeiro was a safe place to host the World Cup 2014 and Olympic Games 2016 (Gaffney 2012: 78). Rocinha's occupation was celebrated as closing a circle in the trajectory of the UPP (*El Pais* 2011; *New York Times* 2011; Veja 2011). It started with the 'pacification' of the favelas that surround Maracanã, the main football stadium in Rio, and those that surround the South Zone of Rio de Janeiro, where the richest neighbourhoods in the city are situated.

The Pacifying Police Unit (UPP) has been regarded as one of the most important programmes of public security in Brazil in recent decades. It was implemented at the end of 2008 and would supposedly reinvent the role of the police force in the country (Gaffney 2012; Costa Vargas 2013; Denyer Willis and Mota Prado 2014). It follows the proposition of a permanent form of community policing inspired by Colombia's experience (Gaffney 2012; Denyer Willis and Mota Prado 2014) as opposed to massive police-military operations conducted by the Special Operations Battalion (BOPE). BOPE is recognised as the world's most highly skilled and lethal urban fighting force, and the favela is their daily training ground (Gaffney 2012; Araujo 2014).

Pacification occurs through police-military intervention to reclaim urban areas from the control of drug cartels (Gaffney 2012; Vargas 2013; Denyer Willis and Mota Prado 2014) and replace them with resident-friendly police units known as UPP (UPP 2014). The World Bank (2011) has also rated the UPP as an example of best practice regarding the interrelation between security and social development. Their operations start with an announcement in the media, which enables armed drug dealers to leave the favela. The BOPE seizes the favela early in the morning, establishes a headquarter unit up on the hill, and hoists a national flag (Gaffney 2012; Denyer Willis and Mota Prado 2014). In some favelas, the first occupation was led by the armed forces. After a few days, the UPP forces occupy the favela and start to regulate the comings and goings of residents, conducting random body and house searches, setting limited durations for dance parties, and settling domestic disputes (Gaffney 2012). As discussed in Alves (2018), what is usually underexplored when looking at public security policies is how much they are linked to the success of neoliberal capitalism in Brazil. Although some may argue that Brazil entered its neoliberal phrase during the 1990s, the selection of Brazil to host the World Cup and Olympic Games can be considered a turning point in the deepening of this process.

Police violence figures in Brazil are astonishing. The average number of police killings in Brazil over six days is the same as the average of police killings in Britain for over 25 years (Amnesty International 2015). The police in Rio alone killed more than 10,000 people from 2001 to 2011. The police in the United States – considered the third most violent in the world – kill on average 200 to 400 people every year (Misse et al. 2013). Quantitative and qualitative research (Misse et al. 2013) used to investigate practices and procedures related to the resistance killings concluded by questioning if extrajudicial killings covered up by the resistance killings are somehow supported by courtroom members, suggesting that the issue may be deeper than a police problem.

The public debate around Amarildo's case fuelled suspicion about the causes that surrounded the gradual increase of disappearances. Two explanations were considered: Firstly, that disappearance was replacing the resistance killings; and secondly, that the increase in disappearances was a consequence of the implementation of the UPPs, that is, of a more permanent presence of military forces in the favelas. Disappearances in the context of Brazil and more specifically, Rio de Janeiro, call for many layers to be explored. There is a critique formulated by many entities related to human rights which claims that *autos de resistência* creates a grey zone covering the police violence.

Second, there is not a broad debate and recognition in society that discusses violence as an issue. Instead, in general, those who are disappeared, or *autos de resistência*'s victims, are under suspicion; and third, enforced disappearances as a category is primarily related to military regimes, because of the political disappearances that occurred during the dictatorship in the country, but not in democracies, which I argue lead to problematic invisibility. Far from being a political dissident, Amarildo was a black male dweller of Rocinha favela in Rio.

The way Brazil has governed racialised groups presents two different phases. Before the 1930s, the police were constituted in a way to protect enslavers, the nobility, and the new urban population mainly from first slaves and, later, from newly freed populations. The urban development of Brazil, especially Rio de Janeiro, followed what was being done in Europe. In many ways, there were attempts to recreate European countries, such as the Parisian big avenues and theatre. This logic was applied not only to the organisation of the urban space but also, for example, to ideas of race. After 1930, black communities seem not to be a subject of concern anymore. All the police attention goes to the communist groups. Over the 1950s, black communities were displaced to favelas where the lack of health service or economic condition leads them to death – a rationale that can be linked to a sovereign decision of letting die. Following the re-democratisation in the 1980s, the 'war on drugs' turned the annihilation of black communities even more dramatic and accounted for 70% of homicide victims – a rationale that can be linked to a sovereign decision of making die. It is important not to forget that the 'war on drugs' is fought between drug cartels and the police – the state apparatus more directly involved with the issue. I argue that the killing and disappearance of marginalised groups are not just an effect of the 'war on drugs', but also a result of a more systematic and racialised logic that has its roots in the colonial past. In that sense, the 'war on drugs' framing is insufficient to understand a more fundamental logic at work.

In the 1930s, Brazil has claimed to be a 'racial democracy'. The term is commonly used to describe peaceful racial relations in Brazil in which gender or class, but not race, constrain social mobility. It also argues that the country has overcome the violence that the slave trade has caused by structuring socio-economic relations during the colonial past. The idea of racial democracy was crucial to Brazil's assertion of itself as a *modern* nation-state, consolidating its position as a modern country. At the time, the migration of (white) Europeans, especially from Portugal, Spain, and Italy, was part of a broader project to *whitening* Brazil's population. However, the violence that was made visible was the one against a communist threat, very similar to the later process of the military regime (1964–1985).

More recently, violence is applied in the context of the 'war on drugs', and although it targets black communities in favelas, poverty and inequality are pointed out to explain urban violence. In the scenario of constant confrontations between the police and drug cartels, the killing of peripheries' dwellers is a casualty of war. In that case, the metaphor of war not only legitimises death, but also locates the conflict in specific areas. Favelas or peripheral areas then become a space where death is expected to happen in what I will be calling necro-geopolitics. The 'war on drugs' is used both to justify the high figure of homicides as well as to associate the death of black population and favelas inhabitants as a war casualty.

The persistent denial of the role race plays in debates about urban violence in Brazil reinforces the myth of 'racial democracy' which was created and reinforced during Era Vargas. It also renders invisible patterns of state violence towards black populations. When looking specifically at cases of disappearance, the invisibility is layered with the crystallisation of the 'political disappearances' from the dictatorship and with different ways to class contemporary disappearances. As disappearance has been highly politicised as an expression of the dictatorship, cases that continue to happen after the dictatorship are not understood as such. Since re-democratisation, disappearance cases have been reported, by the media and elsewhere, as slaughter, massacre, or simply killings. It is only with the worsening of police violence, meaning when police violence overflowed favelas' borders, that disappearances have once again gained public attention.

Concerning more recent research produced in Brazil about disappearances, this book aims to complement recent research produced by Fabio Alves Araujo (2014) and Leticia Carvalho de Mesquita Ferreira (2015). Ferreira's work presents the pathways of those who are searching for missing persons through state bureaucracy. Fabio Alves Araujo's work looks at the collusion between police, militias, and drug dealers on disappearances. Araujo (2014) departs from a socio-anthropological framing to analyse the relationship between suffering, violence, and politics from the perspective of the families and relatives of the enforced disappeared. He concludes that this type of violence is a *dispositif* that has, on the one hand, police officials, militia, and drug dealers; and, on the other side, its victims, who are more likely to suffer this type of violence because of a correlation of factors, such as spatial and social conditions and activities that can place them under suspicion. Araujo stated that disappearances as a practice are a common strategy by actors who work on opposite sides, such as police and drug cartels; that is, certain individuals are disappear-*able*. Ferreira (2015) departs from an anthropological perspective to explore the totalising role of the state in the search for missing persons, and how those cases are subject of a set of *dispositif* that manages missing persons' cases from the perspective of the state bureaucracy. In that sense, this research does not present the perspective of the relatives in the search for a missing beloved, or with the difficulties presented by state bureaucracy in that search. Instead, my aim here is to explore possibilities in terms of different frames of analysis, such as the 'war on drugs' as a narrative that legitimises killings and disappearances, in particular of those who are associated with the drug cartels and problematises this association itself by discussing racialised practices of the police as a representative of sovereignty.

The present book explores different aspects of disappearances in Brazil during the re-democratisation period (1985–2015) in which the police are involved. The book asks why contemporary disappearances in Brazil are not problematised, and more particularly, how the 'war on drugs' reproduces a colonial logic. Regarding the police's action, I examine how the security apparatus has developed over time in Brazil. My broader aim is to show how continuous notions of race and space are implicated in the action of security apparatus in the country.

Conceptual framework

The critiques offered by postcolonial and de-colonial thought are diverse. Postcolonial thought has remained firmly in the realm of culture, although it has also addressed socio-economic issues (Bhambra 2014: 115). It has entered in IR in the 1990s and highlighted how, by not considering other voices, the discipline was less global than it claimed. From there, many other contributions have been added to IR. For example, the work of Gayatri Chakravorty Spivak and Homi Bhabha refers to the history of colonialism in India. Spivak's work (1983) has become influential to what is called Subaltern Studies. Edward Said (1978) is also relevant for presenting 'the West' representations of 'the East' particularly in the Arab world. And Frantz Fanon (1952, 1963, 2004) discussed the mechanisms of colonial control through which the minds of both colonisers and colonised are involved. Fanon argued that European colonisers would see their role as justifiable, while colonised societies would come to internalise their subordinate status. The main contributions of postcolonial analysis have been threefold (Sylvester 2017: 175): a critical perspective taking into account the experience of other countries that are not only the U.S. or in Europe; to incorporate historical relations of colonial powers within the study of IR; to reject the idea that nation-states are the only key actors in IR, and emphasising that there are other relations that can be considered, or impact, international relations.

De-colonial thinking was promoted mainly by Latin American scholars based in the U.S. such as Arturo Escobar, Walter Mignolo, Ramon Grosfoguel, and Anibal Quijano. Their project is to provide a distinguished critique from postmodern, poststructuralist, and postcolonial projects following the justification that postmodernism and poststructuralism are still Eurocentric while postcolonialism is heavily grounded in European authors such as Michel Foucault, Jacques Lacan, and Jacques Derrida, in which a critique comes from within.

Following the Latin American approach, a critique to imperial structures of power emphasises the need to de-colonise, meaning to detach from a colonial power. This detachment would occur through, for example, what is called border thinking as a way to consider alternative knowledge tradition and perspectives to be incorporated as well as other cosmologies outside of European thought (Mignolo 2007, 2011) as well as creating alternative epistemic pathways to western modern thought (de Paula 2015). Another concern of de-colonial thinking is that modernity and coloniality are the two pillars of western civilisations supported by a complex structure of knowledge. As rhetoric, modernity has justified the colonial expansion of Europe to the colonies (Quijano 2000). De-colonial thought also discusses the role of the elites in creating hierarchies using categories of class, race, and gender in the process. Walter Mignolo introduced the 'logic of coloniality' accounting for this discussion, as a logic that created structures of hierarchy based on race and class (and gender) but that is usually legitimised in the name of modernity and development. Although addressing a vast range of concerns, postcolonialism and de-colonial thought are interested in persistent colonial structures of power, and both advocate that we are all living now in a postcolonial society.

To analyse contemporary killings and disappearances in Brazil, postcolonial and de-colonial thought are important for a few reasons. Firstly, because it is crucial to take into account Brazil's history – not only its colonial past but also as an Empire, that I argue and will discuss – it is an important feature of how the local elites perceived themselves in the structure of the plantation in which they were living. Secondly, the social and economic structure of plantations themselves is fundamental to understand how contemporary notions of race are very similarly interplayed, as it was at the plantation socio-economic structure. The plantation and the colonial past rationale, I argue, is still present in the contemporary socio-economic structure, and follows three different aspects: the use of the security apparatus to kill those whose life is considered unworthy; the racialisation attached to the sense of unworthiness; and the sense that those killings and disappearances tend to be located in specific places. By exploring these three elements, I argue that when considering killings and disappearances perpetrated by state officials, it is necessary to step outside of the common lens of disappearance as dictatorship tool – as I explain in Chapter 1. The colonial roots of Latin America are central to understanding how power takes place in Brazil and how certain lives are considered unworthy to be lived.

Anibal Quijano (2000), considering the colonial history of Latin America, highlighted the link between democracy at stake in the continent and its configuration of power. According to him, the modern nation-state is marked by 'a society where, within a space of domination, power is organized with some important degree of democratic relations (as democratic as possible in a power structure), basically in the control of labour, resources, products, and public authority' (Quijano 2000: 557). When considering Quijano's ideas of democracy within a power structure, I would like to highlight Gatti's observation (2014) of a politics over life and death not related to a specific political regime; but instead, exacerbated by those regimes.

If the problem is not the political regime, it is worthy to take a look on discussions on sovereignty as a form of power. When discussing the relationship between sovereign power and life, Foucault (2009) has conceptualised biopolitics to examine mechanisms in which life is an integral part of regimes of knowledge, power, and processes of subjectivation. To Foucault (2009), the process by which biological life has become included within state power marks the transition from politics to biopolitics. Giorgio Agamben, who dialogues with Foucault's work on sovereignty and life, among others, discussed sovereignty through an exception. To Agamben (1995), life has been separated into its political and biological aspects, aiming to make certain lives bare or unworthy. This process happens through the logic of exception according to which this separation is justified and legitimised. In that sense, bare life cannot be considered outside sovereign power relations. More on the implications of life and sovereign power as articulated in contemporary politics will be discussed in Chapter 2.

When discussing 'logic of exceptionality', Giorgio Agamben has used at least three important concepts to explain it: state apparatus, bare life, and camp. His conceptualisations provide key elements to analyse the implications of sovereign power in different realms, such as security and understandings on *dispositif* (borrowed from Foucault); subjectivity based on his conceptualisation of 'homo sacer', and notions of space following accounts on 'the camp'. However, Agamben did not take into account the imperial/colonial dynamics and seemed to locate 'the West' not as a political project but as a geographical area. As developed by Simone Bignall and Marcelo Svirsky (2012), a postcolonial critique of Agamben's work is necessary. While Agamben is concerned with the origins and development of Western political and legal thought and how it supports exclusionary structures of sovereign power and governance, he has not explored how the geopolitical entity of 'the West' emerged, as such, through its imperial domination of others. Also, while Agamben explains aspects of Greek political thought using the formal separation between *bios* and *zoe* to define the capacity of some subjects to live as citizens, 'he does not dwell on how this was predicated on the fact of slavery as a condition for the realisation and operation of the polis' (Bignall and Svirsky 2012: I).

Agamben has discussed the state of exception as a post-Auschwitz era, according to which we are all living in a permanent state of exception, as it will be discussed in depth in Chapter 2. A postcolonial critique, as made by Bignall and Svirsky (2012: I) argued that Auschwitz was based on the colonial experience of Namibia. Whereas Agamben (1995) recurred to the camps created by Spanish colonial power in Cuba, in 1986, or in the context of British domination of Boers settlers in Southern Africa during the 1800s, to help him in his formulation, Casper W. Erichsen and David Olusoga (2011) indicated a previous use of camps towards colonised population in Africa. Their book *The Kaiser's Holocaust: Germany's Forgotten Genocide* addresses the history of a concentration camp erected by Germans on the coast of South-West Africa, the Shark Island, in present-day Namibia. The acknowledgement of coloniality as part of exception is relevant because it locates death not only with the exception or only within coloniality, but it shows how central it is in both 'logic of coloniality' and 'logic of exception'.

An important postcolonial critique based on Agamben's work that is central to the present research was developed by Achille Mbembe (2003) on necropolitics. Mbembe took a further step in the formulation of biopolitics to affirm that sovereign power dictates not only how some people may live but also *how some people must die*, including how some people are exposed to death. Mbembe derived his formulation from studies on slavery, apartheid, and Palestine to analyse contemporary forms of subjugation of life that reduce people to precarious conditions to the extent that some beings are located between life and death. In that sense, the disappeared in contemporary contexts can be related to these individuals analysed by Mbembe, who have to inhabit the liminal space between life and death.

The literature that links forms of sovereignty to forms of life, as well as the literature on sovereign power operating at different spaces, speak to the problematisation of violence towards favela dwellers. Mbembe (2003: 12) discussed modernity as the origin of multiple concepts of sovereignty (and biopolitics) and linked the mechanisms of biopower to the function of racism allowing the state to regulate the distribution of death. Drawing to Foucault, Mbembe stated that the complete example of a state exercising the right to kill is by managing, protecting, and cultivating life at the same time with its sovereign right to kill (2003: 17). The discussion is expanded to the territorialisation of a sovereign state when it assumed the form of a distinction between parts of the globe available for colonial appropriation in opposition to the parts considered part of empires (2003: 23).

Questions of racism have often been sidelined in the discipline of international relations. Different efforts, however, were made to bring 'race' to the fore. A few examples can be found in studies of identity politics (Doty 1998), in discussions on the ethics of representation in security studies (McMillan 2017), or in debates on U.S foreign policies (Lauren 1996), among others. Anievas, Manchanda, and Shilliam highlighted, however, that IR was founded, in large part, 'to solve the dilemmas posed by empire-building and colonial administration' (2015: 2), making race and racism an integral part of the discipline.

This sidelining can also be observed in Brazil, where the idea of racial democracy gives the impression that racial issues have been overcome. As mentioned before, the myth of racial democracy as a product of miscegenation and transculturation has defined how the history of Brazil has been narrated since its colonisation by Portugal in the 1500s. Benito Cao (2011) highlighted that the idea of Brazil as a hybrid nation is central to the denial of racism because it rejects 'racial differences sustained by the social construction of a supra-racial national identity that defines Brazilians of all colours as only Brazilians' (2011: 709). The national identity is supposedly revealed in a Brazilian *way of being* that superimposes racialised identities, preventing racism from emerging. I argue that the invisibility rendered to race as a hierarchical category of social, economic, and political organisation makes it more difficult to problematise violence towards racialised communities. The consequence of taking racialised hierarchies for granted is enormous. One example is that the disappearance and killings of subjects from racialised communities are normalised through the narrative of the 'war on drugs' and explained by class inequality.

In conceptual terms, by relating the elements discussed by Giorgio Agamben building up a postcolonial critique of his work, this book presents

Introduction 11

an original contribution by addressing *dispositif*, racialised bodies, and abject space. In substantive terms, this book contributes to a dislocation of the problem of disappearances from authoritarian regimes or dictatorships in Latin America to locate it in a more contemporary context in which disappearances are still happening. In a nutshell, as will be explained in greater detail later, the difference between the dictatorship and contemporary cases is that during the dictatorships, as Gatti (2014) conceptualised, disappearances happened following a logic of 'detained-disappeared' in which someone was detained for interrogation and tortured, and there was a denial by the state forces of someone's fate. In our contemporaneity, however, disappearances have changed to practices of extermination and abandonment of the body. As I argue later, it can be theorised as a sovereign practice of 'letting disappear'. The book grounds the discussion on contemporary police violence in an analytical framework that encompasses notions of race, postcolonial rationale, and the homogenisation inside the borders of a sovereign state, not because of the nation-state, but showing how the nation-state follows racialised notions of life and belonging.

Considering the disappearance as an expression of sovereign power over life and death, it is marked not only by violence but also by a lack of accountability regarding the resulting impossibility of including the disappeared in official figures and public memorialisation. The disappearances this book deals with are of people who have not been targeted as political enemies, but whose lives are simply considered unworthy. In contemporary urban Brazil, the idea of degraded life is related to the 'war on drugs' that follows racial and spatial logics usually targeting the poorest and black communities' dwellers of favelas. Indeed, it is possible to find the roots of such politics in the colonial process in the country. The present book intends to converse with the debate on sovereign power represented by the nation-state and operated by forms of policing that pushes certain (racialised) bodies to the liminal space of in-between.

Challenges in dealing with the (in)visible

The use of the term 'disappearance' in Brazil maps different historical periods. The way disappearance is understood under the period researched (1985–2015) – under the democratic regime, follows the same meaning as 'missing'. In Portuguese there is no equivalent to the English term 'missing person' as a way to account for those who disappear by free will. In that sense, to simply put 'disappearance' under the democratic rule (1985–2015) accounts for what reads as 'missing' in English – someone who may have decided to leave their social network. Therefore, the fact that someone has disappeared does not lead to a police investigation. An exception to this understanding is when the person disappeared is a minor. In that case, an investigation needs to be carried out by the police since, legally, minors do not have free will to leave their home. Another important aspect of current cases of disappearances is how they are classed as massacre and slaughter, making disappearances even more difficult to grasp.

12 Introduction

When discussing disappearances under the dictatorship (1964–1985) a different interpretation emerged. Under the dictatorship rule, those who were disappeared by the regime and were part of leftist guerrillas are known in the country as 'political-disappeared', highlighting their struggle in fighting against the military regime. Enforced disappearance as a term follows a juridical definition provided by the United Nations and Inter-American Commission as it will be discussed in greater detail in Chapter 1. Nationally, the term 'enforced disappearance' was adopted by the National Truth Commission, as well as by the local commissions, to designate all different groups who were also forcibly disappeared by the regime, having as the most poignant example indigenous peoples and peasant groups. I argue that the differentiation in the understanding and uses of these three terms reveals a narrow understanding of political as encompassing only the political struggle in favour of democracy, and consequently a depoliticisation of land struggle, as well as of the killings and disappearances of indigenous populations and peasants.

As the cases of enforced disappearances that have happened during the dictatorship become broadly discussed in Brazil known as 'political disappearance', this is the only category available to discuss the phenomenon, making the term my starting point. The National Truth Commission Report (2014) pointed out that the Brazil armed forces focused their operations in Rio de Janeiro, São Paulo, and Pernambuco (2014: 532). Regarding contemporary police violence, the Public Security Forum organises an annual survey on police killings. In 2016, São Paulo was number one on that list, followed by Rio de Janeiro. Pernambuco nevertheless was the 70th on the list. In that sense, I have focused on the major three cities – Rio de Janeiro, São Paulo, and Recife – where the armed forces were based and pointed out by their victims as a place for torture and possible disappearance. The fieldwork conducted in this research was spent at each of these cities doing interviews,[3] but also identifying possible networks in which relatives, NGOs, and the police were working together to solve cases of missing persons (in that case, outside of the frame of political disappeared from the dictatorship).

I have divided my interviews into two different historical moments – dictatorship (1964–1985) and re-democratisation (1985–2015) – to identify groups and individuals with whom I could talk. This division was made based on the idea that having two groups would make it possible to identify more clearly which were the fundamental differences and similarities regarding both political contexts but also the dynamic of the violence. About the dictatorship period, the National Truth Commission, in place from 2012 to 2014, named many of the former members of the armed forces who perpetrated killings and disappearances. Some were summoned to testify. A few did. Almost none admitted having taken part in processes of disappearance and avoided giving details on how it worked. In the case of former colonel Paulo Malhães, his detailed testimony was published through an official document introduced by a contextualisation. For example, the document stated, 'it is worrying to read this testimony without bearing in mind the possibility of its being a trap'

(NTC file 2014, iii). Because there are many documents and testimonies from perpetrators available from the Truth Commissions, I would not have anything new to ask them. Thus, I decided not to interview former perpetrators.

Regarding the cases of 'political disappearances', I have researched first the literature based on the reports produced by the National Truth Commission and local commissions of Rio de Janeiro, São Paulo–*Comissão Rubens Paiva*, and Recife–*Comissão Dom Helder Camara*. The reports produced by those four truth commissions presented detailed descriptions of the state apparatus in place at the time to erase any traces of those who were part of the guerrilla; the list of the dead and political disappeared, along with personal histories; and the places where they were tortured, killed, and, in some cases, buried in clandestine graves. They were crucial to identifying possible common patterns, differences, and rationalities when comparing cases that occurred after the military regime. I have also used other reports, such as the 'Dossier on Political Deaths and Disappearances from 1964' (1995) by the Special Commission of Relatives of Political Deaths and Disappearances and Torture Never Again; and '*Direito a Memoria e a Verdade*' (2007) by the Special Commission on Political Deaths and Disappearances created by the Special Bureau on Human Rights of the Presidency of the Republic of Brazil in 1995.

When considering that someone could be *disappeared* by the police in Brazil, the present research seeks to create a juxtaposition between state violence, here in the form of disappearance, and the police killings. By doing so, it is expected to disrupt a historically contingent accepted knowledge position (Shapiro 2012: 28) that informs that disappearances are related exclusively to the dictatorship in the country. In that sense, questions about disappearance have the potentiality to break those stable boundaries and bring to the fore features of a state that deals with its citizens by making some of them disappear(able). In the Brazilian context, the combination of a word that does not indicate the type of disappearance, and an analytical frame that only considers disappearances to be political in the context of a dictatorial government, adds further uncertainty to a phenomenon that is already entangled with ambiguity.

Contemporary cases

My aim was to interview those who deal with the issue of disappearances such as police officers, relatives who became activists, and other researchers – who are researching related themes as urban violence, police violence, or *autos de resistência*; as well as those who were part of the truth commissions at the local and national levels. It was also possible to interview members of the three local truth commissions as well as members of the national truth commission. Because of the highly sensitive subject, in all the interviews I have followed a semi-structured format, allowing for the emergence of subjects in which the interviewee felt comfortable to speak. It is important to highlight that the contact with relatives of those who went missing before or after the dictatorship was established through NGOs and other associations, and I have only interviewed those who have already made their story public. The aim was not to cause secondary traumatic stress experience among the interviewees.

The semi-structured questionnaires started with the question: 'Do you think enforced disappearances are still going on in the country?' Michael Shapiro (2012) reminded us of the importance of political critique to avoid reproducing common sense and the explanatory apparatus of 'representational practices that already exist'. Our aim should be to 'seek to displace institutionalised forms of recognition with thinking'. On more than one occasion I felt that by simply posing that first question, a new critical enquiry was taking shape.

When answering this question, interviewees displayed distinct body reactions and facial expressions, and often other questions emerged. One of the most important answers was a question posed by a police officer interviewed in Rio de Janeiro. He asked, 'If we can kill them why to disappear them?', as will be further discussed in Chapter 3. His question is extremely relevant first because it can be related to the idea of a highly visible 'war on drugs' – as an exceptional measure that takes many lives. Secondly, we can refer back to Mbembe's critique on necropolitics about *how* some people will die. At the same time, it renders invisibility to the slow and dismissive ways that some representatives of the state apparatus deal with the life of black bodies that live in the peripheries of Brazil.

Because disappearance cases as a result of police violence, and subject of this book, are not particularly accounted for in Brazil, there were two ways that I could approach them while in fieldwork. One was following the institutions that somehow deal with missing persons. To follow public institutions proved to be a difficult task. I could not identify where to go first to search for someone. Then, I decided to include the question in my questionnaire: 'Where should I go if someone disappears?' The answers were vague and varied, from 'to the closest hospital' to 'the morgue'. The misguidance on where to go when someone goes missing was pointed out by some of the projects which are dealing with missing people and have been already explored by Leticia Ferreira and Fabio Alves Araujo in their books. Ferreira (2015) described and analysed the search for the one who is missing by the police as a matter of filling in a form. The family searches in the friends' houses, hospitals, and the morgue before they go to the police station and make a formal notification of 'missing person'. After the formal notification, the police start an investigation by calling people who are part of the social network of the missing person and often the same hospitals and institutions already contacted by the family. According to Ferreira, the search is often carried by the family and not by the police. Araujo (2014), while researching how mothers try to find their missing children, also described how it is unclear where to go when someone disappears, even for institutions involved with the task.

Nowadays, there is a police station in Rio de Janeiro specialising in missing person cases. The unit serves only the metropolitan area, which concentrates most of the white middle class and wealthy neighbourhoods. As will be discussed later in Chapter 1, when discussing the data available, the metropolitan area is not where most of the cases happen or are known by violence spread by militias and by the police (G1 2017). The special unit in Rio de Janeiro was created in 2014 following pressure from social movements especially claiming immediate search to cases of missing children. The former police division for missing persons was inside the structure of the Homicides Division, contributing to the idea that disappearance and murder are closer (G1 2015). Part of the demands from relatives in having a special unit dedicated to the search of those who are missing was to feel that their notification was treated with respect and not received as a homicide case. Although the unit allegedly solved 88% of the cases (State of Rio de Janeiro Press 2016), it is the only unit exclusively dedicated to missing persons in the country. It is important to note that most missing persons cases happen in East Zone neighbourhoods such as Campo Grande, Santa Cruz, Bangu, and Taquara, followed by Bonsucesso at the North Zone, thus out of the special police station jurisdiction.

Non-governmental groups seem to vary in their position towards disappearances depending on whom they work with and who they represent – as we cannot consider the non-governmental groups a homogeneous entity. As expected, groups that are constituted by mothers of missing people are more critical of the role played by the police in the search and acknowledge that sometimes police officials are involved in the disappearances. The point that these two groups – relatives and the government – seem to agree on, however, is in the reproduction of moralities, usually voiced by government representatives. For example, when asked if a police officer could be involved in contemporary cases of disappearance, the answer is usually that it could be the case, but on the disappearance of someone else 'because my son/daughter was never an outlaw!' When working close to the state institutions, it was common to find the same discourse stating that those who disappear are problematic youths involved with drugs, sometimes highlighting that they are from broken homes. This kind of narrative only reinforces the depoliticisation of disappearances, reframing them as a social problem.

Because of the way disappearances are classed after the dictatorship, I have also searched for cases known as slaughter or massacres, reading them attentively to understand whether the body was found or not, and when. Also, because I am working with cases where police officers are somehow involved, I have also engaged with the issue of police violence. In that sense, I looked for articles published by the mainstream newspapers nationally such as *O Globo*, *O Estado de São Paulo* and *Folha de São Paulo* in Brazil, and internationally at *The Guardian* and *El Pais*. Amarildo's case, for example, was in the media for three months (from August to October 2013), and it is still mentioned in other reports about police violence in Rio de Janeiro. In the case of non-governmental organisations, I had access to in-depth reports on police violence published by Amnesty International and Human Rights Watch. Also, in many of the public universities in Brazil, there are clusters dedicated to the issue of urban violence as well as police violence. This is the case of the *Nucleo de Estudos da Violência* (Violence Studies Research Centre) at the University of São Paulo (NEV-USP); *Núcleo de Estudos da Cidadania, Conflito e Violência Urbana* (Citizenship, Conflict and Urban Violence) da Federal University of Rio de Janeiro (Necvu-UFRJ), and *Laboratório de Análises da Violência* (Violence Analysis Lab) at the University of the State of Rio de Janeiro (LAV UERJ).

Because of cases that gained wide media attention, like the Acari Massacre and the May Crimes, I was convinced that disappearance was a highly sensitive topic; hence, the expectation that my interviewees would probably be afraid to speak out. Respondents' safety was of paramount concern, and all measures were taken to ensure the data was collected and stored securely and with due consent. Following the instructions by the Ethics Committee through the University of Manchester, I could talk only to those who had publicly discussed their stories. The measure was to avoid re-traumatising former victims and to ensure my safety as a researcher. I was surprised to find out that most people were not afraid to talk about it. In fact, disappearances – apart from Amarildo's case – are not a concern. When referring to the threat of talking about police killings, a common reference was the case of Edmea da Silva Euzébio, the Acari's mother leader who was murdered by the police officer accused of killing and disappearing the group in Acari. A possible explanation of this unawareness of disappearances and lack of concern with the killings may be explained by the way these cases are classed. As it will be further discussed in Chapter 3, disappearances in Brazil do not account for a specific type of violence. As can be observed in the Acari and May cases, disappearances in the post-dictatorship period are equated with death, making it difficult to determine what happened to the victim. It is interesting to observe, however, that the association between disappearance and death started during the dictatorship and might still be under its influence.

After Amarildo's disappearance, as discussed in this chapter, newspapers showed many other cases of disappearances that had happened before him. Also, the mainstream media seemed to be more attentive, for a while, to cases of children's disappearance, for example in the case of Juan, which will be discussed in Chapter 5. I have also analysed cases listed by the two other authors that work with the issue in Rio de Janeiro, Araujo (2014) described in his book *Das técnicas de fazer desaparecer corpos* (*Of the Techniques of Making Bodies Disappear*). I did not include the cases presented by Leticia Carvalho de Mesquita Ferreira (2015), *Pessoas Desaparecidas: Uma etnografia para muitas ausências* (*Missing Persons: An Ethnography of Multiple Absences*), because they mostly refer to cases of missing persons and not to homicides followed by disappearance or cases involving police officers. I have also included cases classed as 'massacre' and 'slaughter', such as the Acari and May Crimes cases. I have given particular attention to cases that have gained more attention in the media because of years of impunity that perpetrators have enjoyed. One may ask why the mainstream media gives more attention to some cases and not others. The reason varies, and it is not a subject of analysis here; still, some cases seem to gain notoriety when they are perpetrated against those who cannot be portrayed as involved with drug activities, either trafficking or consuming, when the person cannot be attached to favelas, and underaged people, as it will be discussed in greater detail in Chapter 6. Another reason why a case gains notoriety seems to follow when the killings and disappearances involve more than one person – then the case is portrayed as 'slaughter' and 'massacre' even when no trace is left behind. Still, as I will further discuss in Chapter 1, it is undeniable from the scarcity of data, for example, how many missing people were, in fact, victims of executions. The classification adopted by newspapers also does not help.

Regarding cases that happened in other states, it was more difficult to find accounts, whether in research or in newspapers. An interviewee stated that it is becoming more difficult to research police violence in Brazil. According to this person, in the past one could see accounts of such cases and get a sense of the ongoing violence perpetrated by the police simply by following the section on crime in the newspapers. With this type of news becoming rarer in mainstream newspapers, it is harder to have access to cases of killings or police violence. At the same time, there are increasingly more videos of police violence in the social media, such as Facebook and independent blogs. Those videos again give visibility to police killings, while disappearances are less noticeable.

A book on disappearances in contemporary Brazil: what was possible to investigate?

I was in São Paulo when the elected president, Dilma Rousseff, was judged by the Congress for corruption charges. The political process that resulted in Rousseff's impeachment in September 2016 was already in motion during my fieldwork. She was the first female Brazilian president, and the fourth president to be elected by direct popular ballot since the military coup. Sectors of the society consider Rousseff's impeachment as a new *coup*. Because those claims were taken to the streets, along with protests asking for a new military intervention against corruption, the dictatorship was a very lively topic in public discussions. Amidst the political climate, contradictory voices were strong. While there was a clamour for military intervention, there was also indignation caused by the killing of Marielle Franco, a councilwoman in Rio de Janeiro, and her driver Anderson Gomes, both shot to death with bullets that had been identified as being sold to the police.

The political moment in Brazil while I was conducting interviews impacted the way that my interviewees reacted to my question. All the imagery related to the dictatorship was brought back and was immediately associated with my question on disappearances. Many of my respondents, especially those connected to the dictatorship as former guerrilla members and their relatives, answered my questions by affirming that disappearance is no longer happening. Because they are part of the narrative of 'political disappearances', their answers included advice on the importance of fighting against the conservative wave and conducting research such as mine to prevent disappearances from happening again.

When I started my fieldwork in Brazil, I was convinced that some unresolved past was being acted out by security forces and that Amarildo's disappearance would bring those repressed memories to the surface. The figures that followed Amarildo's case showed that disappearances cases were rising while police killings were dropping. Brazil at the time was in the final preparations to host the 2014 FIFA World Cup and the 2016 Summer Olympic Games, the culmination of a foreign policy articulated by the former president Lula (Luiz Inacio da Silva). Since 2004, Lula had started to shift the distribution of power between the states of the Global North and emerging powers in the Global South (de Paula 2018: 1–2). Police killings did not fit into this new role, and for the first time, there were federal investments in public security. In 2007, Lula created the Pronasci – a project of $3 billion to develop a range of new preventative and deterrent strategies for policing, among them, the UPP that killed and disappeared Amarildo. This project was intimately related to Lula's commitment to making Brazil secure enough to host the World Cup and the Summer Olympic Games. When it was created, this initiative represented an innovative, even radical new direction for the criminal justice system, and one that was a novelty for the federal government. As in many federal systems, public security in Brazil had been largely a prerogative of state governments. The federal government had previously avoided direct intervention in policing in the large metropolitan centres.

It was interesting to observe that 'disappearance' was so tightly attached to 'dictatorship', making it almost impossible to discuss in the contemporary context. When disappearance makes sense, it is assumed as death. The void caused by someone's absence is immediately filled with an explanation. When the person missed is a favela dweller with a particular racial background, the general explanation is 'it was probably killed by the police somewhere'. If the victim was female and not a favela dweller, the explanation goes as 'she is probably in a relationship with some drug baron living in the favela'. Comments often conclude with 'someone will find the body before too long'. If I arrived in Brazil focusing on disappearances alone, I left the country convinced that this book would need to engage more with *death*.

The (de-)politicisation of deaths caused by the police in contrast to deaths caused during the dictatorship is a key concern in this book. Apart from racialised and spatialised notions, it is important to highlight what Gabriel Gatti defined as *epistemicide* – the killing of the epistemology that would allow the investigation of disappearances by state forces outside the historical frame of dictatorships. Pita (2010) discussed a similar de-politicisation of police killings in Argentina. In a country where public mobilisation and demonstration are part of its culture and tradition, death caused by the police is not considered *political*. Pita highlighted that the politicisation of one's death is attached to the meaning of one's life. If life was dedicated to political resistance or activism, its death is political. By contrast, to kill or to *disappear* with a bare life is not political.

Another important point is that a general account of the police violence in Brazil is associated with the dictatorship. Although it is broadly recognised that a military regime strengthens what can be called a militarisation of social relations by creating a culture of brutality among state defence institutions and normalising law enforcement measures in the everyday life of populations, little attention is given to the racialised rationale in the state apparatus. It was interesting to observe that despite the effort by the Truth Commission Research Group to acknowledge that violence was also perpetrated against favela dwellers, such as in the stop and search of vehicles for no reason, or the surveillance of favela association groups and forced displacement, favela dwellers were nevertheless kept at the margins of the political struggle. The regime believed that favela dwellers were somehow unable to organise themselves as a resistance group, considering that these communities only ran the risk of being co-opted by communist groups or international organisations which worked for racial equality, a narrative that persisted more generally.

What is crucial in our contemporaneity is to highlight a general understanding that some lives are *killable*. This notion and decision embodied by the police are endorsed and legitimised by the silence around violence. To Pita (2010), who used Foucault's and Agamben's conceptual frame, there is a way out. To her, in the condition of being *killable* resides a potentiality to expose the need of limiting sovereign power at the hands of the police. My focus, however, is different. Upon meeting a group of mothers whose children were killed by the police, I asked if any of their children had disappeared. They responded by stressing that their sons were not criminals. I realised that the sovereign embodiment of killings and disappearance also works as a boundary that delimits whose lives are *killable*. As Mbembe (2003) pointed out, a sovereign decision over death is about not only deciding who dies, but also exposing certain populations to death, and mostly in determining how some populations will die.

I opted for a 30-year temporal frame, namely the period between 1985 and 2015, which stands for the re-democratisation of Brazil. During this period, militias and drug cartels became prominent in the urban context, as criminality, police killings, and disappearances, classed as massacres and slaughters, rose. Yet, this period does not represent a formal state of exception. Instead, it presents a body of exceptionalities framed as a war against drugs. In this war, nobody seems to agree about the strategy of occasional intervention in peripheries – as discussed in Chapter 3. As a result, injury, or deaths on those who are closer to *the war zone* – the favela dwellers – are considered to be collateral damage.

To think about the disappearance and police killings in racialised terms is important for a few reasons. Firstly, when looking at figures on disappearance as police killings in urban areas of Brazil, the vast majority of victims are from black communities. However, because Brazil proclaims itself as a 'multiracial democracy', the racial aspects of social relations and consequently institutional violence, even if discussed, are deemed unproblematic. By neglecting race in analysing police violence, the criminalisation of black bodies is perceived not as a problem of race, but only as a problem of poverty that would lead young lives to be involved with drug cartel activities. If one returns to the response of the police and authorities when a 'white' body disappears or is killed by the police, it is more difficult to deny how race interplays a crucial role. When bringing Agamben's ideas on how some lives are deemed unworthy as well as Mbembe's work on the centrality of death to sovereign decision, I expect to discuss the centrality of race in the rationale of sovereign decision.

Secondly, by discussing state violence in racialised terms, this book also engages with a broader issue – the criminalisation of black bodies which, I argue, is deeply rooted in postcolonial societies where social and economic relations were based on the slave trade. It is important to highlight that the structures that make racialised communities more vulnerable need a constant feed-in. As I mentioned before, it was only when turning the thesis manuscript into a book that I encountered a different literature that links the racialisation of security apparatus to Black Capitalism, showing how ultimately the security apparatus also becomes a neoliberal dispositive that works against poverty, inequality, and racialised subjects. In that sense, this book also reflects my attempt to bring more clearly how the security apparatus in Brazil also reflects a rationale based on a neoliberal logic that pushes racialised communities to death.

Thirdly, state violence in Brazil follows a gendered distribution in which 94 per cent of people being killed by the police forces are male bodies (AI 2015). By discussing the specific type of violence in which black males are outstandingly the foremost lethal victim, this work can contribute to discussions which adopt a gendered perspective. However, this book does not present a discussion on how masculinities – or, more specifically, how hyper-masculinity in a context of urban conflict plays a role in Brazil.

The manifestation of gendered racial violence in urban Brazil is rather complex. Alves (2019) points out that in order to produce a satisfactory analysis taking into account a gendered perspective, it is necessary first to recognise black women as also victims of the police instead of framing their experiences as a by-product of black men's fate. There is a group of black feminists[4] in Brazil who point out the specificity of women's violence in Brazil in the context of the militarisation of the everyday lives of favela dwellers. In their work, they highlight from domestic violence to being dismissed by the police when willing to register a crime or the disappearance of a beloved one. Rocha (2012, 2014) claims that one of the many acts of violence perpetrated against black women, for example, is to live with the consequences of the loss of a father, son, and/or brother. It is not uncommon for these women to develop deep distress resulting in depression and other health conditions. In that sense, an analysis which enriches the debate does not need to equalise men's and women's experiences as the type of violence perpetrated against each gendered group differs drastically.

When looking at death distribution in gender terms, resistance movements have women as protagonists as they are the ones left to speak on behalf of the victims of state violence. An interesting aspect of what can be considered a limitation of resistance groups of mothers and daughters in Brazil, as well as on the type of narrative they are enacting, is that their claims very often follow the same morality discourse used by the state to justify the death of favela dwellers. It is common to observe the claim that the police have no right to kill those who are not involved with the drug cartel's activities. The flip side of this argument is the legitimisation of the killings of those who are part of it. However, Rocha (2012, 2014) explains that it would be even more difficult for them to dislocate from heteronormative mainstream discourse when fighting for access to social care, institutional justice, or sometimes the acknowledgement of the crime perpetrated.

Structure of the book

In the following chapters, I seek to demonstrate how the state apparatus in Brazil – more specifically, the police – follows a rationale based on racialised notions of life and space. Throughout the narrative, special attention is given to the black communities for two reasons. First, because African populations were enslaved, brought to the country during the colonisation of Brazil, and later were expected to mix into the white population through eugenics ideas of mixed race. Secondly, because in urban areas of Brazil, black communities are by far the population most targeted by police violence in the 'war on drugs'.

Although indigenous populations are not part of the contemporary killings and disappearances in urban areas of Brazil – and especially in Rio de Janeiro and São Paulo – I will refer to this group in three particular moments. Firstly, when discussing how race was categorised and made up into hierarchies during the colonisation – strongly following notions articulated by the Church. Secondly, when discussing the dictatorship policy for enforced disappearances and the following erasure of this group from the category that became known as 'political disappeared' strictly applied to those involved with guerrilla movements in Brazil during the military regime. Thirdly, indigenous populations come to the fore again when I discuss how colonial ideas on space – and its occupation – are still in place when dealing with peripheries and favelas in Brazil.

As will be become clear, there is a solid historical reason for such methodological bias. Briefly put, the enslavement of Africans was a fundamental reference point for the initial racialisation of (un)worthiness characteristics, as 'slave', and thereby the condition of blackness. At various points in the argument, I shall demonstrate how some features became attached to the idea of blackness being made to carry characteristics that became signals of unworthiness or abjection, although they were first articulated through moral discourses of laziness or vagabond – especially in the First Republic and Era Vargas periods, and more recently articulated as dangerous groups through the criminalisation of drug trafficking. In that sense, 'racial democracy', as it will be discussed, is a myth created to make 'race' and institutionalised racism, invisible. Therefore, and privileging the narrative presented here, although the probability of being killed by gunfire is three times higher for black individuals (UNICEF 2017), those killings are made unproblematic by the criminalisation of their victims.

22 Introduction

The book is divided into six chapters. Chapter 1 provides a background on the context of disappearances in Brazil as it is a common starting point to understand disappearances on the continent. It problematises the current association in Brazil, and more broadly, between 'disappearances' and 'dictatorship'. Chapter 1 starts with the process of dictatorships in Latin America, showing how 'political disappearances' became closely associated with this political process, and then, more recently, was also applied to other contexts. The chapter also discusses the implications and ultimately the limits created by associating disappearances to a very specific political and located experience. It also discusses the implications of only recognising *the political* as the reason for disappearances. In this chapter, I argue that one of the reasons why contemporary cases of disappearances remain unproblematised is the crystallisation of what is understood as 'political' – as a struggle for democracy under a dictatorial regime. Consequently, I argue, contemporary disappearances remain invisible.

Chapter 2 develops a conceptual vocabulary for the book and problematises theoretical frameworks that emerge from the analyses of contemporary disappearances. When discussing the 'war on drugs', it accounts for first considering it a war, in opposition to a general interpretation of it as something else. The chapter also develops, conceptually speaking, an interpretation of Agamben's concepts that emerge from disappearances cases analysed in Rio de Janeiro and São Paulo. It is argued that the concepts of state apparatus, bare life, and camp can be adequately grasped only in the case of contemporary disappearances in Brazil and is situated in a postcolonial context taking into account historical, social, and cultural contexts. In that sense, the three key concepts that I have decided to address following Agamben's work are related to disappearances as a *dispositif* towards racialised bodies that inhabit peripheral spaces. A third step is taken to bring Achille Mbembe's development of Agamben's conceptualisations, providing a critique that opens up an analysis of the implications of sovereign power in deciding how some people must live and how some people must die. By looking at disappearances in Brazil, I expect to contribute to the accounts on 'necropolitics', a concept developed by Mbembe that refers to the sovereign power over life and death. In that sense, Chapter 2 presents an interpretation of Agamben's concepts considering Mbembe's postcolonial thought, each of which will be analysed in more detail in the following chapters.

Chapter 3 discusses how police action was developed over time in Brazil, focusing on different groups considered 'dangerous'. It starts by providing a historical account of the emergence of the police in Brazil and how it developed different roles from helping to build new, urban Rio de Janeiro and keep the streets safe and later from communist groups. The chapter also presents how the military regime made use of enforced disappearances towards guerrilla groups as well as indigenous populations and peasant groups. Following this account, I highlight how the narrow understanding of political excluded the last two groups – indigenous and peasants – from the public memory of 'political disappearances' in Brazil. The chapter also discusses more recently the 'war on drugs' as the ultimate framework that legitimises contemporary killings and disappearances of certain populations, as well as the *autos de resistência* as a dispositive that legitimises those killings. It is worth mentioning that the police here represent an expression of sovereignty and embodies a sovereign's decision, as discussed in Chapter 2.

Chapter 4 specifically develops the argument that following a more visible history of the police leads to a narrative of disconnections. In a first moment, the police consider slaves and black communities as dangerous populations. During the Vargas Era and the military dictatorship, however, communist groups became the so-called dangerous groups, and the concept of race is erased. Race reappears only later, during the re-democratisation, when by conducting the 'war on drugs', not in the awareness of race as an issue that needs to be dealt with but in the figures of police killing that is huge among racialised communities in favelas but remains unproblematised. By normalising that favela dwellers, mostly African descendants, happen to be in the wrong place – the 'war on drugs' are carried in favelas. The most important point made in this chapter is to show how the police had embodied racialised notions from the colonisation and the First Republic when those notions were very clear in the segmentation of African populations in the new urban areas of Brazil. Later, during the Vargas Era, race is erased to give place to the idea of 'racial democracy', when blackness is then associated with poorness first and then an indication of being a criminal.

Chapter 4 explores the concept of bare life intertwined with race in Brazil, making black bodies as disposable life. This chapter presents accounts of the slavery process in Brazil, to the different policies implemented in the country aiming to (racially) whitening its population, and discusses policies that articulated the aim to erase black communities. The importance of this chapter is to complement the previous one showing that there is another apparatus that goes underneath the public memory and outside the locus of 'political disappearances' and communists' threats, in an ongoing process that started with slavery but did not end with it. On the contrary, it has remained strong, especially because it operates outside the categories available that would allow them to be grasped. The chapter also discusses how black communities' inhabitants of favelas and peripheries are associated with drug cartel activities making their lives more likely to be killed following the narrative of the 'war on drugs'.

Chapter 3 and 4 together narrate the racialised embodiment of the police apparatus and argue that the state apparatus in Brazil has developed twofold. First and much more visible is the targeting of communist and leftist groups. This action is visible and celebrated, allowing for resistance and opposition. The second development was the action, first, against black populations, and later when race also became invisible as a category of analyses, and later against the poor, who are associated with the drug cartel's activities. This second action of the state apparatus is more diffuse in its rationale, even if brutal, not allowing to address the problem and making resistance much more difficult to achieve.

Chapter 5 discusses how spatiality is taken into account in the sovereign decision that excludes some people, creating a narrative that makes their lives

24 Introduction

bare. In this chapter, I address how space is deeply connected to apparatus and the politics of death. I argue that the way Brazil deals with space is developed twofold, first following the idea of 'empty space' making invisible those who live at the place – as it was first the central part of Brazil and now the favelas. According to this, space is 'empty', those who live there are not fully subjects, and what happens there is invisible. The second important contribution of this chapter is to build up a link between the plantation and the favela. I argue that both spaces are considered the space of abjection; that is, linked to blackness, criminality, and unworthy life. In that sense, military interventions following the 'war on drugs' is justified because those are the spaces of criminality, and what happens *there* is invisible or unproblematised.

Chapter 6 offers concluding thoughts considering the three elements of state apparatus, racialised bodies, and space. Each of the preceding chapters represents an attempt to present a contribution that builds up, a critique of Giorgio Agamben's works and core concepts from a de-colonial perspective, developed through the work of Walter Mignolo, and a postcolonial perspective, especially by Achille Mbembe. In this chapter, I will also offer some thoughts on a current political moment in Brazil regarding exception, police violence, and military intervention. I finish this chapter with what I consider to be where this contribution leaves us.

In summary, this book narrates a history of political domination that throws certain populations to death. Allying the discourse of criminality to blackness, I argue that the plantation system is still present in the contemporary socio-economic structure, and that it is also reproduced in the 'war on drugs'. These links follow two different aspects: the embodiment of racialised notions by the security apparatus, and the association of favelas and peripheries to blackness. Therefore, the killings and disappearances of favela dwellers remain unproblematised.

Notes

1 Pacification, in the context of the UPP programme in Rio de Janeiro, has been used by the national and international media in quotation marks as 'pacification'. I have decided to follow this convention to highlight the contradiction presented by a policy that intends to promote peace through heavily armed military forces.
2 Although this will be further discussed in Chapter 3, it is important to say, for now, that *Autos de Resistência* is a norm established during the military dictatorship in Brazil, according to which police officers do not commit a homicide crime when acting in case of need or self-defence. The major discussion in the country is if *Autos de Resistência* is being used to cover extrajudicial killings.
3 Because of the confidentiality form that interviewees and interviewer signed, and given the 'uniqueness' of the responsibilities described in each case, all interviews were anonymised. Therefore, it is not possible to reveal in this book whether interviewees occupied the described positions in the past or if they do in the present. Neither is it possible to specify their gender, and therefore they are referred as 'he/she' in the book.
4 See for example, Luciane Oliveira Rocha (2012, 2014) and Polly Wilding (2010).

1 Between a revealed past and a treacherous present

Introduction

The National Truth Commission (2014), as well as local commissions over the country, have promised to unveil the truth regarding one of the most traumatic experiences of the dictatorship, namely, the fate of those who were disappeared by the regime. Until then, the transition to democracy in Brazil happened through the Amnesty Law.[1] Transitional justice, as a framework, is considered key to confront past abuses and to address wrongdoings by exercising justice and repairing violence (Walker 2006: 12). One critique of this framework is that somehow it crystallises violence as belonging to the past, referring specifically to the dictatorial and authoritarian regime, not acknowledging that state violence happens in a liberal market democracy. Referring specifically to the Brazilian experience, Henrique Furtado (2017) argued that the NTC denounced 377 perpetrators portraying them as 'demons' responsible for implementing a state of terror during the last dictatorship (1964–1985). According to him, this narrative depoliticised and victimised leftist militants, the 'dreamers', who fought for liberty and democracy in the past (2017: 1). Furtado has argued that a consequence of the NTC narrative is that it silences the leftist project, as well as the complexities of ongoing violence in the country.

In Brazilian public memory, accounts of 'political disappearance' during the authoritarian military regime refer exclusively to those who were part of the armed struggle to defend a democracy in the country. The National Truth Commission Report (National Truth Commission 2014) stated, 'In Brazil, forced disappearance was the result of a systematic policy by the military regime against political opponents' (p. 501). In that regard, Amarildo's case represents a puzzle given that it was not at all related to a political struggle despite having followed the same kind of pattern of abduction-torture-disappearance, as will be discussed later in this chapter. Furthermore, disappearances perpetrated by members of the armed forces for *political* reasons seemed to have made the struggle for democracy the only theoretical and methodological framework available to discuss such events (see, for example, Brysk 1994; Robben 2005; Mezarobba 2007; Bauer 2011; Edkins 2011; Gatti 2010, 2014).

The present chapter develops the argument that connecting enforced disappearances to a specific understanding of what 'political' means, restricts the

DOI: 10.4324/9781003032519-2

analyses of cases not associated with broader violent dynamics in place during the military dictatorship. Additionally, in either case, whether outside the context of the political struggle or in the aftermath of the military regime, disappearances were de-politicised. In this chapter, I partly answer the question as to *why disappearances in Brazil are currently unproblematised*. To do so, I take into account the experience of 'political disappearances', meaning the disappearances that happened in the country as well as in other countries in Latin America, during the military dictatorship that took over the continent in the 1960s, 1970s, and 1980s. The historical accounts of the disappearances that have happened in that period are crucial because they have deeply affected the way people in Brazil, in Latin America, and, as we will see, in other parts of the world make sense of that phenomenon. I argue that this interpretation of disappearances somehow crystallises its understanding and attaches it to a dictatorial regime in the past.

This chapter starts by presenting the military regimes in Latin America. First, I will discuss how the cases of enforced disappearances became deeply associated with the experience of Latin American dictatorships. The first section aims to present the main features of the dictatorships in Latin America and how *enforced disappearances* became its main policy towards political dissidents. Afterwards, I will present what Gabriel Gatti (2014) and Mandolessi and Perez (2014) have called the 'travelling' of the term aiming to push the government to address wrongdoings in Franco's dictatorship in Spain. At the end of the first section, I briefly present a few other examples of disappearances outside the political framework of authoritarian regimes. These examples are important given that a closer look at illegal arrests and extrajudicial executions helps us to identify new ways disappearances have taken place. Today's disappearances display different features. They are not associated with a political regime acting against its opponents, or with the participation of the armed forces. Instead, it is the police who are taking part in different practices of killing, illegal arrests, and disappearances.

In the following section, I discuss what it means to narrow the phenomena to what is usually called 'political disappearances' and its consequences, as well as what is at stake when narrowing the understanding of political struggle. I develop the argument that what I am calling the crystallisation of 'political disappearances' has led to a conundrum which limits the possibility of acknowledging cases of disappearances outside the chronologically bound and politically situated context of dictatorships in Latin America. The section finishes by discussing the constraints caused by keeping the same understanding of politically enforced disappearances associated with dictatorships to analyse contemporary cases, both regarding its victims and perpetrators.

Disappearances during the dictatorship in Latin America: Argentina as the archetypical case

Among the Latin American countries that witnessed disappearances, Argentina is the most discussed case, while also presenting the highest number of victims.[2] With vast literature on the topic, the amount of information about Argentina is larger than that for other countries. Therefore, much of what is known, as well as how we analyse disappearances, is influenced by the Argentinian experience. Wolfgang S. Heinz (1995), who analysed the motives for disappearances in Argentina, Chile, and Uruguay, highlighted that in Argentina, disappearances became the primary tool of state repression. Caroline Silveira Bauer (2011), in her comparative study of disappearance practices in place by Argentinian and Brazilian dictatorships, explains why, in comparison to Brazil, Argentina presents a more substantial number of victims. If one sees the dictatorship in the South Cone as a process, it is possible to identify its beginning in 1954 in Paraguay. It was then implemented in 1964 in Brazil and Bolivia, in 1973 in Chile and Uruguay, and only in 1976 in Argentina. According to the author, if we follow a chronological perspective, we realise that Argentina was the first option of exile for many who were fleeing authoritarian regimes in their original countries. At the time, the number of people living in Argentina in exile totalled 5,00,000 people (Robben 2005; Bauer 2011: 46).

In 1976, under the Argentinian army jurisdiction, a Condor Operation centre was implemented in Buenos Aires. Under its jurisdiction, 300 kidnapping operations were carried out. Fewer than 40 people survived (Bauer 2011: 46). The Condor Operation was a covert agreement between Argentina, Chile, Uruguay, Paraguay, Bolivia, and Brazil aimed at eradicating communist and Soviet influence from the Southern Cone of Latin America, as well as suppressing active or potential opposition against neoliberal economic policies (Klein 2007: 126). The Condor Operation did not follow national borders. Instead, it followed the idea of an ideological border, affecting all the community of dissidents living in exile.

A significant example is the disappearance of 160 Uruguayan citizens during the 12 years of dictatorship in the country. What is particular in this case is that most of the disappearances – between 135 and 150 people (Mezarobba 2003: 153; Bauer 2011: 46) were kidnapped and disappeared in Argentina by Argentinian officers. Because of its clandestine nature, the number of deaths and disappearances is unclear. The *Archivos del Terror*[3] suggests that at least 30,000 disappearances and 50,000 deaths can be attributed to the Condor Operation. Among the victims were dissidents, left-wing politicians, unionists, peasants, priests, academics, and guerrilla members.

Also, Argentina did not want to repeat the same method used by Chile. The dictatorship led by Augusto Pinochet (1973–1990) institutionalised violence from its first day, beginning with the execution of Salvador Allende, the president at the time, in the presidential palace on the day of the coup (Brasil 2007: 20). Chile became notorious because immediately after the coup, millions of people were imprisoned, not only in military barracks but also in unusual places such as the *Estadio Nacional* or on merchant ships (Mezarobba 2007). People were interrogated and many were tortured to death, making the imprisonments, tortures, and killings a horrendous show. Heinz (1995) highlighted that the main reason for the Chilean government to use disappearance was to hide its responsibility. According to the author, when a political prisoner in the country was sentenced to death by the military courts, which never happened in Argentina, Brazil, or Uruguay, the Chilean government was harshly criticised in the international arena. Furthermore, the secret security agency named National Intelligence Directorate (DINA) systematically planned the killings and kept them in secret to avoid a possible loss of support from the dominant elite. To Heinz, even though the bourgeoisie was appalled by the possibility of losing everything under Allende's government, they would not have been prepared to openly support the gross violations of human rights that were taking place.

Antonius C.G.M. Robben (2005: 277), a cultural anthropologist who has researched in Brazil and Argentina, claimed that enforced disappearance is Argentina's nightmare, just as the Holocaust is Germany's. In the book *Political Violence and Trauma in Argentina*, Robben asks the question: why did the Argentinean military junta decide upon disappearances rather than imprisonment or even execution? To answer this question, Robben highlighted that junta members themselves differed in their motivations to apply disappearance as a method and that the line between premeditation and opportunism is hard to draw.

Robben listed different categories and linked them to distinct motivations – operational, judicial, political, symbolic, economic, historical, pedagogic, psychological, and social, to analyse the rationale behind it. Operationally, it allowed the junta to proceed with the operation without the need for lawful arrest or interrogation with the presence of a lawyer. Also, it spread great confusion among the revolutionary organisations who did not know, at the end of an operation, if their missing members were dead or alive, had defected or deserted, or were being tortured for information by armed forces officers. As a result, guerrilla members needed to change previous plans on how to carry out the operation. Judicially, disappearances destroyed incriminating evidence, making it impossible to trace a person, which would have been the case if he or she was abducted by kidnappers in disguise, in unmarked cars, with authorities denying having them in custody, and bodies being cremated or buried in mass graves. Politically, the disappearances misled national and international opinion. Argentinean diplomats and military authorities denied the disappearances and the existence of secret detention centres, something that Robben pointed out as a lesson learned from Chile in Pinochet's first year in power. 'Yet, the Argentine military did at night what Pinochet's men had done during the day' (2005: 279). Symbolically, the destruction of bodies prevented guerrilla members from becoming martyrs. Economically, the government feared that international opinion would keep investors out of Argentina, which would be a disaster for the modernisation of the country's economy. Historically, military leaders knew that the regime would not last forever, and in that sense, the absence of any trace of violence would protect the reputation of the armed forces. Robben concluded that the absence of a body to mourn prevented the revolutionaries from commemorating their dead: 'disappearances served as a conscious construction of collective national memory' (Ibid.: 280). Pedagogically, military commanders wanted to punish the parents for not instilling in their children values such as patriotism, Christian morals, and obedience to authority. The military blamed parents for their offspring's involvement in revolutionary politics, a book that also justified the kidnapping of babies from revolutionary mothers. Therefore, there was no need to return the bodies of the disappeared since such 'parents did not deserve to mourn their dead' (Robben 2005: 280). Psychologically, the annihilation of the enemies' bodies was a successful measure to inspire a sense of empowerment. 'The enemy had been defined as invisible, subterranean, and fed by foreign world powers' (Ibid.: 280). Socially, many of the disappeared were non-combatants but politically active citizens, and 'the armed forces decided to annihilate, traumatise and re-socialise a politically radicalised segment of society, instil anguish and fear in their relatives and terrorise society' (Ibid.: 280). Robben also observed that 'traumatisation manifested itself at the societal level as a culture of fear in which people shunned most informal contacts outside the family, and consciously cut all ties with relatives of disappeared persons' (2005: 280).

Heinz (1995) stated that the first experience of disappearances took place in Tucuman, a province in Argentine, in 1975. According to him, the Tucuman experience was crucial to establish a pattern of disappearances, to be followed throughout the country. At the time, 387 people were kidnapped and disappeared, 96 people were kidnapped and reappeared, and 24 were assassinated (Heinz 1995). A methodology was applied following a pattern of abduction-disappearance-torture. Within 24 to 48 hours, the decision was taken whether a person should be released or not. General Vilas, who carried out the operation, complained that every time someone was detained, political parties and even the central government would ask them what had happened. The General decided then to apply a new model. If the operation was carried out by men wearing uniforms, there was no other possibility but to hand the prisoners over to the justice system. However, if officers were wearing civilian clothes and driving non-official vehicles, in many cases not registered in the national database, there were no complaints from the justice system or political parties regarding the prisoner. Consequently, the prisoner would be held in unofficial detention centres.

As discussed in the preceding examples, Argentina is constantly used as a reference point in comparative studies on the disappearance. Consequently, it influenced most of what is known about the topic, and how to analyse other cases in Latin America and the world. This section has introduced the dictatorships in Latin America and how disappearance has become one of the most important tools for political repression of communist movements in the region. The following section shows the effort at the international level to create a legal category of 'enforced disappearances' and how cases in different contexts are being framed, or not, following this classification.

Political disappearance: a 'travelling' concept

The Report from the UN Working Group on Enforced or Involuntary Disappearances (Report number 20: 14)[4] affirms that since its creation in 1980, a total of 54,405 cases were referred to them, and 104 governments were registered. The number of cases under active consideration stands at 43,250, encompassing a total of 88 states. The number of cases transmitted to the UN Working Group demonstrates that the crime of enforced disappearances is not isolated in the past but continues to be widely used worldwide,[5] supported by the pernicious belief that it is a useful way to defend national security and to fight terrorism or organised crimes.

The use of disappearances has also brought to the surface human rights violations in other parts of the world. Silvana Mandolessi and Mariana Eva Perez (2014) narrated the process of trans-nationalisation of the category *desaparecidos*. Even though Franco's dictatorship in Spain happened before the onset of authoritarian regimes in Latin America, the category *desaparecido* has increasingly been used to reframe past events. In 2013, the Spanish government was under pressure to investigate the disappearances that occurred during the Spanish Civil War (1936–1939) and during Franco's regime (1939–1975). Mandolessi and Perez (2014) argued that the use of the term '*desaparecidos*', an emblematic figure of Latin America, has been used in the last decade in Spain to refer to the *fusilados* of Francoism, which the authors consider to be illustrative of the process of transnational exchanges using old terms in a distinct context.

Mandolessi and Perez (2014) addressed the struggles and consequences by using the term originally associated with the Argentinian case in Spain. The legal impact using the term *disappearance* in Spanish courts went against the prescription of not pressing criminal charges against the regime's perpetrators. Furthermore, Mandolessi and Perez (2014) unveiled other aspects that are also important in the debate around the use of the term disappearance in the Spanish context. On the one hand, there were emotional reactions, such as discomfort, embarrassment, and even anger expressed in the face of what they called a translation of the term. On the other hand, enthusiasts who encouraged the use of the term strived to demonstrate that both events were not as distinct from one another as they seemed at first glance. The Spanish experience of Franco's dictatorship also relates to an epistemological uncertainty – not knowing what happened, not knowing if the person is dead or alive, and the threat of terror (Mandolessi and Perez 2014).

The interesting point illustrated in the discussion presented by Mandolessi and Perez's article (2014) is that although memory is not a property, Argentina somehow appropriated recognisable images and narratives of what disappearance is and how to act in resistance to it. This narrative can condense and awaken a particular emotion attached to a particular subjective experience. The subjective experience here is related to the social network from where the disappeared is absent. The commonalities between different experiences of disappearances, according to Mandolessi and Perez (2014) present the potentiality of creating a transnational community linked through a particular affection – by sharing those emotions related to absences in the Hispanic world. Certainly, this network is extremely important and enables relatives and friends of those whose whereabouts are uncertain to create a solidarity support system and new ways of remembrance and resistance.

Nevertheless, the representation of '*desaparecido*' associated with the Argentinean context, where this term goes alongside '*politico*', creates a particular representation that excludes other types of disappearances that are not deemed political because they may not follow the same pattern. In that sense, the attempt to find commonalities in different contexts does more than build an emotional network or promoting visibility. It also promotes a hierarchy of experiences and grants a second form of invisibility to a phenomenon which originated from an elusive practice.

Contemporary cases of disappearances which follow different political contexts

The belief that disappearances in democracies are non-political poses significant constraints on investigating disappearances in contemporary democracies. In that sense, Brazil is not an exception. The problem is that this belief de-politicises contemporary political struggles, locating them in the dictatorial past. Also, it follows a western-based dichotomous model insofar as it is predicated on a division between democracies and dictatorial or authoritarian regimes, without taking into consideration more nuanced features. In the following examples, we will see how extrajudicial executions, illegal arrests, and disappearances do not necessarily happen in a context of military regimes and dictatorships.

In Mexico, in September 2014, a group of students were mobilising a social protest. On their way to the place where the manifestation would happen, they were stopped by the police and a group of unarmed civilians. The case became known as the Ayotzinapa because the majority of the 43 students who were disappeared were from the Ayotzinapa Rural Teacher Training College (Talavera Baby 2015: 25). Although the Ayotzinapa gained substantial attention, there are accounts of other cases of disappearance in Mexico (Human Rights Watch 2013: 3). According to Human Rights Watch, there were 149 cases of disappearances where evidence pointed to the participation of state officials also following the 'war on drugs', initiated by President Felipe Calderón, from December 2006 to December 2012. In 2015, the Chicago Police Department in the United States disappeared or detained by forcing 7,000 people in off-the-book interrogations carried out in a warehouse in Chicago. Individuals, in general males from black communities, were kept there without the right to phone calls or a lawyer. Such practices were in place from 2004 to 2015 (*The Guardian* 2015).

When associated with the 'war on drugs' and all the exceptionalities attached to the narrative of war, as will be discussed in greater detail in the following chapter, disappearances can be a consequence of extrajudicial executions. In the example of the Philippines, after winning its election in 2016, the country's president, Rodrigo Duterte, urged citizens to kill suspected criminals and drug addicts (*The Guardian* 2016). Following an investigation, Amnesty International published a report (2017) detailing how the police have systematically targeted mostly poor and defenceless people across the country while planting evidence, recruiting death squads, and multiplying the number of victims of enforced disappearances. In contrast to Chicago's case where disappearance was connected to illegal arrest and detention, in the Philippines case, disappearances were carried out by death squads. In those cases, disappearances tend to occur as a result of killings that make identification of the body impossible or by dumping the body in remote places difficult to locate.

These two examples are important given that a closer look at illegal arrests and extrajudicial executions helps us to identify new forms of disappearance that differs from the pattern of kidnap-torture-disappearance that was common during the dictatorship, or how it was theorised by Gatti (2014) as *detained-disappeared*. In this new contemporary form, disappearances are not associated with a political regime acting against its opponents and the armed forces are not usually the main perpetrator. The contemporary form of disappearance legitimises the irrelevance of one's life by associating the act with criminality, duly supported by the 'war on drugs' and is usually marked by *killing-abandonment* (of the body). The differences between forms of disappearance, both from each other and from 'political ones', provide a map where the embodiment of sovereignty is articulated in a specific way. The challenge resides in the type of lenses we use to look at this phenomenon. Once it becomes visible, it raises a new sort of provocation.

This section has discussed 'political' disappearances in the context of military dictatorships in Latin America and how they became closely associated with this regime and with the fight against communism in the region. I have also discussed how the phenomenon created a legal framework during the dictatorships. I have addressed how disappearance travelled as a concept to put pressure on the Spanish government for the persecution of perpetrators during Franco's dictatorship. The three examples presented aimed at showing how disappearances have gained different contours in the contemporary context. The Ayotzinapa case in Mexico, the illegal arrests in the United States, and the Philippines' 'war on drugs' are but a few examples of how disappearances are shifting shape.

Disappearances: an elusive practice

A disappearance brings a lot of uncertainty, and the ways of referring to it are similarly imprecise. In the Portuguese language, for example, *disappearance* has the same denotation as *missing* in the English language. In the Cambridge Dictionary, *missing* stands for 'someone who has disappeared and is no longer in communication with family and friends'. To Jenny Edkins (2011), there is always a tension when someone goes missing. From a biopolitical governance perspective, a missing person is just an impersonal absence. The absence is acknowledged, but it has no deep implication. On the other hand, for a family that lives in anxious waiting, *missing* stands for an irreplaceable person (Ibid.: 12–13). The way that this book refers to the disappeared, as well as to disappearance, is informed by the possibilities and nuances of the term in the English grammar mainly because that is the language used for writing the book.

In Brazil and Portuguese grammar, however, there is no clear distinction, as in English, between *missing person* and *disappearance*. Both phenomena are called *desaparecido*. Because it is not always clear if someone went missing or was (enforced) disappeared, I will use *disappear* interchangeably. It is also important to highlight that in Brazil, there is no specific legislation for enforced disappearances, making the term meaningless regarding accountability. In the case of disappearances in Brazil, the word is attached to two meanings. The first one is 'the political', as it became part of the political claim associated with the military regime. The other one, however, is more subtle. The way political disappearances have been addressed in the country is often associated with the idea of death. This idea is ubiquitous and repeated by different actors. This is clear in Law 9,140 from 1995, which spawned the Special Commission for the Dead and Political Disappeared in the same year; in reactions by victims' relatives who engage in activism; in the way that newspapers deal with dictatorship victims, which was brought back into the limelight during the National Truth Commission work; and also in the very *raison d'être* of the Truth Commission. All those different actors have listed the names of the dead and political disappeared together without, for example, making a distinction of how many were still disappeared and how many were found dead.

I will mark the difference only when, for example, the actors involved classed the person as missing, implying that the person left by their free will, or when referring to cases where there is evidence that the disappearance happened with the participation of police officers. In the latter case, I will then refer to enforced disappearances – as agreed by different international organisations, such as the United Nations, the Organisation of American States, and the Inter-American Human Rights Commission, of which Brazil is a signatory. At the international level, the United Nations Declaration on the Protection of All Persons from Enforced Disappearance (1992), the Inter-American Convention on Forced Disappearance of Persons (1994), and the International Convention for the Protection of All Persons from Enforced Disappearance (2006). The Organisation of American States has pushed for a commitment from all the signatory countries to prosecute and punish those responsible for the violations that took place under the military dictatorships.

The Declaration of the Protection of all Persons from Enforced Disappearance adopted by the UN General Assembly is quite similar to the Inter-American Convention on Enforced Disappearance of Persons, except that the Inter-American declaration includes normative enforcement, as it is possible to see in their description.

> Forced disappearance is considered to be the act of depriving a person or persons of his or their freedom, in whatever way, perpetrated by agents of the state or by persons or groups of persons acting with the authorization, support, or acquiescence of the state, followed by an absence of information or a refusal to acknowledge that deprivation of freedom or

to give information on the whereabouts of that person, thereby impeding his or her recourse to the applicable legal remedies and procedural guarantees.

(Article II OAS 1994)

Brazil signed the Rome Statute[6] in 2002 and the Inter-American Convention in 1994 but ratified it only in 2013. About the Inter-American Convention on Forced Disappearances of Persons, the Inter-American Commission advised Brazil, in 2010, to put in place the necessary measures to ratify the convention. Although the document was submitted to the National Congress and approved in 2011, as of this writing, it had not yet been enrolled.

The bill (PL 6240/13) was passed by the Senate and, in December 2013, it was approved by the Human Rights Commission at the Lower House or Chamber of Deputies with a few changes to the original text. The bill defines enforced disappearances as 'any act of arrest, detention, kidnap, or any other way to constrain someone's freedom, be it by state officials or by any other state institution, armed or paramilitary groups' (PL 6240/13).

The debate, which emerged from the process of implementing the legislation on enforced disappearances at the national level, is pervaded by the notion that enforced disappearances are a practice that happened in Brazil during the civil-military dictatorship (1964–1985), as implied in the interview with the lawyer Luiz Flavio Gomes given to the Chambers of Deputies' Press. According to the interviewee 'This bill fills a gap in the Brazilian legislation, although, in practice, enforced disappearances were carried out more frequently during the military regime. Besides, Brazil is following a recommendation from the international Human Rights entities'.[7]

Some researchers in Brazil have used the term 'civil-disappeared' (Oliveira 2007; Freire 2013), thus making a distinction between the cases that happened during the dictatorship, known as the 'political-disappeared', and cases that happened after it ended. I reject this distinction because it reifies the boundaries that contribute to a misinterpretation of the phenomenon nowadays. The use of 'civil-disappearances' reinforces the idea, largely disseminated by the police (Ferreira 2015: 16), that although disappearances may be potentially the result of homicide, it is most likely to be the outcome of a family drama, which is then related to the private sphere or an extraordinary event.

To discuss disappearances in contemporary Brazil, meaning after the dictatorship which took over the country from 1964 to 1985, the present book aims to address cases that happened in the 30-year period that followed it, namely from 1985 to 2015. As mentioned earlier, Amarildo's disappearance haunted Brazilian society by reminding it of the violence inflicted by the military regime during the dictatorship. One reason may be the way it happened – kidnapping, torture, and disappearance. The level of consternation caused by an event that demonstrates the excessive use of force by the police when dealing with the riots in the country, and which is normally associated with authoritarian regimes, revealed a brutal face of the state. The desire by part of the population to put an end to the militarised police forces, perceived as a residual feature from the dictatorial past, is not new. Nonetheless, to consider the dictatorship as a starting point and to deem it the only regime in which disappearances occur needs to be reconsidered if we are to examine contemporary cases.

Certainly, the limitation regarding vocabulary has practical implications. When not by free will, disappearances are classed as murder followed by the concealment of death, largely associated with drug cartels. Revenge carried out by drug dealers gained notoriety when Tim Lopes, an investigative journalist for *Rede Globo*, was reported missing while working as an undercover reporter. Drug dealers from Vila Cruzeiro, who identified him as a reporter, kidnapped and judged him in a mock trial, before torturing him and burning his body inside some rubber tyres. This manner of enacting a parallel legal system that includes a mock judgement of the offender followed by death penalty was known for being carried out by drug dealers who terrified favela inhabitants and rival drug cartels. In Amarildo's case, the initial chief of police in charge of the case accused Amarildo and his wife of cooperating with drug dealers. According to Elisabete, Amarildo's wife, the chief of police was convinced that Amarildo was killed by drug dealers and was about to close the case after one week of investigation (Carta Capital 2014). The consequences of detaching disappearances from the dictatorship context, in theoretical and practical terms, will be discussed in the following sections.

It would not have been possible to discuss disappearance in Latin America without referring to the military dictatorship because of the way the regime impacted how disappearances came to be interpreted. As an example, the dictatorship memory created proximity between death and disappearances. In contemporary cases, however, I am arguing that there is a new twist in its understanding, whereby disappearances have been classed as a 'massacre' or 'slaughter' by the media. It is possible to find many occasions where cases of disappearances were described in the media as a massacre, as for example, in the Acari Massacre, in 1990, when 11 people disappeared (Araujo 2014; Oliveira 2014; Misse 2018). Another example is known as the May Crimes, in 2006, when 505 people were killed, and four people went missing (IHRC 2011; Araujo 2014; Comparato 2014; Guerra 2016). Although the details of each case will be discussed later in this book, for now, it is important to highlight that one way to render contemporary cases of disappearances invisible is to call them by another name.

Between the 'wrong' victim and the 'wrong' perpetrator

The 'wrong' victim

As mentioned in the introduction of this chapter, the framework where disappearances are constituted is the one associated with military dictatorships in Latin America. This perspective was reinforced by the NTC as well as by the other local truth commissions that have applied the same framework to analyse cases of enforced disappearance. A case that has been rendered invisible through the collective memory of the country is the enforced disappearance of indigenous communities, peasants, and favela dwellers. Their struggles were only partially brought back into discussion following the work of the truth commissions[8] in the country. According to these commissions, at least 8,350 members of indigenous communities and 10,000 rural workers went missing. Still, they were not included in the final account of 434 victims of killing and *political* disappearances. As mentioned elsewhere, the term 'political' here has gained a very narrow connotation, according to which it means to be involved in the struggle for democracy or being a member of a communist party. The first political recognition regarding the victims of the regime happened only in 1995 with the Law for the Disappeared, the outcome of a long struggle that started in 1979. Mezarobba (2007) highlights that in that same year, the Lower House deputy Octacilio Queiroga proposed an amendment to the law whereby the family of the disappeared would receive a monthly pension.

Other law amendments were proposed as well as the investigation of disappearances by the Federal Police, without success. Mezarobba (2007) highlights that during the entire military regime, the families focused on having access to the truth regarding the fate of their loved ones. They wanted to find out what happened to them, the circumstances of their disappearances, and who the perpetrators were. Differently from those who went into exile and were able to later return to their country, or those who were arrested for political reasons and were later discharged, much less was known regarding those who disappeared.

The Amnesty Law (1979) does not mention cases of disappearance, only including information on how families may be able to order a 'declaration of absence to those who, involved in political activities and disappeared from the family realm for more than one year without any note to the family' (Amnesty Law, 6.683/1979). This document stands for a presumed death that allows for marriage dissolutions and inheritance arrangements. It is important to note that despite the existence of the Amnesty Law, the military regime did not admit that those who disappeared had been the subject of the repression apparatus, nor had those tortures occurred. In the few occasions when the Army Forces talked about them, they focused on disseminating the story that those who disappeared were hiding in unknown places or living in another country. For that reason, in many cases, the families opted for not requiring this declaration (Mezarobba 2007: 38). Only in 1987 did the Brazilian state recognise its responsibility for the imprisonment and death of Mario Alves.[9]

The first time the Army Forces assumed their responsibility for enforced disappearance happened during the 1990s. In 1991, the External Commission to Find Political Disappearances was created. The commission, composed of 15 deputies, aimed at finding the fate of the political disappeared. Commission members could not oblige anyone to testify, but they were able to listen to the families and search for information by contacting the Brazilian President and the armed forces. The Navy Forces sent to the commission a report communicating the death of 43 people during the Araguaia Guerrilla.[10] It was the first time that the Navy recognised not only the death of those people but also, and significantly, the guerrilla itself.

In 1994, the Commission of Dead and Political Disappeared and the organisation Torture Never Again demanded the official recognition of 144 resistance members. They decided to write a Commitment Agreement to give to all candidates during presidential elections. The letter called for an agreement between all candidates to 'formally recognise the responsibility of the Brazilian state in the detention, torture, death and disappearance of political opponents, and the immediate creation of a special commission of investigation and restitution at the federal level' (my translation, Mezarobba 2007: 48). In May 1995, the Ministry of Justice finally announced that the Brazilian state had decided to recognise the deaths of the political disappeared and was committed to pay compensation to the families. However, the Brazilian state did not investigate the circumstances of the disappearances. The National Truth Commission, established more recently (2012–2014), was able to investigate the disappearances but was denied the power to enforce punishment of the perpetrators through legal processes.

The concept of enforced disappearance adopted by the National Truth Commission in Brazil follows the parameters from international law in Human Rights. The definition adopted by the NTC in Brazil is as follows:

> This violation occurs from deprivation of freedom (even when legally applied and outside official establishment) perpetrated by state agents – or other people with their authorization, support or acquiescence – followed by the refuse in inform the imprisoned destiny preventing the exercise of juridical guarantees.
>
> (National Truth Commission 2014)

The report also highlighted that enforced disappearance involves the transgression of many rights, including the rights of freedom, of life, and of personal integrity, as well as the violation of other human rights, such as kidnapping, torture, homicide, and concealment of bodies.

To deal with the issue of classification of enforced disappearances, the NTC decided to include only cases where the detention was recognised but no other information was provided in the follow-up, as well as cases when there was recognition regarding someone's death but the remains were never found. The NTC Report pointed out that between 1964 and 1985, 243 people in Brazil were 'political disappeared'. The number represents more than half of a total of 434 fatal victims of the regime. However, the NTC adopted a third category of cause of murder during the Brazilian dictatorship, namely the enforced disappearance; but concluded that only 33 people were victims of enforced disappearances (National Truth Commission 2014)

The silence from the part of the state was not only related to the practice of torture, killing, and enforced disappearance. The NTC report included a clarification regarding the classification of victims of enforced disappearances. It states that the historical-social context to which the victim belonged was taken into consideration, as well as the modus operandi applied by state officials to establish the criteria determining who was regarded as a victim of the dictatorship (National Truth Commission 2014: 295). This clarification gave grounds to exclude indigenous communities, peasants, and favela dwellers in the figures of political disappearances. In the case of indigenous communities, it was alleged that they did not acknowledge that a dictatorship was in progress and that because they were living in tribes and reservations, they were not aware of the existence of a nation-state (interviewee number NTC01, 2016). In the case of rural workers, the commission claimed that they were not included in the national figures of deaths and political disappearances because they were victims of private police forces or militias (National Truth Commission 2014). It is important to note that the report (2014: 329) pointed to militia groups and death squads acting with acquiescence and support from the Brazilian armed forces.

The category of enforced disappearance is not recognised as a widespread practice, being restricted to the dictatorship. By adopting the third category of *enforced disappearance*, the NTC followed the dominant narrative and kept the category of *political disappearances* as an exclusive classification, thereby silencing once again victims of enforced disappearance. Following that reasoning, one can conclude that a particular understanding of political – being affiliated to a guerrilla organisation, being a communist, or being involved in the struggle for a different political regime in the country – overrode international conventions in the decisions made by truth commission members on how to proceed with the classification of the victims of the regime.

According to the Working Group on Enforced or Involuntary Disappearances of the United Nations (UNWGEID), it is also important to highlight some elements that characterise enforced disappearances. They are the deprivation of liberty against individual will; the involvement of government officials, even if by acquiescence; the refusal to acknowledge the deprivation of liberty; and concealment of the fate or whereabouts of the disappeared. This definition is broadly used by other international organisations, such as the Organisation of American States and the Inter-American Court of Human Rights.

Regarding the experiences by favela dwellers during the dictatorship, the Truth Commission Working Group of Rio de Janeiro (*Comissão Estadual da Verdade do Rio de Janeiro*) and São Paulo (*Comissão da Verdade do Estado de São Paulo 'Rubens Paiva'*) did consider forced displacement. In Rio de Janeiro, people were forced out from their homes following the urban reforms by Governor Carlos Lacerda, who wanted Rio de Janeiro to stand as an example of the modern city after it lost its position as the Brazilian capital. The Working Group of Rio de Janeiro also highlighted the incursion of military forces in favelas, which, despite not being a new practice, was justified by the need to exercise surveillance over a population that was considered both dangerous and easy prey for recruitment by communist groups. The chapter on racism and dictatorship in the Truth Commission Report in Rio de Janeiro (2015) challenges the supposedly neutral narratives of political resistance during the dictatorship, which usually describes the movement as being organised by the educated elite (2015: 125). Although the Truth Commission Team of Rio de Janeiro addressed cases of forced displacement, military incursions, and slaughter, it did not include favela dwellers who were not engaged in political activities. Nor was that their aim. Consequently, the extent of other experiences by favela dwellers outside the dictatorship context was rendered invisible, making it difficult to trace, for example, cases of enforced disappearances.

Here I want to highlight that the narrative of the dictatorship in the country, recognised as the moment of exception, has marginalised other groups and struggles to create new exceptions. The 'wrong' victims here are those who, despite being recognised by the Truth Commission as victims of the military dictatorship, were not incorporated into the final number encompassing killings and political disappearances. Those exceptions have also been approached by Caroline Silveira Bauer (2017). Bauer argued that although the effort of truth commissions was important in bringing to the fore aspects of the military regime, such as economic support and cooperation by private companies, and the participation of civil elites in its structure, the NTC still focused on the dynamics played between militaries and guerrilla members. According to this author, such a narrative reified the silence around other social sectors during the period. What the NTC did not do was to bring to the fore those who were not part of the political struggle.

The 'wrong' perpetrator

An important difficulty in researching contemporary cases of disappearances is to identify who is the perpetrator, or if the perpetrator would be the 'right' one to make a case of enforced disappearance. It is important regarding accountability and the promotion of justice, but it is also crucial to determine whether the disappearance in question is *enforced* – perpetrated by state officials or by another actor. In the case of Brazil, drug dealers and militias are usually blamed for such acts. As will be discussed in more detail in Chapter 3 on the police apparatus, acts by militias and drug dealers cannot be categorised as such.

To start with, many militia members are in fact members of the military police force, fire officers, or armed forces, who may be retired, but not necessarily. Although they are not acting in the name of the state, as some of my interviewees pointed out, they have received training and weapons from the state. There have been cases in Rio de Janeiro, analysed by Alves Araujo (2014), where the police, drug dealers, and members of militias exchange 'prisoners' who are never seen again. This messy context further complicates the recognition of a crime as 'enforced disappearances', although the participation of a state official should be enough in accordance with the legal framework available, as discussed earlier in this chapter.

The messiness comes from a context of urban violence perpetrated by different actors, such as militias, police officers, and death squads. Messiness, as elaborated by Aradau (2017), is caused when multiple rationalities cannot be aggregated into a single coexisting reality. Multiple realities can be partially connected, but they lack the significance normally gained through a single narrative.

Regarding temporality, messiness emerges when time becomes 'tidal' rather than 'linear' – i.e. situations in which things come and go and then go or come again, instead of moving on. What seems momentary – as in the case of a state of affairs – may not be there at the next moment but could return at another moment (2017: 131). Aradau (2017: 131) highlights that messiness is not the same as ambiguity. Instead, messiness comprises situations in which multiple rationales coexist, not as order and disorder, nor as domination and resistance, but as diffused realities and moments that are connected but remain dispersed.

Acts of alliance between the police and drug dealers contribute to stability in the management of crime and accountability in peripheral areas of the city. In the example of Rio de Janeiro, the perpetrators of disappearances are observed by Fabio Alves Araujo (2014). He describes cases when someone is under arrest, but instead of being directed to a police station, the person is taken to local drug dealers (2014: 118). Graham Denyer Willis (2015) described a similar scenario in São Paulo. According to him, it was possible to establish links between forms of violence and consensual governance among the police officials and organised crime groups, making violence more stable. Acts of a partnership between the police and drug dealers can also hinder accountability, and the way data is produced. In the following section, I explore a few links between the police and the militias.

This messiness is also reflected in the way Brazilian society has addressed the issue over the years. Five years before Amarildo's case, in 2008, a protest organised by the NGO Rio da Paz placed dozens of car tyres on the sand of Copacabana Beach. The intervention was called 'Micro-wave Demonstration'. Dolls were put inside each tyre to depict a practice used by militias and drug dealers to murder their enemies using carbonisation. Posters were displayed with the words 'Nine thousand people have disappeared in the last two years. It is suspected that 6,300 of them were murdered' (Jornal do Brasil 2008; Ferreira 2015). After Amarildo's disappearance, another demonstration was organised by the same NGO, again on Copacabana Beach. At that time, however, the protesters suggested that many of the disappeared were, in fact, victims of police violence (Ferreira 2015).

Araujo (2014) defined enforced disappearance as a governmental *dispositif* that mirrors the action of police officers, militia, and drug dealers. According to Zaluar and Conceição (2007), paramilitary groups or militias follow the same reasoning of death squads and 'corrupted police' or *policia mineira*, which emerged in Rio in the 1960s, 1970s, and 1980s at Baixada Fluminense – an area to the west of the city and a fair distance from the wealthy southern area (Zaluar and Conceição 2007; Cano 2008; Cano and Duarte 2012). In the early 1990s, there was a change with regard to the way the *policia mineira* controlled their territories after disputes over territories and waves of violence that left many bodies in the streets (Zaluar and Conceição 2007). The new group that took control adopted a less aggressive and arbitrary posture with a decrease in murder figures. An analysis of the data from The Public Security Institute of Rio de Janeiro (ISP-RJ) shows that figures on missing persons have been increasing since the 1990s. While in 1991 there were 2,616 cases, in 2003 those figures went up to 4,800 (ISP-RJ 2009). A less aggressive approach in combination with an increase in the figures of missing persons reinforces Araujo's (2014) argument.

As discussed so far, contemporary forms of policing represent a relevant aspect of a contentious context characterised by the 'war on drugs' in Brazil. It not only expresses the sovereign's desire/power but also reveals a subtle dynamic between police forces and organised crime groups. In this context, disappearances emerge as a practice that poses a high level of uncertainty in the accounts of its responsibility. However, it is possible to determine who is more likely to disappear and where. As will be explored in the development of the book, many cases of disappearances have been portrayed in the media as 'slaughter'.

Lucia Eilbaum (2017), an Argentinian anthropologist, discusses the 'new' meaning of disappearance. For the author, 'disappearance' is related to a particular context that belongs to a specific political and social tradition, intimately related to human rights movements; to evoke 'disappearance' is a political act referring immediately to crimes committed by the military junta (1976–1983). Elibaum also describes her encounter with a new series of meanings connected to disappearances in Rio. There, disappearances refer 'to "vanished" bodies in carioca favelas, either as a result of police action or as a result of drug cartels' (2017: 551).

This section has discussed the challenges resulting from the use of a narrow category of political disappearances in Brazil. It has led, I argue, to the invisibility of other victims of the same phenomenon, because they were out of the context of the leftist guerrilla. By crystallising the right victim and the right perpetrator as well as the right historical and political context, contemporary cases of disappearances are classed as non-political. The absence of national laws, a context of public security characterised by different actors, and the absence of a normative framework also contribute to a scenario in which cases of disappearance do not have visibility. In that sense, it is possible to affirm, echoing Gabriel Gatti at LASA 2018,[11] that the way disappearances became associated with dictatorships in Latin America has led to an absence of theoretical and epistemological tools to deal with the issues raised by cases of enforced disappearances. In the following section, I will discuss how this messiness reflects on the data available in the country regarding police violence preventing the accountability of cases of disappearance.

Messy data for a messy reality

In Brazilian law, there is no classification of enforced disappearance as a crime. As Ferreira (2015) pointed out, disappearances are considered a minor occurrence among others, and it is commonly related to family issues. Araujo (2014) highlighted that the police tend to generalise the cases affirming that the person who disappears did it deliberately because of a family disagreement or because of mental health problems. It is true that in many cases, disappearances occur because of this kind of issues; however, this is not the full picture. A common complaint from families is their mistreatment by the police when they go to register a missing person. As 'gone missing' is not classed as a crime, families are often told by police officers 'no body, no crime', which is perceived as an excuse to avoid investigation and dismiss the case. The same logic was applied during the dictatorship.

Notwithstanding, the government showed concerns about the rise of missing persons even before Amarildo's disappearance. In 2009, an event was organised by the Public Security Institute of Rio de Janeiro (ISP-RJ), a research institute that provides training for public employees from the security sector, including police officials. For the first time, there was a study focusing on the figures for missing persons. The 2009 survey[12] presented the result of a survey from 2007. The research aimed to create a profile of those who went missing and the possible causes of their disappearance. The data analysed showed that 71 per cent of people who disappeared were eventually located. The incidence of missing people was concentrated outside the capital (ISP-RJ 2009a, 2009b) and consisted mainly of males between the ages of 10 and 19, and senior adults who are suffering from mental health issues or addiction to drugs and/or alcohol. These figures were seen as being crucial for comparison purposes. Differently, from missing people, victims of murder are usually between the ages of 20 and 29. Moreover, while in the category of missing people 60 per cent are male, among victims of homicide, 80 per cent are male. This difference was emphasised to contrast the profile of missing people and that of homicide victims.

The survey (ISP-RJ 2009a), however, generated discomfort among those whose research focuses on public security. One of the aims of the survey was to verify if the category of 'missing person' was being used to cover up extrajudicial killings in Rio de Janeiro. Four hundred families were contacted by phone, and the following figures emerged: 71 per cent of those who disappeared were eventually found alive, 15 per cent did not reappear, and 7 per cent were found dead (Carta Capital 2014).[13] The location of 70 per cent of those who went missing was used to conclude that missing persons and victims of murder belonged to different categories. However, according to Ignacio Cano (Carta Capital 2014), senior lecturer and coordinator of the Laboratory of Analyses of Violence (LAV) at the State University of Rio de Janeiro, the study presented some flaws and methodological limitations, such as the use of a small sample and phone interviews. According to him, the absence of further investigation in the survey made a conclusive result impossible.

Leticia Carvalho de Mesquita Ferreira (2015) recounted her first impressions when the research was made public, and the optimism generated by the results. According to her, the idea that it is possible to identify who disappears and their whereabouts brings some comfort, both to know that those who went missing are not vulnerable to specific types of crime and to be reassured that in most cases, people come back home after a while. However, Ferreira also sensed that the research exposed a need for certainty and the avoidance of other scenarios. She has reflected on a few questions, such as 'Which discomfort were those results seeking to attenuate? If there was optimism by publicising it, which would be the pessimistic scenario the data was confronting?' (2015: 22). To answer those questions, Ferreira (2015) conducted ethnographic research on violence, social suffering, and the state bureaucracy embedded in the politics of searching.

Michel Misse, the scientist in charge of the Research Centre for Citizenship, Conflict and Urban Violence – Necvu-UFRJ in its acronym in Portuguese – located at the Federal University of Rio de Janeiro, decided to look at the figures from the ISP-RJ survey more carefully. Misse took into consideration the number of people found dead and observed that among them half could be classed as executions because of the circumstances of their death, such as the type of injury presented. Because there is no investigation when someone is reported missing, these deaths are not accounted for by the police or by the health system. Misse et al. (2013) claimed that if one takes into consideration the 60,000 people who disappeared between 2000 and 2012 only in Rio, this percentage will correspond to around 600 deaths without any records. Contrast this with the total figure of 243, the number of political disappeared during the dictatorship in Brazil, which lasted for 21 years.

Fabio Alves Araujo (2014) also shared some discomfort and stated that only research on the ground could partially solve the problem of researchers interested in public security. He has analyses of narratives told by relatives about the disappearance of their loved ones from a socio-anthropological perspective. From these accounts, Araujo accessed moral and political grammars by which 'disappeared', 'victim', 'relatives', 'violent death', 'favela', 'police/state violence', and 'militia', among others, constitute a range of meanings. Araujo (2014) concluded that the intricate range of meanings informs and reifies the type of vulnerability, which is affected by space, social class, and activity – making some bodies disappear(*able*).

Daniel Cerqueira, a senior researcher at the Institute for Applied Economic Research (Ipea), highlighted that those who are investigating are also the most interested in achieving specific results. For example, the first source of data is the Missing Person's Report, known as *Registro de Ocorrencia*, and the first step in the police inquiry. It is the *register* crucial to get raw data identifying the profile of victims and perpetrators, the type of crime, and whether or not an investigation or criminal cases were followed up. One of the strategies by the public security bodies is to pay a cash bonus to police units with decreasing rates of unsolved crimes. Daniel Cerqueira points out that the payment of this bonus is potentially problematic because those who receive it are also the people who produce the data (Carta Capital 2014).

The research conducted by Misse et al. (2013) observed an issue regarding the age declared in the Missing Person's Report. They concluded that police officers are not recording data properly regarding the age of those who were killed because of 'resistance killings'. The research points out that there is a higher occurrence of 'no information regarding age' in the general registers from 2004 to 2005, as well as a lower occurrence of minors. When compared to the information available in the following years, the opposite occurred: a lower occurrence of 'no information regarding age' and a higher number of 'minors', leading to the conclusion of an 'extraordinary increase of victims among children and teenagers' (Misse et al. 2013: 35).

In the following years, when there is a lower frequency 'no information regarding age' it is possible to notice a major increase in underage victims (Misse et al. 2013: 35).

It was only after the book was printed that the ISP/SSP-RJ contacted the research team to inform them that there was a mistake in the figures from 2009, 2010, and 2011. Misse et al. (2013) considered it an odd mistake since in the new chart the 'no information regarding age' kept increasing from 2006 onwards, which means that the new chart presents less information than the previous one. It is important to note that, in the cases of 'resistance killing', the register is filled in by the police officer, which means that the perpetrator is identified, the victim is referred to the morgue, and both profiles become known. Note also that one of the allegations made by the ISP/SSP-RJ related to the profile of missing persons was that the ages in the categories of *homicide* and a *missing person* were different.

Ana Paula Miranda, an anthropologist who oversaw the ISP-RJ until 2008, declared in an interview with the newspaper *O Estado de São Paulo* (2008) that the ISP-RJ is manipulating the data released by not including figures from the 'resistance killings' in the final count of homicides. Furthermore, according to her, there are cases where the cause of death is clearly murder, yet it was being registered under 'dead body'. The misclassification of data was also endorsed by research published in 2012 by Daniel Cerqueira from Ipea '*Mortes Violentas Não Esclarecidas e Impunidade no Rio de Janeiro*' (Unexplained Violent Deaths and Impunity in Rio de Janeiro, 2012). Although the number of deaths caused by homicides in the state of Rio de Janeiro declined by 28 per cent between 2006 and 2009, when comparing the figures presented by the police through the ISP-RJ to the figures by the Mortality Informational System (SIM), generated by the Ministry of Health, 'there is evidence that this variation is due to error in data classification' (Cerqueira 2012). Furthermore, the research results were twofold. 'First, the number of fatal violent incidents with an unknown cause in Rio de Janeiro has inexplicably increased since 2007, a fact that completely clashes with the national standard' (2012: 5). Secondly, it was estimated that the number of homicides in Rio de Janeiro from 2006 to 2009 remained relatively stable, but the number of 'hidden homicides' – meaning deaths classed as the undetermined cause – increased sharply during this period. 'It is estimated that 3,165 homicides went unrecorded in 2009, which represents 62.5% of the registered homicides' (Cerqueira 2012: 6). According to Cerqueira (Carta Capital 2017), from 2007, under Sergio Cabral's term in office, there were difficulties in matching the information from the police with that from the Health System, leading to many of the violent deaths being classed under 'death by undetermined cause'.

By observing the variation in the numbers of missing persons following changes in the state government of Rio de Janeiro, it is possible to identify different trends. While during Rosinha Garotinho's term in office (2003–2007) there was a fall of 19 per cent, those figures went up during Sergio Cabral's term in office (2007–2014). The latter implemented the UPP's project when disappearances increased by 32 per cent. The analysis of the data related to murder crimes during these two governments shows that the figures dropped by almost the same percentage, 35 per cent in the last one. An analysis of the figures on *autos de resistência* shows an even greater decrease: they fell by 72 per cent from one government to the next (Carta Capital 2014). In Brazil, the governor holds the highest rank in charge of the elaboration of public security policies.

The peak of *autos de resistência* was in 2007; it then decreased in the following years. This trend was also followed by a decrease in homicides. Misse (2011: 8) among others has considered that the decrease may have followed the implementation of some of the Pacification Units, which in turn led to the weakening of drug cartels and less confrontation with the police. It is worth noting that the confrontation policy that characterised the public security strategy started to be substituted by the occupation of favelas with permanent UPPs. The implementation of UPPs in 2011 also included a programme to reduce criminality including murder and manslaughter, robbery followed by death, grievous bodily harm followed by death, and *autos de resistência*.

The state of São Paulo does not use the classification '*Autos de Resistência*', and the police are considered less lethal in comparison with Rio de Janeiro. Still, research published by a municipal body in São Paulo in 2016 (Gvac in JusBrasil 2014) shows that while homicides are decreasing, the figures for police lethality are increasing. The way police killings are classed in São Paulo is under 'suspicious death'. A series of reports organised by the newspaper *O Estadão* (2015) showed that the number of homicides is higher than the figures presented by the Department of Public Security of São Paulo. In 2015, at least 21 cases were not accounted for in the municipal statistics. Instead of being registered under the category of homicide, those deaths were registered as 'suspicious death', a term that lacks meaning, or as 'body injury followed by death', which also refers to murder but is classed under a different category.

Amarildo's disappearance also raised questions about police brutality whether enforced disappearances were once again being used to cover extrajudicial killings. The report *You Killed My Son: Homicides by Military Police in the City of Rio de Janeiro*, published by Amnesty International (2015), pointed out that police officers in Rio de Janeiro were injuring or shooting people who had already surrendered. According to this report, there have been many flagrant incidents of police violence in Rio de Janeiro over the past few years, often caught on video and disseminated on social media. The Human Rights Watch (HRW) report *'Good Cops Are Afraid': The Toll of Unchecked Police Violence in Rio de Janeiro* follows up previous research conducted in 2009, when the organisation called attention to unlawful police killings being routinely covered up. In the research carried out by the NGO, police officers admitted in interviews that there are officers who threaten witnesses, plant guns or drugs on their victims, remove bodies from crime scenes, or take them to hospitals under the pretext that they are trying to rescue them. Another interviewee described an operation designed to kill suspected gang members as opposed to arresting them (Human Rights Watch 2016).

In another piece of research published by Ipea, '*Mapa dos Homicidios Ocultos no Brasil*' or 'Map of the Hidden Homicides in Brazil' (2013), Daniel Cerqueira analysed data on the deaths classed as 'undetermined cause' in the entire country from 1996 to 2010. Cerqueira pointed out that numbers of homicides in Brazil are 18 per cent higher than the official registers indicate, concluding that every year approximately 8,600 homicides are not acknowledged by the official figures. Also, it was possible to identify seven states with an increase in rates of violent death by 'undetermined cause', namely, Rio de Janeiro, Bahia, Rio Grande do Norte, Pernambuco, Roraima, Minas Gerais, and São Paulo.

Although it is true that life is messy, rather than being a particular feature of disappearances, my argument is twofold. First, disappearances challenge the boundaries between life and death, creating a grey zone that on the one hand makes it difficult to identify the causes of disappearances, which may include an individual free will, accidents, or violence by perpetrators. Secondly, the data generated and made available by the state seems to reflect both uncertainties. The data both mirrors disappearances cases and reflects the lack of more contemporary ways to interpret disappearances.

Disappearances: between life and death

Fundamental to this research and the discussion regarding sovereign power is the possibility of life and death. As discussed in the introduction, differently from disappearances carried out during the dictatorship, those in contemporary Brazil have not been politicised. Another fundamental difference is that while in the past the armed forces were part of the strategy to obtain information from guerrilla members, disappearances now involve the participation of police officers, militia members, and drug dealers who want to spread fear, stigmatise, or simply show that the life of a criminal has no value.

While Michel Foucault conceptualised biopolitics as life deeply embedded in power relations, Giorgio Agamben, formulated a critique of the relationship between life and politics when engaging with Foucault's concept of biopolitics. Agamben drew on the Greek differentiation between *zoe* – as the simple fact of living or as an attribute inherent to animals, humans, and gods; and *bios* – which indicates a form or way of living inherent to an individual or a group, enabling political life, the *bios politikos*. Therefore, the entry of *zoe* into *bios* constitutes a fundamental shift in the relationship between politics and life where the simple fact of life is no longer excluded from political calculations and mechanisms but resides at the heart of modern politics (Vaughan-Williams 2009: 97).

To summarise, while Foucault sees biopolitics because of a political and historical transformation that emerged during the seventeenth century to govern populations through the institutionalisation of medicine and security, Agamben sees the production of a biopolitical body as the original activity of sovereign power.

Vaughan-Williams (2009) highlighted the contentious interpretation surrounding bare life and proposed a reading according to which bare life is the 'form of life produced immanently by sovereign power in a zone of indistinction between *zoe* and *bios*' (2009: 103), a view that opposed the one proposed by Edkins and Pin-Fat (2005). In the latter article, Edkins and Pin-Fat followed Foucault's reasoning whereby violence resides outside relations of power. To them, bare life resides precisely where politics and power relations are no longer an option. Departing from the notion of power developed by Foucault, Edkins and Pin-Fat claim that a certain amount of freedom is needed to enable a relation of power. In opposition, bare life, as discussed by Agamben (1995), could be found only as a submissive relation to the sovereign power.

Adding to those conceptualisations on power relations, Edkins and Pin-Fat (2005) elaborated on the relations of violence in Agamben's work to propose a contestation. According to them, Agamben sees sovereign power as something that leads to the administration of bare life – exemplified by, but not confined to, the concentration camp – which cannot be regarded as a power relation in Foucauldian terms but as a relation of violence. Edkins and Pin-Fat show how Agamben's analysis of sovereign power reaches an impasse where there seems to be no way out.

But the role of the subject is not static. In colonial societies, for example, members of the slave patrol were often former enslaved persons themselves. Similarly, contemporary discussions about making the police a more diverse institution do not necessarily lead to a less lethal use of force (Vitale 2017). A more useful way to elaborate on this conversation is through the concept of ambivalence. In Agamben's (1995) conceptualisation of sacred life, he reminded us that ambivalence is not simply a matter of secrecy or impurity. Sacredness is not related to a sense of original divine status – as in a religious sense in which man was created in God's image; or in Latin ancient cultures where those who were offered to the gods were sacred. Instead, homo sacer is the one that can be killed but not sacrificed. This means that this life may lack meaning or political agency, but still, it is a life worth living.

Agamben (1995) introduced those ambivalences to demonstrate that the structure of sovereignty is connected to that of *sacratio* through the conceptual association between sacredness-sovereignty-life. In that sense, the function of sovereignty is to delimit exceptionality, or a zone of indistinction, to create the borders that constitute life as sacred or bare. Agamben proposed an analogy between sovereign exception and sacred life where life is that which can be killed and is politicised precisely because of this potentiality. Life becomes subject to practices of securitisation and exceptionality defined by norms and can be politically (dis)qualified by sovereign decision (Vaughan-Williams 2010: 1078). In this sense, one important role of sovereignty in contemporary politics consists in deliberating about what forms of life qualify as politically relevant.

While Agamben's work focused on the Holocaust, his understanding of life as ambivalent could inform analyses of race-related decisions. Although

Judaism is not considered a race, it is possible to affirm that it was through the idea of a race that anti-Semitic feelings were disseminated. Du Bois, for example, after spending two formative years at the University of Berlin after the Second World War, suggested that an understanding of the 'Jewish problem' afforded him a 'real and complete understanding of the 'n-word problem' (Du Bois, quoted in Anievas, Manchanda, and Shilliam 2014).

When examining the data on disappearances and police killings in urban areas of Brazil, it becomes clear that most victims come from black communities. However, because Brazil proclaims itself as a 'multiracial democracy', the racial aspects of social relations, including institutional violence, are denied. By discussing the disappearances and police killings, this book also engages with a broader issue – the criminalisation of black bodies in societies where colonial socio-economic relations were grounded in the slave trade. If we continue with the discussion generated by Agamben's ideas on life, it is possible to conclude that the way some lives are deemed unworthy results from a decision that remains uncontested. As this book focuses on the action of police officers who sometimes act in collaboration with other groups – militias and drug cartels – it is noteworthy that the police embody sovereign decision over which life matters, and which is disposable. I argue that the decision over life follows a racialised rationale informed by slavery.

Foucault (1992) defined sovereignty as the power to take life and let live. However, sovereignty in the West has become, since the seventeenth century, expressed by what Foucault calls 'biopower', whereby the ancient right to take life and let live is replaced by to make life and let die. Giorgio Agamben (2002) relies on the context of the state of exception, where those who are considered out of the norm are deemed (un)worthy. Taking Hitler's policy towards mostly Jews into account, Agamben flipped the Foucauldian formula to reconsider sovereign power as making life and making die, as he analysed the production of bare life in the camp. He identified a distinction between early-modern forms of spatial occupation – when enslaved life was a form of death-in-life, to late-modern spatial occupations – where disciplinary, biopolitical, and necropolitical types of power are combined (2002: 16). As a result, there is a shift from policing and discipline to an alternative and more tragic form of power based on terror. In that sense, to Mbembe, death can ground a form of politics – necropolitics, which re-structures life around the exposure to death.

As put by Brassett and Vaughan-Williams (2012: 22) the relation of violence between sovereign and individuals is grounded in the exclusive inclusion of bare life within the state. Bare life is included in the exclusion – the state of an exception – because in the last instance the sovereign state can kill, and such an act would not be considered homicide. Another possibility to think about life is through death. However, as death has been considered in western thought as the end of the line, not much concern has been devoted to it. Achille Mbembe has also engaged with Foucault and Agamben to discuss the role of the sovereign power not only to determine who will die, but how one will die. The perspective offered by Mbembe is extremely relevant here because it opens the possibility to think about disappearances and extrajudicial killings not simply as the end of a life that was deemed disposable, but as two ways of dying that marks which lives are disposable. In that sense, some populations become aware of the disposability of their life not while living (a very difficult life), but now when one of them is killed. In that context, the uncertainty of a disappearance only lengthens this moment of awareness and the uncertainty of one's fate.

Mbembe (2003) developed the idea of necropolitics to talk about sovereign power, not as the power that governs life or decides which life is unworthy, but as the political power that exposes some people to death. Having as an example the experience of slavery, apartheid, and Palestine, Mbembe notes that the sovereign decides not only who will die, but also how they will die, and by deciding how some people will die there is also a decision on how they will live until then. He highlighted that instead of looking at a society's capacity for self-creation through institutions, he is interested in how sovereignty instrumentalises human existence and the material destruction of human bodies and populations (2003: 13–14), seeing sovereignty as an expression of the right to kill. Mbembe's ideas resonate with how people living in favelas and peripheries are supposed to die. In that sense, police killings followed by the disappearance of the victims' bodies can be considered the precise moment when those who act in the name of sovereign power draw the lines of exclusion.

Conclusion: expanding the conceptualisation of enforced disappearances

This chapter started by discussing how disappearances became directly associated with the experience of Latin America dictatorships. The term, however, has 'travelled' to Spain, to put pressure on the government to recognise the past wrongdoings and the victims of Franco's regime. I also mentioned more recent examples of disappearances elsewhere, such as in Ayotzinapa (2014), Chicago (2015), and the Philippines (2016), the latter in a very similar context to the 'war on drugs' in Brazil, which will be discussed later in this book. I then discussed how the legal framework concerning enforced disappearances was implemented and incorporated by the National Truth Commission in Brazil as well as by local initiatives. I have argued that the way the term 'enforced disappearances' was interpreted by the NTC in Brazil, which follows a widespread national narrative, has crystallised the concept. Indeed, in opposition to the term 'political disappearances,' the NTC has reinforced the invisibility of those who were placed outside of what is considered the political struggle. This view sustains a narrative about the military dictatorship in the country that narrows down broader dynamics in place when the country was under a dictatorship. It also undermines struggles over land. Struggles over land have played an important part in the development model adopted by the country. This model privileges agribusiness, benefitting big landowners to the detriment of family farmers and land reform. As for the indigenous populations, the development model translates into struggles over natural resources.

The danger of a single narrative about the military regime that focuses on the political struggle over democracy has many consequences. It de-politicises

50   A revealed past and a treacherous present

other struggles in the country – such as the struggle for land and the consequences of a development project based on the exploitation of huge extensions of land by large corporations and makes victims who were part of other tensions invisible, as well as crystallising particular understandings of victims and perpetrators. By focusing on the struggles for democracy, considering similar struggles in neighbouring countries, the military dictatorship in Brazil, controversially called *ditabranda*,[14] is sometimes perceived as a softer version of dictatorship as opposed to the more violent versions elsewhere in Latin America.

The chapter also discussed the difficulties and limits of acknowledging perpetrators in contemporary cases of disappearances (and killings), in the messy context of public security after re-democratisation. This challenge is reflected in the last section of this chapter where I discuss and interpret the data on police (and state) violence. It is also important to highlight that denying the existence of enforced disappearances in a highly violent context, including the 'war on drugs', is a way of undermining the subjective experiences by the families and communities from where the person was taken. This chapter does not attempt to reconfigure a methodological or epistemological tool to analyse enforced disappearances in Brazil, or elsewhere. Instead, it problematises the existing framework adopted and its interpretation by the Truth Commission in Brazil. It also problematises the qualitative analyses of episodes of state violence, challenging the general assumption that violence is organised rather than messy.

The following chapter outlines the theoretical framework developed to account for cases of disappearances. Although the focus is on contemporary cases during the re-democratisation period in Brazil (1985–2015), it is important to note that the decision over the value of human life follows a colonial rationale. Following that reasoning, the politics of killing and the fixed boundaries of the term 'disappearance' are expressions of sovereign decisions, legitimised through discourses of exception.

Notes

1 Created in 1979 by the military regime, the Amnesty Law marked the transition to democracy in Brazil. The law allowed exiled activists to return to the country, but it has also shielded human rights perpetrators from prosecution. In 2010, the Inter-American Court of Human Rights declared Brazil's amnesty law illegal because of the provisions that prevented the investigation and punishment of serious human rights violations and demanded that the nation should act upon those past violations.
2 Argentina has officially recognised 8,368 people as victims of disappearance, murder, or kidnapping during the military regime. This figure is disputed by social movements, who claim the total number of victims is 30,000. Apart from Chile, where 4,299 people were recognised as victims of the regime, the Brazilian official numbers, 434, are close to other countries in Latin America which also went through authoritarian regimes, such as 425 in Paraguay, 350 in Bolivia, or 300 in Uruguay (Folha, de São Paulo 2016a), although the Brazilian population is at least ten times bigger then these other countries.
3 The *Archivos del Terror* (Archives of Terror) were found in 1992 by Martin Almada, a lawyer, and Jose Augustin Fernandez, a judge, in a police station in

A revealed past and a treacherous present 51

Paraguay. They were looking for files on a former prisoner when they found the archives describing the fate of thousands of Latin Americans. The discovery of the archives helped to expose the vast operation run by the security service of Argentina, Chile, Uruguay, Paraguay, Bolivia, and Brazil who had secretly kidnapped, tortured, and killed hundreds of people with CIA cooperation (available in English at http://www.unesco.org/new/es/communication-and-information/memory-of-the-world/register/full-list-of-registered-heritage/registered-heritage-page-1/archives-of-terror/, accessed on 20/02/2015).

4 Available in English at the website: http://daccess-dds-ny.un.org/doc/UNDOC/GEN/G14/176/73/PDF/G1417673.pdf?OpenElement accessed on 07/10/2015.
5 In the Report of the Working Group on Enforced or Involuntary Disappearances (2017) stated that from 19 May 2016 to 17 May 2017, the Working Group reported 1,094 new cases of enforced disappearances in 36 states of which 260 were considered urgent (2017: 4).
6 Available in English at the website: http://legal.un.org/icc/statute/romefra.htm (accessed on 07/10/2015).
7 Interview available in Portuguese at the website: http://www2.camara.leg.br/camaranoticias/radio/materias/RADIOAGENCIA/460126-CONGRESSO-PODERA-TIPIFICAR-E-TORNAR-HEDIONDO-CRIME-DE-DESAPARECIMENTO-FORCADO.html (accessed on 07/10/2015).
8 The NTC published a thematic volume (2015) dedicated to groups particularly affected by the dictatorship: members of the military forces who did not agree with the regime or refused to engage in torture, urban workers, peasants, indigenous communities, and homosexuals, among others. As a result of their work, those groups were for the first time also acknowledged as victims of the dictatorship.
9 Mario Alves de Sousa Vieira was a politician and one of the founding members of the Brazilian Communist Party in the early 1970s. He was very active in the party, having worked there in different capacities. He was also a specialist in Marxism, having travelled to the Soviet Union in 1953 to take part in a course on Marxism-Leninism. Mario Alves disappeared in 1970 after leaving his house in Rio de Janeiro and was taken to DOI-CODI, where he was brutally tortured and murdered.
10 The Araguaia guerrilla was an armed movement in Brazil (1967–1974) against the military dictatorship (1964–1985), which was based in an area adjacent to the Araguaia River. The militants of the Communist Party (PC do B) aimed to establish a rural stronghold informed by the experiences of the 26th of July Movement during the Cuban Revolution, and by the Communist Party of China during the Chinese Civil War.
11 XXXVI International Conference for Latin America Studies Association, Barcelona, Spain 2018.
12 In 2011, the same institute conducted new research based on the cases that occurred in 2010 and verified some common features in comparison with the data analysed the year before. One commonality was the victims' profiles between 2007 and 2010. However, the last study showed an increase of 832 missing people whose fate remains unknown.
13 There was no information about the remaining 8 per cent.
14 The newspaper 'Folha de São Paulo' published an opinion article at its editorial in 2009, naming the dictatorial regime in Brazil from 1964 to 1985 as *ditabranda*, meaning a soft version of dictatorship characterised only by institutional disruption, while access to Justice and political dispute were maintained (*Folha de São Paulo*, 17/02/2009, 'Limites a Chavez').

2 Between nation-building and modernity

Introduction

In the discipline of international relations, questions about sovereignty and power have shifted focus. The relation between sovereign power and subjects has invited inquiries following critical, post-structural readings of state sovereignty not only regarding biopolitics (Edkins, Pin-Fat, and Shapiro 2004; Edkins and Pin-Fat 2005; Zevnik 2009; Walker 2010) but also regarding geopolitics (Bigo and Guild 2005; Bigo 2006; Vaughan-Williams 2009; Minca 2015). Drawing on Agamben's work, Edkins, Pin-Fat, and Shapiro investigated persistent relations and expressions of power and how they operate (2004, 4) when discussing the relation between sovereign power and life. The authors focused on sovereign lives and how they contest sovereign power. They argued that sovereign power could extend the limits of politics to establish relations of violence. As a result, life follows the rule of a technologised administration. Andreja Zevnik (2009) engaged in the debate exploring the forms of life that thrive in the current mode of sovereign power.

Achille Mbembe (2003), also drawing from Agamben's work, has built up a critique to discuss the exercise of sovereignty as the control over mortality. He uses the example of late modern colonial occupations, such as Palestine and the apartheid regime in South Africa. Mbembe (2003: 12) discussed modernity as the origin of multiple concepts of sovereignty (and biopolitics), linking the mechanisms of biopower to the function of racism as a means to regulate the distribution of death. According to Mbembe, the most extreme example of state sovereignty is when power is exercised by managing, protecting, and cultivating life while preserving its right to kill (2003: 17). When discussing the territorial aspect of sovereign power, Mbembe considered the global project of colonisation where a distinction was made between parts of the globe available for colonial appropriation in opposition to the parts considered part of Empires, such as Europe – where sovereign power operated in a different manner (2003: 23).

With regard to studies of sovereign power in contemporary urban contexts, the problematisation of violence towards favela dwellers speaks to the aforementioned body of work by linking sovereignty to forms of life, and by exploring how sovereign power operates in different spaces. State violence against

DOI: 10.4324/9781003032519-3

these populations is somehow naturalised by the assumption that black communities are more likely to be subjected to shoot-to-kill police operations, as they live in favelas and peripheries where drug activities are rampant. These assumptions tend to forget that black communities ended up living in favelas and peripheries due to decades of lack of housing policies in Brazil's urban development, or the abandonment of these populations after the abolishment of slavery. The criminalisation based on racialised and specialised bias also usually make it difficult to favela dwellers to access the formal labour market.

Theoretical accounts such as Marxism would explain black communities as the mostly probable target of police violence in favelas by the precarity of the 'working class', making race completely absent in the analyses. Such analysis obscures differential impact on racialised populations in terms of both security and neoliberalism. More than that, it obscures how security is also tied up to economic aspects of the state rationale. The present section addresses how state and economy are intertwined in necropolitical terms. Most of the literature in IR and especially in critical security studies currently based on Foucaultian accounts keep the state at the centre of its analysis, never the market. At the same time, neo-Marxist accounts such as the critique of David Harvey (2007, 2015) often presents social struggles along axes such as race, or gender as a major hindrance to successful leftists' class struggle against neoliberal hegemony. Those theoretical boundaries create a faulty understanding of violence and neoliberalism that prevents analysis on the state and market rationale at once, shedding more light in its differences than in their commonalities, or interconnections.

The assumption that either the state or the market appeared first also prevents us from centring what I argue is an important element that transformed the world to the way it is, and that made possible both the state and the market as we know to (co-)exist. I argue that looking at colonialism to both the emergence of the modern state and capitalism can help us in this analysis. I suggest that the concept of racial capitalism helps to theoretically ground and connect the histories of slavery and colonialism with contemporary forms of violence towards racialised populations in Brazil. I also argue that among many different forms of violence, police killings, and disappearances present a particular form of violence and necropolitics that places the lives of racialised communities in Brazil as 'excess', a saturated form of life that can be dispensed in a superpopulated and therefore, with a high availability of bodies and labour force to the neoliberal market.

This chapter examines two different processes regarding police killings and disappearances in Brazil. One of these processes is the contemporary struggle of the 'war on drugs' and the discourse of exception attached to it. Since the 1990s, the rationale of war, and the exceptionality that it represents, has been used to legitimise the killing of those who are supposedly connected to drug activities. The 'war on drugs' helps to explain how a state apparatus was put in place that marginalises certain types of life through its criminalisation. It is important to note that the 'war on drugs' mostly targets black communities in favelas and peripheries, associating them with the idea of dangerous populations.

Although the war on drugs can explain police operations in favelas and has been used to legitimise the killing of drug dealers, it does not explain why those killings remain unproblematised. I argue that when analysing the criminalisation of black bodies, one must consider the colonial past and its legacy. In that sense, the logic of exceptionality presented by the work of Giorgio Agamben needs to be combined with the logic of coloniality introduced by Walter Mignolo and with the postcolonial critique of Achille Mbembe. By looking at the convergence of exception and colonial reason, it is possible to explore the variables that have resulted in the criminalisation of those who are linked to drug activities and in the annihilation of black bodies.

After exploring coloniality in the process of state formation, this chapter explores Agamben's work about the logic of exceptionality. It discusses the state of exception and bare life in the context of the 'war on drugs' in Brazil. From the perspective of the mainstream literature on security, the 'war on drugs' should not be considered a war. This perspective focuses on related threats and is based on two assumptions, first that threats originate outside the state's borders, and second that these threats are primarily military. I argue, however, that the 'war on drugs' presents many similarities with the 'war on terror' – the American-led global counterterrorism campaign, a subject that has attracted a great deal of attention in IR. To list a few commonalities, both the 'war on drugs' and the 'war on terror' associate racialised subjects with dangerous subjects, legitimising the use of exceptional measures – including gross violations of human rights – in response to an imminent threat. An important specificity of the 'war on drugs' is the use of the police, which in Brazil is a highly militarised force. Although police forces do not usually take part in wars, the 'war on terror' has also witnessed an increasing use of police forces. The importance of the use of the police in both cases will also be discussed.

After discussing the 'war on drugs' and the exceptionalities that therefore arise, I will engage with the theoretical debate on life and death. The specific discussion that the present research engages with is the one regarding aspects of modern sovereign power, to investigate which type of life emerges under sovereign power. This discussion will later address the role of racism in the calculation of biopower and as a condition for the acceptability of death. I bring Achille Mbembe's conceptualisation of sovereign decision when analysing the death of sections of the population, and his perspective on how race (or racism) and spaces are both interrelated in the decision-making process. The discussion moves to the theoretical debate brought by Agamben, now on space and territoriality. The section aims to open the discussion of how contemporary camps reproduce imperial/colonial mapping of the world, which presupposes that some people are incapable or unworthy of citizenship. The last section of this chapter discusses the process of nation-building in Latin American countries marked by the need to leave behind the colonial past and assert itself as a modern country. In this first section, I will introduce the concept of the 'logic of coloniality' developed by Walter Mignolo, which has deeply influenced how the elites in these countries articulate race and class. I finish the section by discussing the implications of such a project.

There are some possible frameworks to discuss contemporary killings and disappearances in Brazil. The chapter relies on Agamben's concepts of state of exception, bare life, and camp to explore the 'logic of exceptionality' that is currently happening in Brazil, which legitimises exceptional measures against imminent threats. The 'war on drugs' is crucial in this discussion because it is constantly mentioned in discussions about police violence in Brazil. However, the 'war on drugs' alone does not explain why police operations target black communities in favelas and peripheries. For that reason, the logic of coloniality is also important as an overlapping rationale when discussing killings and disappearances in Brazil, as well as Mbembe's critique of Agamben's work, which brings the discussion on death and on the right to kill to the debate.

This chapter initiates the discussions that will be further elaborated in the following chapters. Chapter 3 will focus on the police as the state apparatus that represents the immediate response to the 'war on drugs'. The police are a militarised force that focuses on different groups considered 'dangerous'. Chapter 4 will focus on the embodiment of racialised notions by the police as part of the colonial structures in the country even though race is constantly claimed to be invisible as a category. Chapter 5 will analyse how race and space are intertwined and reproduce colonial structures.

Nation-state: a project between coloniality and modernity

Ideas on belonging are important in this discussion if we consider sovereign decisions on who may live and who may die. Although this book does not focus on nation-building, it is important to briefly contextualise how Brazil has articulated the notion of modernity, following what Walter Mignolo has called 'the logic of coloniality' (2000: 11). The logic of coloniality has deeply influenced how the elites in these countries articulated race and class. The last section of this chapter discusses the process of nation-building in Latin American countries marked by the need to leave behind the colonial past to assert itself as part of modernity.

This discussion is related to the rationale that legitimises the killings and disappearances of racialised groups. I argue that while the 'war on drugs' may legitimise killings in favelas and peripheral areas, it cannot explain why its target is mostly racialised groups. As I will develop in the following chapter, the 'war on drugs' and the colonisation process in Brazil have to be considered to address why the killings and disappearances of certain populations remain unproblematised.

Poststructuralist inquiries into the sovereign nation-state tend to follow two main interrelated historical trajectories. One is the process of state formation, and the other is the process of nation-building (Shapiro 2008: 269). Regarding the process of state formation, the emphasis is on the process by which states monopolised violence within a bounded territory. In order to do so, it was necessary to disarm sub-national groups, assert fiscal control over the population, create armies, and institute bureaucracy (Shapiro 2004: 34). 'As a result, states are understood primarily as territorial entities with exclusive, coercively and legally supported sovereignty' (Shapiro 2008: 269). These measures aimed at securing territorial boundaries and governing all aspects of the population.

The process of building a *nation* has also been articulated regarding 'modernity'. Shapiro (1999) relied on Eric Hobsbawm and Terence Ranger's (1992) conceptualisation of 'invention of tradition' to discuss the invention of stories that operate as a basis to forge allegiances. As part of the same debate, Benedict Anderson (1991) claimed that 'imagined communities' were made possible by the modernisation of communications and the spread of literacy. Shapiro argued (1999: 47) that the complex set of forces responsible for assembling 'people' in groupings identified as 'nations' are underpinned by cultural governance. To Shapiro (2008: 270), nations are understood as peoples who belong to a shared cultural community with a historical trajectory concerning/regarding citizen-subjects, and there are many ways to give this sense of a community that shares both a cultural and historical trajectory, thus creating a bond between people and state.

Despite having 'identity' as the main category of analysis, Heather Rae (2002) discusses different cases of state formation, observing that strategies of pathological homogenisation constitute an integral part of the state system. She claimed that in Europe, the process of state formation was religiously motivated, as in the case of Spain expelling Jews and Moors in the late fifteenth century. The narrative that the nation-state as a political project expanded from Europe to Latin America and other parts of the world does not acknowledge how the process, in many cases, was marked by violence. A very important and distinctive feature is that while in Europe,[1] religion was used as a homogenising strategy for the nation-state, in Latin America, colonial domination was based on distinctions of race in which the Church played a fundamental role. At the time of the colonisation in Latin America, the Iberian region, ruled by Catholic monarchs, was expelling other religious groups, such as Jews and Muslims, thus placing religious identity at the centre of the foundation of the colonies that later would also become nation-states. At that moment, Christian representatives in Brazil were protective towards Amerindians. Seen as naïve and without any culture or religion, Amerindians were considered as a *tabula rasa* and were forced to convert to Christianity during the sixteenth and seventeenth centuries (Duviols 1971; MacCormack 2021; Mignolo 2000: 21).

Walter Mignolo (2000: 21), whose conceptualisation follows a systemic[2] point of view, pointed out that with the 'discovery' of Latin America, Christianity became the first global project, articulating westernisation and colonisation, and enforcing the boundaries of colonial difference. According to Mignolo (2000: 29), the 'discovery' of new lands allied to the expulsion of the Moors from the Mediterranean laid the groundwork for the re-articulation of racial imaginary based on the two central ideas of 'purity of blood' and 'rights of the people'. While purity of blood drew on the three religions of the book – Judaism, Christianity, and Islam – the rights of the people emerged from early debates on the humanity of the Amerindians in the Spanish colonies in the Americas. The rights of the people did not involve African slaves.

While the Church had the duty to educate and catechise the Amerindians, who were considered vassals of the king and servants of God, African slaves were part of the Atlantic 'commerce' (Manning 1990, in Mignolo 2000: 30). Thus, slavery was equated with Africanness and Blackness, and race became a determining variable when mapping regions, establishing social strata and structuring work relations.

The process of Brazil becoming a nation-state is marked by the transference of the Portuguese Crown in 1808 to the then colony, when the Braganza royal family left Portugal just a few days before the invasion by Napoleonic troops. If the change gave place to an unfamiliar situation, whereby Brazil was both an Empire and House of the Crown, it did not, however, change the plantation as a system of production fuelled by the slave trade from Africa. Lage (2016: 20) pointed out that the Portuguese transference to Brazil led to a 'liberal revolution' in Portugal a few years later, aiming at a 'political regeneration' of the country (see Neves 2011: 81–95, in Lage 2016). In a manifest released in the Portuguese city of Porto in 1820, one reads that 'the idea of the colonial status to which Portugal has been effectively reduced deeply afflicts all those citizens that still preserve the sentiment of national dignity' (Manifest of the Portuguese Nation to the Sovereigns and Peoples of Europe, 1820, quoted in Maxwell 1999: 188, in Lage 2016). The coloniser claimed to have been colonised, while the colonised remained dependent, even if independent (Lage 2016: 20). The year 1822 marks the official declaration of the independence of Brazil, as well as the culmination of a process that had begun in the eighteenth century through which Brazil became increasingly independent from Portugal and increasingly dependent on England (in Lage 2016: 20; apud see Maxwell 1999: 183–184; Santos 2003: 24–26; Weffort 2006: 166; Ricupero 2011: 125–128; Caldeira 2011: 181–195).

Mignolo's (2005: 65) observation about the new Creole elites in the Spanish and Portuguese former colonies is relevant, even if the process of independence was different in each of the former colonies.[3] While in Brazil the independence process was made by Dom Pedro I in negotiation with Portugal, England, and internal elite groups, in the Spanish part of the continent independence was through military action. The Creole, who went from being a subaltern group to becoming the dominant elite, looked towards France for political ideals, emphasising republican values based on the state to build a just and peaceful society (Mignolo 2005: 66). Creoles of Spanish and Portuguese descent were closer than they imagined to African slaves and Creoles of African descent. However, Creoles of Spanish and Portuguese descent lived under the illusion that they were Europeans too, although they felt their second-class status. By the mid-nineteenth century, the historical foundation of Creole identity under colonial rules was quickly stored away, and the Creole elite alienated itself in its effort to adapt, and to adopt republican and liberal projects.

Shapiro (1999: 47) pointed out the role of national narratives in forging original myths, offering a historical trajectory that testified a collective belonging. In telling the story of the creation of *The Idea of Latin America* (2005), Walter

Mignolo discussed the processes that led Creole elites of Spanish and Portuguese descent to express their identity as 'Americans', and how the process of emancipation followed the rise of a new social class – the bourgeoisie, whose members were mostly white Christians, educated at universities in Europe. But while this new elite celebrated economic and political emancipation from both the monarchy and the church, they saw themselves as part of modernity in a continent inhabited by people of European descent, and where Indigenous peoples, Africans, and poor Mestizos became poorer and more marginalised.

Mignolo defines the logic of coloniality as an ideology that works through four broad domains of human experience. It operates, first, in the economic domain in which the appropriation of land, exploitation of labour, and control of finance are justified; second, in the political domain, where there is a control by authority; third, in the civic domain, with the control of gender and sexuality; and fourth, in the epistemic and the subjective/personal domain, with the control of knowledge and subjectivity. Each domain is interwoven with the others, since appropriation of land or exploitation of labour also involves the control of finance, of authority, of gender, and of knowledge and subjectivity.

Mbembe (2003) calls attention to the relation between modernity and the multiple concepts of sovereignty which derive from the first, showing how the territorialisation of the sovereign state made a distinction between parts of the globe available for colonial appropriation versus Europe itself. Following this distinction, colonies were supposedly inhabited by 'savages', not organised as a state, not part of a human world, and a place where armies are not an entity, making it impossible to differentiate between combatants and non-combatants. As a result, colonies became zones where war and disorder coexisted, where the controls and guarantees of the juridical order could be suspended, the zone where the violence of the state of exception operated for the sake of 'civilisation'.

The building of a nation-state in Latin America and Brazil was deeply marked by Creole elites asserting themselves as decedents of Europeans. During the 1930s, the project of whitening the Brazilian population reinforced race as an important category in the imaginary of what a Brazilian population *should* be. Such reasoning not only pertains to the past but still plays an important role in the local imaginary. It is important to notice, that although perceived as a mixed-race region by outsiders, members of the Latin American elite see themselves as white. This self-assertion has been problematised by Quijano (2000) and recently evoked by Argentine President Mauricio Macri when he showed his support for a Mercosur-European Union trade agreement at the World Economic Forum in Davos 2018. At the event, he claimed, 'we are all descendants from Europe' (Telesur 2018). The declaration shows not only how elite members perceive themselves but also how members of other communities are rendered invisible. In the case of Argentina, over 30 indigenous nationalities live in the country, and they account for roughly one million people (World Bank Group 2015: 22). The population identifying themselves as Afro-Argentine is close to 150,000 (INDEC Censo 2010).

When discussing police killings and disappearances that target mostly black communities and favela dwellers in Brazil, the link between dictatorships and enforced disappearances does not give a full picture of the problem. Gabriel Gatti (2014), a sociologist who undertook substantial research on the theme, has produced interesting work developing the argument that the detained-disappeared emerged from a continuum that goes back to the colonial rationale, rather than constituting a distinct historical moment (2014: 158–161). In contrast to general correlations between disappearances and authoritarian regimes, Gatti (2014) considered disappearances not as a barbaric act, but as a civilising project. In that sense, enforced disappearance was not an exception resulting from the dictatorship in Latin America, but a *raison d'état*.

This section discussed how the project of nation-building in Brazil and Latin America, which was deeply influenced by the European understanding of sovereignty state in territorial terms, was pursued by local elites. I have demonstrated how first colonies were considered a place of exception, as formulated by Achille Mbembe (2003). I have argued that the logic of coloniality as a mirror of modernity presents similarities to the logic of exception as discussed by Agamben. I have argued that the colonial view of territories is still reproduced in our days. This argument will be further developed when I discuss racialised notions applied by the Brazilian state apparatus in the logic of the 'war on drugs' – as the sovereign right to kill in favelas.

Between the logic of exception and metaphors of war

Accounts about a re-emerging state of exception gained attention, in international relations and elsewhere, after 2001 following the terrorist attack on September 11. Using the response to the attack by the U.S. government, observers examined how exceptionalism was expressed in its aftermath (Graham 2006; Bigo and Tsoukala 2008; Debrix and Barder 2009; Huysmans 2006, 2008; among others). This discussion is relevant to this research because it is possible to trace parallels between the 'war on terror' and the 'war on drugs'. For example, both have presented a tendency to use the metaphor of 'war' to justify a call from the executive power to hijack the decision-making process from the other powers – judiciary and legislative. It concentrates power in the hands of the executive using the frame of need or exception.

As a consequence, laws and norms are changed, and exception becomes the rule. Here, I will present a closer look at the 'war on terror' and on drugs, the metaphor that enables a range of norms to be put into place. I will also draw on the commonalities between both wars, even if tangentially when duties carried out by armed forces and the police change hands; when 'exception' is used to make decisions about peoples' lives; and when actors attach life to certain specific places. These issues are also related to Agamben's conceptual frame because they reflect ways through which exceptionalities are expressed in our political system.

The way Giorgio Agamben enters in the theorisation about sovereignty is by the logic of exceptionality. He departed from the concepts of sovereignty and exception developed by Carl Schmitt (1922, cited in Agamben 1995), stating that the sovereign is the one who decides when the exception needs to be applied, and that exception 'consists in nothing other than the suspension of the rule' (Agamben 1995: 18). Agamben developed these concepts further, invoking Walter Benjamin's critique of Schmitt to affirm that 'the tradition of the oppressed teaches us that "the state of exception" we live in is the rule' (Benjamin 2018: 392).

Agamben (2005) traced a parallel between the Nazi state and 'the so-called democracies', where he identifies characteristics of authoritarian and totalitarian regimes as those present at the beginning of the twentieth century. Agamben claims that the Third Reich was a state of exception that lasted 12 years, arguing that 'since then, the voluntary creation of a permanent state of emergency (though perhaps not declared in the technical sense) has become one of the essential practices of contemporary states, including so-called democratic ones' (2005: 2). The logic of exception as the foundational assumption in the existing system creates the condition of possibility for exclusionary policies on a permanent basis. These policies reflect the changes faced by the militarisation and politicisation of issues such as terror and drugs, and how life is inscribed in the sovereign realm and attached to specific spaces.

Logics of exceptionality in the context of the 'war on terror'

Although in general, common sense associates the state of exception with dictatorships, whether constitutional or unconstitutional, to Agamben, the major risk nowadays is the state of exception in democracies. Understood as a technical state of exception, following the 'metaphor' of war, it can be considered less dangerous. In that sense, the state of exception is not related to a political regime, but to 'a space devoid of law, a zone of anomie in which all legal determinations – and above all the very distinction between public and private – are deactivated' (Agamben 2005: 50). Thus, the essential task of a theory of the state of exception is not only to clarify whether it has a juridical nature or not, but to define the meaning and modes by which exception, law, and politics are related.

Notwithstanding Agamben's constant mention of law (1995), he is not referring to the juridical rule applied in a trial or to individual cases. By 'law', Agamben refers to language and norms. Language, in Agamben's terms, is a grammatical tool used to create meanings to maintain a subject in infinite suspension in relation to law. Law is related to the technical administration of life that, when hijacked by the political, works as a mechanism of inclusive exclusion that the sovereign power can deploy to place life both inside and outside the juridical order. Norms, as technocratic forms of governance, were interestingly captured by Michael Dillon (2003), who analyses how the sovereign apparatus has become more and more complex in recent times, potentially connecting the juridical realm to people's lives, for example, in the state's right to survey.

The use of war as a metaphor has many implications. Rainer Hülsse and Alexander Spencer (2008) discussed the process through which Al-Qaeda was constructed as a military group by the German popular press to justify the need for counter-terrorism practices in the aftermath of terrorist attacks in New York and Washington (2001), Madrid (2004), and London (2005). The metaphor, however, has shifted from 2004 onwards constructing Al-Qaeda as a criminal group, thereby changing the threat from external (war) to internal, now in need of a juridical response.

In the context of war on drugs in Brazil, Leite (2012) has explored the representations of Rio de Janeiro as a city under war. According to her, the consequence of this representation is of favela dwellers as ambiguous entities, which puts their civil and human rights in jeopardy by depicting them as irreconcilable with public security. The metaphor of war gives legitimacy to policies supported by 'operations' in favelas, whereby the police can confront drug dealers without taking local residents into consideration, leading to what I will call space of exception. This metaphor also legitimises the use of armoured vehicles and heavily armed police during incursions in favelas. Known as the 'big skull',[4] the black armoured vehicles are perceived as lethal. Again, there is a consequence associated with this narrative. Framing the issue of drugs as war leads to a militarisation of social relations between state and citizens, creating a risk to everyone whether they are criminals or not. By choosing to deal only with the supply side of the drugs market, following international security and market logic, the state perpetuates the problem. It ignores its responsibility in reducing the demand for drugs and considering other relevant aspects in this intricate dynamic. According to Dalby (1997: 14), the drug war militarises social relationships in areas that receive military assistance to tackle drug production, processing, and distribution without necessarily solving key problems such as poverty and underdevelopment.

An important aspect of the discourse of exceptionality is how it is articulated regarding security. Rens Van Munster (2004) argued that the semiotics of the war on terrorism represented a shift in discourses of security in the United States, leaving behind the frame of domestic or international law in order to consolidate a permanent state of exception. This shift regarding a narrative that creates a permanent state of exception has implications in different realms. Didier Bigo (2002, 2006, 2014) has problematised what he identified as a shift from war, defence, international order, and international security to strategies regarding crime or public order and police investigations to bring together defence and internal security. Amongst its many consequences, there is the formation of police networks at a global level and an increase of police duties being transferred to the armed forces.

Mark B Salter (2008) reflected on the shifts in the aftermath of September 11 and on the logic of exceptionality, arguing that borders are a political space where sovereignty and citizenship are performed by individuals and sovereigns regarding who is admitted in and who is not. He also highlighted that the use of emergency powers and the use of 'all means necessary' in the 'war on terror' support Agamben's claim that 'the state of exception tends increasingly to appear as the dominant paradigm of government in contemporary politics' (Agamben 2005: 2).

I bring these considerations on the 'war on terror' to show how both 'wars' operate following a similar framework. To recap, the implications of the 'war on terror' can be perceived in the way exceptionality is located inside the logic of sovereignty; in how it demands action in terms of military response to the threat; and in the manner it changes the lives of those who live in a 'permanent state of exception', namely, those who are seen as the potential perpetrators.

Another important implication in the framework of the 'war on terror' and on drugs is the articulation of threat regarding danger. Campbell (1992) highlighted the role of interpretation when considering what a threat is and the association between danger (1992: 350) and specific identities. Andrew W. Neal (2006) has discussed the importance of Guantanamo Bay as the exemplary empirical site of exceptionalism involving exceptional practices and dangerous identities. According to him, Guantanamo represents a far-reaching array of exceptional practices, varying from the securitisation of immigration and asylum, the extraordinary rendition of terrorism suspects, and the practice of torture. Andreja Zevnik (2011) also referring to the Guantanamo detention centre, followed Agamben's reasoning to claim that although the place has been seen as a symbol of human rights abuse, if one thinks of the history of the western world, this situation is not exceptional but in fact symptomatic of the very nature of the liberal democratic system and the liberal notions of human rights. Zevnik (2011: 156) presented how the idea of legal subjectivity encompasses a particular notion of the subject according to which, to fully account as a human, one must also be recognised as such, implying the need for more than a biological definition. This observation is fundamental in the discussion here once inmates, drug dealers, and favela dwellers are constantly constructed as less than human.

Logics of exceptionality in the context of the 'war on drugs'

A less common frame to discuss exceptionality in the discipline is the 'war on drugs'. In the following paragraphs, I will introduce the context where the 'war on drugs' emerged and how it spread to Latin America, in light of the discussion on the concept of the state of exception used as a framework to analyse the 'war on terror'. I argue that although the wars on terror and drugs affect different regions of the globe and have different scales of impact, they also present some commonalities. I will discuss the array of practices, justifications, and resignifications, articulated and legitimised through claims of need or exception to the norm to fight drugs in Latin America, and how the U.S. agenda on the 'war on drugs' was internalised in Brazil. The 'war on drugs' helps us to understand the context where the exception is articulated, legitimising disappearances and police killings in contemporary Brazil.

The 'war on drugs' emerged during the election campaign of 1968, in the United States when Richard Nixon centred his campaign on the need to restore law and order. At the time when Nixon became president, there was a domestic and foreign campaign against the international illegal drug trade. At the national level, legislative changes were necessary to allow the federal government to intervene in the control of urban criminality (Baum 1996: 14; Feitosa and de Pinheiro 2012: 68), which resulted in tighter control of the drugs entering the country, mainly through the Mexican border, and massive incarceration of dealers and consumers.

At the international level, military interventions and aid were offered to suppress the production, transportation, and distribution of drugs and to repress narco-cartel activities in Latin America and the Caribbean. In some countries, military operations were carried out, such as in Panama (Just Cause Operation; Karam 2003), in Colombia (Colombia Plan; Feitosa and de Pinheiro 2012; Rodrigues 2012), and in Bolivia and Peru (Huskisson 2005; Feitosa and de Pinheiro 2012; Rodrigues 2012; Martins 2013). Criticisms of the military aid offered by the United States to Latin America signals hidden motives, such as the fight against leftist guerrilla groups (Weeks 2006: 62; Peceny and Durnan 2006).

A decade after Nixon's call against drugs, Ronald Reagan deepened the emphasis on the militarised aspect of the fight against crime (Campbell 1992: 173). The activities of drug cartels associated with leftist guerrillas brought about what became known as narcoterrorism (Feitosa and de Pinheiro 2012). Narcoterrorism is considered the attempt by narcotics traffickers to influence governments or society through violence and intimidation. Emma Björnehed (2004: 305) explained that the concept of narcoterrorism originates from an understanding that the two phenomena, narcotics trafficking and terrorism, are interconnected, leading to anti-drug and anti-terrorism policies to face a threat. The liaison between drug cartels and leftist guerrilla groups is generally perceived as a reason to legitimise the use of military measures against the drug cartels by the United States, pre-empting the strategy by Andean governments of adopting exceptional military measures of repression, thus turning the 'war on drugs' into an issue of regional security (Rodrigues 2012: 17).

A continental effort underpinned the National Security Directive Administration 221 (NSDD 221) on Narcotics and National Security. Following its rationale, the Secretary of Defence and Attorney General in conjunction with the Secretary of State, 'should develop and implement any necessary modifications to applicable statutes, regulations, procedures and guidelines to enable U.S. military forces to support counter-narcotics efforts more actively, consistent with the maintenance of force readiness and training' (NSDD-221 1986: 3). The counter-narcotics efforts were contentious in many respects, not least of which was the role of the U.S. Army, because of their interventionist nature. The militarised feature of the 'war on drugs' was taken to another level in 1989, during the mandate of George Bush (1989–1993), when a new directive was published highlighting the need to focus on Colombia, Peru, and Bolivia (Feitosa and de Pinheiro 2012). The Andean Strategy policy promoted cooperation between these countries to stop the production of drugs by focusing on different areas of concern, such as economic assistance to major cocaine-producing countries, disruption of activities by trafficking organisations, and military involvement in counter-narcotics operations to provide additional support. However, only financial support for military assistance was provided (Rodrigues 2012: 17).

Some authors have reflected on the reasons for the United States to use the frame of war. Jeremy Elkins (2010) called attention to the fact that the analogy of war has marked the last 50 years, which saw the United States declaring war on many different issues such as poverty, cancer, crime, drugs, and, lastly, terrorism. According to him, the impact of the use of the analogy of war reinforces a dichotomy between the national and individual realm, which are both perfect and healthy, and the foreign otherness, underpinned by notions of 'friend' or 'enemy'. Feitosa and de Pinheiro (2012) reflected on the need by the United States to redefine national security priorities after the end of the Cold War, as well as to justify the budget earmarked for military forces, by identifying a new enemy. Interestingly, Campbell (1992: 175) called attention to the discourse of danger linking drugs to black communities. With a drop in drug consumption over the years, the National Institute on Drug Abuse report from 1990 showed that drug consumption was greatest among single white men (Campbell 1992). This result contradicted the grounds that justified the 'war on drugs' based on the perception that high levels of drug consumption among certain groups and areas constituted a particular form of danger. Campbell (1992: 180) observed similarities between the discourse of danger associated with communists and that being used to refer to drug users, producers, and pushers.

Following the foreign aid provided by the United States to countries in South America, Brazil started to reformulate its anti-drugs apparatus in 1996, characterised by the creation of the National Secretariat for Drug Policy (SENAD), initially linked to the Ministry of Defence. The problem of creating an agency at the national level following the same model as in the United States was that in the Brazilian constitution, policies on drugs are attributed to the Federal Police. Even though giving the responsibility of fighting drugs to the armed forces would, therefore, be unconstitutional, a colonel was designated as the head of the new agency (Rodrigues 2012: 28). Later, that agency went to the Ministry of Justice, and its main role became that of coordinating and integrating actions related to drug-related prevention and repression, which started overseeing the non-authorised production of narcotic substances and drugs that may cause dependency, as well as those related to the recuperation of dependents (SENAD). During the 1990s, the new policies targeting drug trafficking reached the Amazon region. Considered by the United States as a porous border, specific policies were designed by the Brazilian government. The Amazon Surveillance System (SIVAM, in Portuguese) was created to control air, soil, and subsoil in the state of Amazonas reinforcing the national sovereignty in the region (Herz 2006; Rodrigues 2012: 29).

It is important to note that policies on the 'war on drugs' did not follow a political regime or different political positions of presidents in charge. The first version of the Law on Drugs (Law 6,386 issued in 1976, *lei de tóxicos* in Portuguese) in Brazil was passed during the dictatorship and followed the Single Convention on Narcotic Drugs from 1961 by the United Nations, which extended prohibitions and created an international regulatory framework on illicit drugs. According to Rodrigues (2002), the UN convention was taken as a base to update national legislation on drugs, giving the state greater autonomy to use coercive means against drug traffickers (Forte 2007: 195). From the 1990s onwards, after the country's democratisation, presidents of the centre-left and centre-right showed similar inclinations regarding policies on drugs and related legislation, mirroring the North American agenda on the matter.

The last update of the Law on Drugs, issued in 2006 (Law number 11,343), introduced alternative penalties to drug users. However, none of the updates in Brazil specified the quantity that would differentiate a drug user from a drug trafficker. It is important to note that the first law regarding drugs issued in 1976 already specified a difference between consumers and traffickers without elaborating on how to make this differentiation. Critics of this law claim that this imprecision opens the door to penal selectivity and places the decision on the difference between a consumer and a trafficker in the hands of police officers (Forte 2007: 195; Rodrigues 2012: 30).

As previously pointed out, parallels can be made between the 'war on terror' and the 'war on drugs', as seen in Salter's (2008) argument on the embodiment of sovereignty and citizenship, and how these performances relate to a permanent state of exception. Firstly, it is possible to argue that in the context of the 'war on drugs', the sovereign decision over who represents a criminal is also taken by duly authorised individuals – namely, police officers.

The issue here is that, as pointed out by Forte (2007) and Rodrigues (2012), the decision tends to follow sensitive parameters, such as a social origin or skin colour, affecting the relationship between sovereignty and citizenship. Brazil has the third largest number of people arrested in the world, following closely behind the United States and China, and ranking above Russia in fourth place. The rate of prisoners per 100,000 inhabitants increased to 352.6 individuals in 2016. In 2014, there were 306.22 prisoners per 100,000 inhabitants. Taking into account skin colour, the survey shows that 64 per cent of the prison population is made up of black people, even though black people represent only 54 per cent of the country's population. Crimes related to drug trafficking account for the highest number of incarcerations, representing 28 per cent of the total prison population.

With regard to the legal system, drug-related activities follow the general rule for any other type of crime. The Federal Police act in instances of international trafficking, the police investigation is conducted by the Civil Police, and the immediate repression is made by the Military Police, who is responsible for ostensive patrolling. A complementary law (Art 16A, Complementary Law 97, issued in 1999 and later altered through Complementary Law 136, issued in 2010) established rules regarding the use of the armed forces in the 'maintenance of law and order', impacting urban areas in Brazil. At that time, it was established that operations regarding public safety needed to be limited regarding time and space and had to be led by a military authority, nominated by the President. Rodrigues (2012: 31) called attention to the fact that the first action was carried out in Favela do Alemão–Rio de Janeiro only three months later. The operation aimed to consolidate state authority in the favela and prepare the place to be occupied by the Pacifying Police Unit (UPP). Since then, on many occasions, the armed forces have been used as a first step in the occupation of favelas.

Although the 'war on terror' and the 'war on drugs' have different targets and impacts, both have helped to create similar grounds on which exceptionalities are built. The war as analogy also indicates the role played by the juridical realm. In the United States, the term 'war on drugs' meant a series of changes in legislation. At the international level, those changes allowed the United States to offer military aid in operational and financial terms resulting in military operations in many countries in the South Cone, such as Peru, Colombia, and Panama, among others. Further research will be necessary to investigate how changes in U.S. legislation laid the groundwork for military operations, including the financial aid provided for the 'war on terror'. Both 'wars' avoid calling against a specific subject. Terror is a feeling, and drugs, a generic substance. The lack of precision, however, leaves the door open to a constant making, unmaking, and remaking of tactics and targets.

Police as apparatus

Whereas sovereignty has been widely discussed in international relations, as we have seen so far, those discussions tend to focus on the role of a militarised apparatus, following the context of wars and not necessarily including the police. On this issue, Didier Bigo (2014) has precisely discussed the use of armed forces in the fight against terror and to maintain law and order. Bigo (2014) claimed that by propagating the idea of 'global (in)security', the conventional line that distinguishes the constellation of war defence, including international order and the constellation of crime, public order, and police investigation, became blurred, facilitating the alignment between defence and internal security to face global threats. One important consequence, according to him, is the polarisation of military functions of combat, and the criminalisation and judicialisation of the notion of war. In Brazil, the 'war on drugs' has evolved in tactic terms regarding how the military and police apparatuses have been used. It is possible to observe a process characterised by the army taking over police duties in urban areas of Brazil as in the military pacification intervention at favelas on the one hand, and the enhancement of the lethal capacity of the police, on the other.

Here, I would like to push those disciplinary boundaries further. I will first present the notion of *dispositif* or apparatus in the context of police killings and disappearances in Brazil. After, I will explore the role of the police as an institution that embodies sovereign decisions. It is important to bring the role of the police to this discussion given how they decide over life and death. By introducing and presenting the topics just described, I will develop the theoretical frame discussed in this research on the role of the police as an expression of sovereignty.

The relation between sovereign power and life, which is mediated by the *dispositif*, is addressed in the debate on how exception structures sovereignty.

Agamben's use of the term was informed by Foucault's definition that refers to the *dispositif* as heterogeneous ensembles, such as institutions, discourses, regulatory decisions, and laws, which maintain the exercise of power within the social body (Foucault 2007). Agamben works with the idea of apparatus

> in which and through which, one realises a pure activity of governance devoid of any foundation in being. This is the reason why apparatuses must always imply a process of subjectification, that is to say, they must produce their subject.
>
> (2009: 11)

Drawing on the example of Brazil's 'war on drugs', it is important to explore the role played by the police as one of the main actors in the apparatus network. Here I argue that because of some drug-related lacunas in the law, decisions are made by police officers in their daily and routine activities. After introducing some of these lacunas, and how they can be related to the discussion by Agamben about law and norms, I will elaborate on how police officers are embodying sovereign decisions over life (and death).

The legislation in Brazil does not make a differentiation between a drug dealer and a drug user. As discussed earlier, this lacuna in the law leaves the first decision to the police officer, who has to decide every single event. I would like to unpack this decision using different layers of analysis. First, there is the discussion about the lacuna in law, already made by Agamben. Secondly, I would like to explore the position occupied by the police officer as the one who decides who is a user and who is a trafficker of drugs. While a lacuna is not a suspension of the order, it can be used to justify a technical state of exception. Agamben's conceptualisation of sovereignty and exception (1995) implies a juridical order that works with the duality, rather than two concepts related by presence or absence, constituting what he described as 'the paradox of sovereignty' (1995). This inter-changeability between sovereignty and exception allows an interpretation that sees the exception as part of sovereignty.

To Agamben, a lacuna in law will always be present because it is inherent to the relationship between law and reality, the norm and the world, and this lacuna brings into focus the absence of an internal nexus between the norm and its application or realisation. A lacuna also leaves space for individuals to make a decision, which is why Agamben identifies a tendency towards an undifferentiation between the legislative, executive, and judiciary roles in the western political-juridical tradition, and the subsequent need for someone in power to make a decision. The centralisation of power in the legislative with the support of the judiciary is vital to the development of Agamben's conceptualisation on sovereignty and exceptions. Agamben warned that when the lacuna represents a risk, a rectification by the executive will be necessary. The dynamics of deciding over a lacuna or an ambiguity in law can be related, for example, to the imprecision in the case of the 'war on drugs' regarding the authority of police officers in deciding who is a drug user and who is a drug dealer.

Agamben (1995: 64) pointed that the 'state of nature', postulated by Hobbes, in a war of all against all is still present in the sovereign structure and that an important feature of the sovereign is precisely the indistinction between humans and animal, civilisation and nature, law and violence. Although different aspects of exception operate in democratic states in a more restricted way, Agamben associates the state of nature, which in Hobbes is part of a contractual tradition, with the state of exception, to show how the exclusion of liberties is part of the sovereign logic. According to Agamben (1995), the state of nature is not a pre-juridical time but a principle that is part of the sovereign state. In saying that, the organisation of biological life was not solved with the end of the state of nature. The administration of biological life is a vital part of the sovereign state and, crucial in Agamben's thinking, the production of bare life is the original activity of the sovereign power. In the case of Brazil, it is also important to observe that the head of the chief of the police is the state governor, who occupies an executive position. The tendency is a scenario of a police state where the exception is the rule.

This section aimed to introduce and discuss the state apparatus in Agamben's terms and how it is related to the role of law, norms, and, ultimately, to the sovereign power and logic of exception. It presented the role of the police as the institution which deals more directly with the 'war on drugs' and translates the sovereign decision into practice. I also discussed that such rationale – the paradox of sovereignty – is not necessarily related to specific political regimes, such as dictatorships. Thus, contemporary nation-states recognised as democracies are characterised by technical regimes of exception in which the aim is the political-technical administration of biological life. In the case of the 'war on drugs', a militarised police force responsible for law enforcement is central to the idea of a state apparatus that focuses on the technical administration of life. The following section will focus on the idea that in Brazil, as in many countries nowadays, instead of a totalising state of exception, the suspension of personal liberties aims at specific groups.

Governing death and racial capitalism

This section starts with a historical account developed by Cedric Robinson and his discussion on 'racial capitalism', in which Robinson proposed to highlight the ways racism permeates the organisation and development of capitalism. Robinson (2020) brought the emergence of capitalism way before the British Industrial Revolution that is claimed to be the birth of capitalism. What Robinson left behind, however, was how colonialism enters in this process following the same rationale of racialising populations to justify their subjugation. The systemic world view presented by Anibal Quijano has showed us that capitalism did not start with the Industrial Revolution in 18th-century Britain, and it pushes our understanding of capitalism back to colonialism. According to Quijano (2000), the Industrial Revolution was made possible by the extraction of raw resources from various parts of the world, starting with Latin America.

Between nation-building and modernity 69

Although Robinson does not link much of his discussion to the extraction of raw materials from Latin America, adding the context of Latin America colonization to this discussion shows the beginning of a new rationale and ethical justification of violence and subjugation of populations based on their racialised features. Let us not forget that at the time of colonisation, although the state was not existing yet, the Church was the sovereign actor and player who would provide legitimisation to the killings and subjugation of certain people. In Chapter 4 I present the religious fundamentals based on sacred strictures that legitimised enslavement of those with darker skin.

Therefore, this section starts with Cedric Robinson and his looking back at history to pinpoint racialised aspects that are in the roots of capitalism in Europe. By offering a historical account of the development of colonialism and its links to capitalism, I point to the necessity of historicising state violence and neoliberalism within racial capitalism's long effects, drawing attention to continuities in capitalism, and that racialised exploitation and violence are intertwined. Then, I make the link with Latin America through the contribution of Quijano. Both authors destabilise established assumptions concerning the Industrial Revolution as a starting point to capitalism. Destabilising these notions is important because it sets the ground to analyse how state security apparatuses are not at all dissociated from the market and to show both rationales operating following necropolitics. After presenting the state and market links in a historical account that tell us a story of power and subjugation, I will return to the discussion on the sovereign power and production of life (and death) as conceptualised by Foucault, Agamben, and Mbembe, to discuss how necropower interplays with economic factors. The section proceeds by bringing the conceptualisation of Warren Montag as necroeconomics – the nexus between economics and necropolitics to show the underlying necro logic of capitalism.

The theoretical and historical discussion introduced here is the background to the book project as a whole and speaks more particularly to Chapters 4 and 5, which discuss the governmentality of black lives in Brazil from the plantation system to the favelas. Linking necropolitics to necroeconomics, this section fills two important gaps. The first is Marxist literature's neglect of the racial background of economically disenfranchised populations. The second is the lack of understanding of the specific logics of state violence through the police, that targets specifically this part of the population, and not all economically marginalised communities. By discussing the role played by the security apparatus in this context, I expect to highlight the link between security apparatus and economic dispossession. The literature on police violence in the United States focus on how the police apparatus leads black populations to the incarceration system and how prisons became a central policy to deal with black lives in the USA (see Gilmore 2007). I argue that in Brazil, although the incarceration system is as perverse as in the USA with 34 per cent of its population consisting of black people,[5] the 'war on drugs' provides a further legitimisation for the annihilation of black communities. In that sense, it is possible to observe that the security apparatus is a state mechanism that fulfils the function of annihilating what is considered 'excess' of life, constantly regulating an economic system, which created, commodified to later annihilate what is considered saturated. The mechanism applied to 'regulate excess' depends on the country in question. This section speaks directly to the discussion on racial capitalism and draws on the plantation system situating the Iberian slave trade in the context of necroeconomics.

Racial and colonial capitalism

Robinson (1983) used historiography and archaeology research on black radical tradition to map a (dis)encounter between Marxism and Black radicalism. Based first in the experience of South Africa's economy under apartheid, Robinson historicises enslavement as part of the European feudal mode of production and interrogates why Marxism forgot to include slavery in the emergence of capitalism over the Industrial Revolution in the United Kingdom. His argument challenges many of the current assumptions on the field of political economy, which very often fails to take race into question and marks the Industrial Revolution as the starting point of capitalism with no past. Much of Marxist theory does not consider the different processes in Europe and elsewhere, or does not make a direct link of these processes, which happened outside Europe, that allowed the Industrial Revolution to happen.

The impact of Robinson's work takes multiple directions. Firstly, he argued that capitalism did not emerge in the Industrial Revolution but permeated much of the feudal system back to the European Middle Ages and trade relations in Genoa, both a much earlier process that is consolidated hand in hand with the consolidation of the nation-state itself. According to him, the subjugation of Irish, Jewish Roman, Gypsy, and Slav communities – who suffered dispossession – is a deep mark of the trade relations in Genoa during the Middle Ages and indicates the first attempts to racialise certain populations. According to Robinson, racialisation is deeply rooted in Europe and can be traced back to the first modes of trade. Secondly, Robinson argued that Marxism overlooked racialised structures in European industrial capitalism. According to him, capitalism was not the great moderniser which gave birth to the European proletariat as a universal subject. On the contrary, Robinson pointed out a tendency of European civilisation that does not homogenise but does differentiate – by exaggerating regional, subcultural, and dialectical differences into racial ones, there was a justification towards 'enslavement' of certain populations. Thirdly, Robinson showed how medieval cities in Europe already implemented slavery as a form of domination and hierarchisation, based not on skin colour at first, but that later would serve as a model for Atlantic slavery. A fundamental implication of Robinson's argument is not only to centre race, capital, and the formation of the nation-state, but also to tighten them up in a way that is not possible to consider one without considering the others.

Robinson's view pushes back the emergence of capitalism before the Industrial Revolution and can be complemented by the work of Quijano (2000) and Mignolo (2005), who centre the experience of European capitalism on coloniality and its racial axis in the colonisation of the 'New World'. Quijano argued that capital as a social relation is older than the Americas, and although it was based on the commodification of the labour force born at some moment around the eleventh or twelfth century in the Iberian and Italian regions, it was in the Americas and during the colonisation that capitalism was structured and articulated as a form of social organisation and control of labour linked to commodities production. Quijano's world-system theory challenges the Marxist view that much of the historical, social, and economic processes that happened during the colonisation of Americas is precapitalism. Instead, Quijano argued that although from a Eurocentric point of view, reciprocity, slavery, and independent commodity production are all perceived as a historical sequence prior to commodification of the labour force, and therefore, precapital, slavery in America was deliberately stablished and organised as a commodity to produce goods for the world market and to serve to the purposes and needs of capitalism. Quijano concluded that all the forms of labour and control of labour not only were simultaneously performed in America, but they were also articulated around the axis of capital and global market. Together, slavery as a form of labour configured a new economic system: capitalism.

In this colonial and capitalist system, Quijano argued (2000), Western Europe was in a privileged position that allowed for the control of gold, silver, and other commodities produced by unpaid labour of indigenous groups, African enslaved populations and mestizos granted with a decisive advantage to compete for the control of worldwide commercial traffic. Apart from Western Europe, all the rest of the regions and populations were under some form of colonial subjugation and incorporated into the New World market under European domination and under non-waged relations of labour. Under this process, Europe concentrated for almost two decades the control of waged labour (of white Europeans) and industrial production.

The account of capitalism as pre–Industrial Revolution is neither a matter of accounting to another historical version nor an attempt to advocate to a different starting point for the emergence of capitalism. The importance of including colonialism in the Americas and trade relations in Genoa is to look at capitalism in its necro aspect as well as the intertwining between capitalism, necropolitics, and race. Quijano highlights that the vast genocide of indigenous populations in Latin America in the first decades of colonisation was not caused by the violence of the conquest nor by the plagues brought by the conquistadors, but because American Indigenous groups were used as disposable manual labour and forced to work until death. The way life and death are intertwined with capitalism is central in this section. As it will be explored in greater depth in Chapter 4, Quijano argued that a racial axis, as we know, marked by phenotypic differences and biological structures between conquerors and conquered, does not have a known history before the colonisation of America and worked to grant legitimacy to the relations of domination imposed by the conquest. If we consider racism as an intrinsic part of capitalism, we can also see it as a structuring force that would push difference to create hierarchisation. In that sense, as Robinson explained, Western Europeans were not interested in homogenising difference in the continent, nor as a single labour force as Marxism defends, but quite the opposite. The interest was to highlight difference in others to justify a system of otherness resulting in a condition of poverty and dispossession. Following this rationale, the othering process in the emergence of capitalism tied up to the emergence of nation-state led to the legitimation and yet hidden necro relations between former empires – now modern nation-states – and former colonies – now the so-called underdeveloped parts of the globe.

From biopolitics to necroeconomics

My aim in this section is to juxtapose the discussion on biopolitics – especially necropolitics – to the necro aspect of capitalism. I will elaborate in the following paragraphs how capitalism commodifies and reduces life in the labour force. Once life cannot be absorbed into the labour market, they become 'excess'. This is the precise moment in which state and economy work together to regulate the excess of life. While economy pushes some groups – currently mostly racialised groups – to the margins, making these groups an 'excess', the state – through the violent action of police apparatus, regulates this same 'excess' through death. To do so, I will start by bringing back the discussion on biopolitics and its critique in Agamben, followed by the necropolitics elaborated by Mbembe, and finally I will elaborate more on the economic implications of the nexus between power relations and violence by bringing Montag to this conversation. By adding Montag, I explore the underlying necro logic of capitalism.

As introduced in Chapter 1, Foucault's formulation of sovereign power has been contested and developed through a long discussion on biopower. To Foucault (2019), there was a shift in the way power is exercised and experienced throughout the eighteen centuries while there is a consolidation of the nation-state and the decline of empires. Before that, according to Foucault, power was from above to below, exercised by the sovereign and followed the now-fashioned formulation of 'take life and let die'. To Foucault, this shift made power relational, meaning that it happens through relations of power. Another important discern in this shift is discipline. Disciplinary power aims to make populations to flourish instead of punishment in which death was the result – in this shift, sovereignty is lived through 'making live and letting die'.

Agamben (1995, 2002) contested the idea that there was a shift and, based on the experience of the Holocaust, argued that sovereign power is very much alive, still exercising the old formulation of 'take life and let die' – a decision that, according to him, occurs based on exception. Agamben's ideas influenced much of the literature on the 'war on terror' given the similarities between the state of exception declared by the United States in the aftermath of September 11 and his philosophical framework. Following the debate on biopower, Mbembe brings a postcolonial perspective and introduces the term necropolitics. Mbembe's contribution is based on the examples of the

Palestinian conflict with Israel and apartheid in South Africa to point out that sovereign power is very much alive. According to him, however, the decision is not based on how to make a population flourish. Instead, sovereign power is marked by the decision on who is going to die and – very importantly – how.

Montag's (2005) work perceives death as a requirement to economy and defines necroeconomics as an inheriting side effect of capitalism which continually justifies it. He first engages with the discussion on biopower, following Foucault, Agamben, and Mbembe, to then show how the work of Smith (1863) and Hegel's (1977) (both in Montag 2005) already presented a necro aspect of economics (and capitalism) in it. Montag argues that death was already at stake in Smith's position on the requirements to the flow of wealth across society as well as in the subsistence of a population. Smith defended that 'specific circumstances, require the death of a significant number of individuals: to be precise, it requires that they be allowed to die so others may live' (2005: 14). According to Montag (2005: 14), the rigour found in Smith places the market as a mechanism that adjusts the proportion of labourers to the fund available for wages as it distributes malnutrition to the social ranks whose numbers exceed their ability to obtain subsistence. In the example, children would be the first to perish under malnutrition. In engaging Smith's ideas with the biopower debate, Montag (2005: 12) points out that if societies must exercise, and not merely possess, the right to kill, the market, understood as the very form of human universality as life, must necessarily, at certain precise moments, 'let die'. In that sense, the market regulates mortality (Montag 2005: 15) as death establishes the conditions of life, death as by an invisible hand restores the market to what it must be to support life (Montag 2005: 16). Montag argues that, by making death a necessity in the production of the life of the universal, Smith's economics is a necroeconomics.

The governmentality of life and death in Montag also places the sovereign decision in this regulation. Montag (2005: 15) observes that the market reduces and rations life; it not only allows death, but it demands death to be allowed by the sovereign power. Montag continues,

> it is at this point that the state, which might appear to have no other relation to the market than one of a contemplative acquiescence, is called into action: those who refuse to allow themselves to die must be compelled by force to do so.
>
> (2005: 15)

It is important to acknowledge at this point that the 'let die' formulation that Montag observed in Smith is abandoned as part of the population will be forced to die, by the state. The biopower formulation of 'letting die' assumes a more straightforward position, as in Mbembe's formulation of necropolitics.

While Montag's point is highly relevant to understand the necro aspect of economics, Robinson makes the point of a process of racialisation of subjugated population as an intrinsic aspect of an economy that made possible capitalism as theorised by Marx to emerge a few centuries later. However, if

Robinson's work is eye-opening by bringing racialisation and slavery to the core of capitalism and economy, it fails in addressing how the relationship between colonies and empire was also a fundamental part to the process of slavery and racialisation of black bodies as is currently presented and expressed. To Anna More (2019), it is fundamental to consider how the transatlantic slave trade can inform our understanding of necroeconomics and its history; for that, she argues, we must turn not to industrial England but to the 'so-called primitive accumulation' of capital as conceptualised by Marx. Violence was not only in 'dispossession' but also in the 'subjugation of life to the power of death' (2019: 82) as it was in the transatlantic slave trade. More (2019) argued that the relationship between Europeans and Central African subjects was approached through political negotiations based on a matrix of theological, legal, and cultural understandings and practices.

While most of the Eurocentric literature tends to focus on the Industrial Revolution as discussed in the previous section, historical accounts of the colonisation process in America and the transatlantic slave trade open the possibility of deepening our understanding of what is called racial capitalism to include theories and practices already present in the context described by Marx as originary accumulation or precapitalism by Quijano. More (2019) analysed Gil Eanes de Zurara's *Chronicle of the Discovery and Conquest of Guinea* (1453), which describes one of the first large-scale sale of enslaved Africans in 1444. This event marked one of the first raids in which the capture of Africans was linked not to wars between Portuguese and northern Africans, but an expedition coordinated by the Infante himself aiming to provide labour for Portugal and profit to the traders and the Crown. More (2019: 76) argued that Zurara's unique recording of the sale at Lagos, which Zurara himself emphasised as commercial ventures, makes clear that the origin of the slave trade was already marked by the racialisation and commercialisation of human captivity.

Life as excess: securitisation as excess regulation

As has been presented in this chapter, racial capitalism centres race in the development of capitalism and challenges the Industrial Revolution as the starting point to capitalism and neoliberalism. By doing so, racial capitalism dislocates the emergence of capitalism from the Industrial Revolution to relocate it in the plantation system. This dislocation is not entirely new. Decolonial literature from Latin America (as in Walter Mignolo and Anibal Quijano) has already pointed out to colonialism and the genocide of indigenous communities, as well as plantation and the Atlantic slavery system as processes that gave ground to the emergence, 200 years later of the Industrial Revolution to happen at the other side of the Atlantic. According to decolonial thought, the Industrial Revolution was made possible through the hierarchisation of life through racialisation of different populations, the commodification of life (both indigenous and of African origin) as an enslaved and therefore unpaid working force, the extraction of raw materials as well as the profitable sea transport of enslaved people.

One important direction that recent work on racial capitalism is taking is to conceptualise how some lives are deemed as excess. Mbembe (2019) in his later developments on necropolitics has explored the idea of (black) life as surplus. Here I would like to elaborate more on the links between capitalism and necropolitics considering how the lives of racialised groups has historically gained contours of excess or surplus following the logic of capitalism. Mbembe (2019), as Quijano (2000), argues that historically, in settler colonies and pro-slavery states, racism served as a subsidy for capital. Surplus is an amount of something, usually refereeing to materials, that is left over when requirements have been met. Maybe more interesting to this discussion, surplus is an excess of production or supply. To Mbembe (2019: 177) capitalism is marked by consistently reducing the human person to a thing, an object, a sellable, a buyable, or a possessable commodity and has been impelled by three drives: the constant manufacturing of races or species (of which black bodies are a part); the seeking to calculate and convert everything into exchangeable commodities; and the attempt to maintain a monopoly over the manufacture of the living as such. Although the idea of life as surplus may sound uncanny to some, applying the term 'surplus' to life, instead of to things, highlights the neoliberal and capitalist logic that makes it possible to understand life as excess.

By making this claim, these authors are placing the exploitation of life at the centre of the development of capitalism. As difference was constructed based on racialised notions, what follows is the annihilation of black lives. Examples of how the conceptualisation of life as surplus and its impacts in our contemporaneity are discussed in the work of Ruth Gilmore (2007) on the prison system in the United States and in Jaime Amparo Alves's work (2018) on police violence and black urban life in Brazil. In her book, Gilmore (2007) looked at California's prison-building project to analyse its role in the creation and maintenance of what she calls a workfare-warfare state. According to her, with the end of the golden age of American capitalism, the prison system became a way to deal with four surpluses' forces: financial capital, land, population, and state capacity (2007: 64–78). Although Gilmore's work is outside the scope of this book; it does help us to see how the logic of life as surplus or excess that needs a securitising regulation by the state and its security apparatus occurs with different accents elsewhere. Alves's work (2018) argued that the economy of anti-black violence in the making of urban Brazil includes spatial segregation, mass incarceration, and killings by the police, constituting dimensions of the reproduction of the urban order. To Alves (2018, 4) and de Paula (2015), the so-called Third World cities such as Cape Town, Guatemala City, and São Paulo were turned into competitors for foreign investments; therefore, securing the city has become a matter of securing urban development. Following the neoliberal dimension of securitisation, Tony Samara (2011, in Alves 2018) notes that under the security governance regime, the black urban poor are seen as a threat of underdevelopment; therefore, the police and the criminal justice system are deployed not only to contain 'black crime' but also to enforce development. Here, I would like to highlight that the security apparatus is a fundamental aspect of dealing with what is considered excess of certain lives and argue that police killings and disappearances in Brazil are also a dispositive to deal with the same excess. I argue that the logic of the 'war on drugs', as discussed earlier in this chapter, is a key element in the legitimisation of the security apparatus action in this regulation.

Conclusion: situating Brazil within the conversation between Foucault, Agamben, and Mbembe

This chapter has presented and discussed the theoretical framework of the book following the debate on sovereign power discussed by Foucault, Agamben, and Mbembe. Foucault has explored changes in power, which went from being concentrated in the head of the throne, to a more 'capillary' and diffused manner penetrating the structure of society. Agamben questions whether we have completely overcome sovereign power, reminding us that it is in the domain of exception that power gains legitimacy to kill. Agamben also highlighted the importance of certain subjectivities and spaces, and how they become part of the administration of life. Mbembe (2003) elaborated on the importance of colonies as spaces of exception and race as the subject of violence, both overlooked by Agamben. I argue that in the colonies, power seemed to be more arterial than capillary, concentrated in specific domains, and legitimising decisions over life and death of certain places and peoples.

The chapter started by discussing exception regarding the 'war on drugs' because this is the narrative of exception currently operating in the legitimisation of police killings and disappearances in Brazil. The 'war on drugs' was discussed in light of the 'war on terror', as both create certain conditions whereby some lives and spaces are considered outside the norm. This discussion reveals a context permeated by exception – to echo Agamben. Using the concept of state apparatus, I argue that the police are the authority that embodies sovereignty in everyday Brazil – from stopping suspects in the streets to participating in extensive militarised operations – especially in favelas. The context of the 'war on drugs' is crucial to understanding the level of militarisation of law enforcement in the country, as well as the narratives that make some individuals subject to police action.

The concept of exception is also important in this discussion because the usual frame to discuss violence, including killings and disappearances, perpetrated by state officials, is that of the dictatorship from 1964 to 1985. However, as I have discussed in this chapter, the state of exception also takes place in 'so-called democracies', as Agamben highlighted. Once an exception is in place; life and space are 'captured' on the threshold between sovereignty and exception. As we have seen, the war as a metaphor not only leads to the exception in discursive terms but produces a series of changes in many realms, such as military and police apparatuses, life, and space. It is also important to highlight that in a context ruled by exception, killings and disappearances are legitimised when regarding those whose are considered as part of the abnormal.

Between nation-building and modernity 77

The chapter also discussed disappearances as liminality between life and death. The section introduces the dialogue between sovereign power and which possibilities of life are possible while drawing on the conceptual framework of 'right to kill', as discussed by Mbembe. The section has also introduced the relevance of discussing sovereign decision over life taking racialised notions into account and how they were historically constructed in the colonial process. In that sense, the nation-building process encompassed a modernity project that was different from the European version. While in Latin America and Brazil nation-building is marked by imperial/colonial relations, as discussed by Walter Mignolo and conceptualised as the logic of coloniality, the European process was based on religion (Rae 2002). Later, this process followed racialised notions to classify spaces, and the right to live and to kill (Mbembe 2003).

In this chapter, I argued that police violence is a fundamental dispositive operating to govern death in postcolonial spaces in the Global South. I argue that, in Brazil, the 'war on drugs' provides the legitimation needed to fulfil a rationale of state violence that deals with the 'excess' of life by making racialised populations die. The sovereign decision regulates through the security apparatus life that has been commodified into the economic market. Once certain lives are understood as excess – for example, by not serving as a working force – these lives become also killable. As will be further discussed in the subsequent chapters on state apparatus, life and death and space, which follows a historically grounded analysis in the development of urban areas in Rio de Janeiro and São Paulo, the plantation system is fundamental to understanding how urban areas were developed hand in hand with a racialised security apparatus. In that sense, what we see is the reproduction of colonial order within itself by recreating similar logic of racial and class hierarchies as those implemented during the colonisation of Latin America, including Brazil.

The following chapters follow from the discussion on state apparatus, life and space to analyse the specificities in Brazil. These three realms are crucial to my argument, since they shed light on how racialised notions are appropriated by the police and expressed as sovereign decision through the 'war on drugs'. In Chapter 3, I discuss the police's embodiment of sovereign will. In Chapter 4, I discuss how the police action is based on racialised notions, and in Chapter 5, I discuss the consequences of a symbolic construction of favelas and peripheries as a space of exceptions, following a colonial rationale.

Notes

1 The nation-state articulated homogeneity inside borders in terms of religion and then articulated dominance in terms of social class – as introduced by Antonio Gramsci. One important difference between Europe and Latin America in the process of nation-state building is that in the former, empires were multi-ethnic; consequently, racism and ethnic nationalism reached its height in the continent only during the twentieth century with fascism and Nazism (Mignolo 2000).

2 The de-colonial approach emphasises the notion of a world-system instead of using nation-states as a unit of analysis. It is used, for example, to refer to division of labour across the globe, as well as *coloniality* versus *imperiality* as part of the same logic and not as a separated phenomenon.
3 De-colonial thinkers such as Walter Mignolo, Immanuel Walerstein, Anibal Quijano, and Arturo Escobar, while discussing Latin America, tend to not account for Brazil's historical specificities. When I refer to Latin America, even when citing those authors, it will include Brazil. If there is a specific difference or similarity, it will be pointed out.
4 The armoured vehicle known as Big Skull was analysed by Amnesty International in 2006. The research under the title of 'We Have Come to Take Your Souls: the Caveirão and Policing in Rio de Janeiro' brought important information to discuss the policy of confrontation adopted by the state towards the 'war on drugs'.
5 According to the U.S. Bureau of Justice Statistics (BJS), in 2018, black males accounted for 34 per cent of the total male prison population, white males 29 per cent, and Hispanic males 24 per cent. White females comprised 47 per cent of the prison population in comparison to black females who accounted for 18 per cent of the female population. In 2017, blacks represented 12 per cent of the U.S. adult population but 33 per cent of the sentenced prison population. Whites accounted for 64 per cent of adults but 30 per cent of prisoners. And while Hispanics represented 16 per cent of the adult population, they accounted for 23 per cent of inmates.

3 The police apparatus

Between highly noticeable killings and unnoticed disappearances

Introduction

> Do you think we are disappearing people? This is not a dictatorship. We can kill, why would we make someone disappear?
> (Interviewee RJSO2)

During my fieldwork, to mention the word 'disappearance' generated discomfort. In many cases, the reaction was a look of fear. When the interviewee was a police officer, someone related to police activities, or specialists in public security, the discomfort was palpable. The discomfort was followed by the comment 'disappearance is a militia thing'. It is interesting to highlight that in many cases, the militia is the police – doing off-hours work. I find it puzzling that a police officer is able to change into a different role and act as militia. Although it can be argued that when the officer is performing such tasks, he or she is off duty, they operate having being trained by the state and using the know-how they learnt while doing police work.

Police violence in Brazil is usually associated with the dictatorship that was in place in the country from 1964 to 1985. During the military regime, the *auto de resistência* was created by the armed forces as a way to protect police officers who, under confrontation, killed someone. Later, the *dispositif* was used, and misused, by the police in the context of the 'war on drugs'. As will be discussed later in this chapter, the way the victim was killed in many cases indicated that instead of a confrontation, an execution occurred. Another correlation currently made between police violence and the dictatorship is the action of militias and death squads. Again, during the military dictatorship, São Paulo being only one example, police officers from the Department of Social and Political Order, the DOPS, led an extermination group to track down outlaws. After the dictatorship, militias, extermination groups, and death squads continued to operate, often overlapping such roles with their regular police activities.

To investigate why the killings and disappearances remain unproblematised, it is important to take a look at the *dispositif* that leads to death. This chapter examines the police apparatus in Brazil, combining a historical and

DOI: 10.4324/9781003032519-4

theoretical perspective, and how it developed over time. In historical terms, the chapter starts by focusing on the emergence of the security apparatus in Brazil and its relation to a state of exception. It covers the constitution of the police force in Brazil during the colonial and imperial period when the police helped to build cities, to control vagabonds, and to keep the royalty safe. The first point of inflexion regarding the role of the police was during the Getúlio Vargas government (1930–1945), when the police underwent a process of bureaucratisation and internal re-organisation to face the communist threat – allegedly the reason for the Vargas *coup* in 1937. Then, during the dictatorship, the apparatus built by and for the police was redesigned and passed to the hands of the Brazilian armed forces. The section on the dictatorship will focus on the use of disappearances against leftist guerrilla members.

At the end of the military dictatorship in Brazil in 1985, the 'war on drugs' assumed a condition of exception that was earlier associated with the fight against communism. As discussed in Chapter 2, in the context of the 'war on drugs', exceptionality follows the idea of a war that needs all measures in place to fight a well-armed dangerous enemy. A particular *dispositif* that gained relevance in this context was the *autos de resistência*. The chapter finishes by discussing the action of police killings, death squads, and disappearances in contemporary Brazil. In Brazil, political disappearance accounts only for those who were involved in the fight for democracy in the specific context of the dictatorship (1964–1985). As a consequence, I argue, there is an erasure of the epistemological framing that would have permitted the visibility of disappearance in a different context and scope.

In theoretical terms, this chapter engages with the debate on *biopolitics* and with the politics of death. As discussed in Chapter 2, disciplinary power, following Michel Foucault (2007), does not account for *making die*. On the contrary, disciplinary power is in place to optimise life, and violence occurs in the absence of power relations. Giorgio Agamben (2005) discusses the state of exception as an inherent part of the sovereign power that is still in place, in spite of modernity – especially in the decision over which lives can be made bare. Achille Mbembe (2003) goes a bit further to state that 'to exercise sovereignty is to exercise control over mortality and to define life as the deployment and manifestation of power' (Mbembe 2003: 12). For Mbembe (2003), technologies of control subjugate life to the power of death. In that sense, sovereign power has instrumentalised life and the risk of death as its central project.

In 'Necropolitics', Mbembe discussed the relationship between sovereign power and death, linking notions of modernity and terror, especially in the context of late-modern forms of colonial occupation where terror is used to justifying the 'concatenation of multiple powers: disciplinary, biopolitical and necropolitical' (2003: 29). To link those multiple powers, military presence and regularised warfare lead to totalising forms of control over life and death within a given space. When looking at police action in urban areas of Brazil, it is not difficult to trace a parallel with Mbembe's ideas. There, a colonial rationale based on slavery has confined black communities mainly in what are now favelas. Later, in the historical process of urban development and neoliberalism, favelas became the place for criminality, creating a space of exception within the norm. In this context, the life of black bodies is made bare to the point that the decision to make *them* die is not problematised, nor is one's disappearance.

This is the first of three chapters where I will converse with Achille Mbembe and Giorgio Agamben to analyse cases of disappearances and police killings of favela dwellers in urban areas of Brazil. The following chapter will draw on the racialised notions embodied by the police. It is important to notice that dominant narratives about the development of the police do not take 'race' into account. While this chapter presents dominant historical narratives on the development of the police in Brazil, the following chapter adds racialised accounts to the development of police action as the embodiment of sovereign decision.

Roots of an institutionalised police

From colony to empire (1500–1888)

There is controversy as to when the security apparatus was introduced in the new colony. Raymundo Faoro (1958) claims it happened during the process of colonisation, having its roots in the conquest of the territory. According to the website of the Regional Secretariat of Public Security of São Paulo, the idea of police emerged in 1500 when Dom Joao III adopted the system of hereditary captaincy, giving to the dignitaries (the owners of the land) authority 'to establish the administration, promote justice and organise public order as he wished' (Regional Secretariat of Public Security of São Paulo 2016). The captaincies of Brazil were an administrative landed division created by Portugal. Each was assigned to a Portuguese nobleman who became the Captain General. The captaincies were a hereditary possession, and the dignitaries had civil and criminal jurisdiction over all inhabitants in their captaincy following the Portuguese code of law.

Whereas in Faoro's viewpoint the security apparatus arose in the country with the aim of conquering the territory, it is important to highlight that this process did not take place in an empty space. On the contrary, as observed by Enrique Dussel (1995) and Tzvetan Todorov (2003), the domination of colonised territories first occurred through a military intervention that soon started to pervade the everyday lives of indigenous peoples, turning them into slaves and confiscating their land and resources. In many cases, the intervention *in the land* led to episodes of resistance organised by indigenous groups. One example is the Massacre of Saltpetre River in 1676 (Silva Pessoa 2006), a task force organised by the dignitary to punish a group of indigenous rebels, which resulted in the killing of 400 natives. In the example of Cariris Resistance (Moraes, 2001) a confederation of indigenous tribes was organised against the occupation and exploitation of their lands. However, in 1713, military forces killed most of the natives, putting an end to the movement.

Thomas Holloway (1997) opposes Faoro's (1958) argument that the police have their roots in the colonisation process. Holloway claimed that the

82 The police apparatus

expedition and military forces present in the colony could not be recognised as a police force, given that they did not perform what was considered to be basic police activities, such as repressing and preventing crime to protect persons and property and fighting internal or external threats. Holloway (1997) argues that police activities started when the Portuguese Royal Court was transferred to its first and largest colony, in 1808. Once the Court was established, mainly in Rio de Janeiro, Portuguese bureaucratic institutions were also reproduced in the new empire. The role of Superintendent of Police was created in 1808 and the Real Military Police Guard in 1809.

The Superintendent of Police, in charge of semi-urban areas, oversaw petty crimes, assured the ideological conformity of intellectuals, provided security for the royal entourage, built roads and waterworks, and so on (Cabral 2011; Schultz 2005; Silva 1986). The Real Military Police Guard was created by recruiting impoverished free males born from illicit relationships among white men and black women (Algranti 1988a). In many cases, without having many work options, they were forced to fulfil the position of police officers. With the growing concern about the need for a security force, military training was offered to those who worked part-time.

The Superintendent of Police at the time insisted on the creation of a sentry with military training to control enslaved populations, as will be further discussed in the following chapter. Police duties and roles have changed a great deal since their initial configuration. From 1808 to 1827 the judiciary and police duties overlapped, which changed only with the promulgation of the Imperial Penal Code decentralising police activities. Despite having administrative roles, the police was targeted as part of constitutionalist efforts to constrain royal authority in 1821 (Schultz 2005). In 1841, the Superintendent role was abolished, and each province started to have a chief of police. In 1842 a regulation defined the duties of the administrative law enforcement and the judicial police, both under the leadership of the Ministry of Justice. In 1871, the judicial sector was separated from the Police and the 'Police Inquest Department' was created, establishing a set of investigative actions to be performed by the Judicial Police to check the existence and authorship of a criminal fact, and to enable legal action. It is defined as a persecutory administrative procedure. Misse (2011) discussed in depth the implication of the police inquest department in Brazil, as well as the experience of other countries such as Argentina, Spain, and France.

In 1873, the Brazilian National Guard started a process of demilitarisation as an attempt to take back power from the private sector and concentrate it in the hands of the state. Also, after the Paraguay War, many soldiers who took part in the conflict were recruited all over the country. The last decades of empire were marked by a growing interest by the provinces in the use of police forces.

The security apparatus in Brazil was developed with the perspective of defending the nobility and aiming to expand agricultural lands owned by oligarchies. Holloway (1997) explained that when the colony was turned into an empire and Rio de Janeiro became its urban capital, the security apparatus was more concerned with the nobility's welfare rather than that of the populations.

Lemos (2012) highlighted how the new official role was concerned with organising the bureaucracy in the Department of Public Security and guaranteeing public security. In that sense, the police played two different roles: protection against private violence – the classical monopoly of violence – and a form of bureaucratic governmentality. Because it was through the police that a sense of hierarchy was established, with the introduction of wages, orders, and surveillance measures, Marcos Luis Bretas and Andre Rosemberg (2013) argued that police activities promoted the implementation of bureaucracy in Brazil, giving embodiment to a state-building process in the country.

The First Republic (1889–1936): Police action in semi-urban areas

The Proclamation of Republic in 1889 also marked the end of the Atlantic slave trade in Brazil. The end of the empire was caused mainly by lack of political support. The First Brazilian Republic was mainly articulated by the militaries in the country. Nevertheless, da Costa (1998) claimed that the First Republic was not a result of a tension between modern, liberal, and democratic values represented by the new urban middle class versus the rural oligarchies with their totalitarian politics. Instead, it was caused by a tension between traditional oligarchies in the Northeast, which were economically bankrupted but politically strong, and new oligarchies in São Paulo, which despite being wealthy had little political power. The Republic brought a new political alignment marked by decentralised federalism and by the idea of public order. The decentralised federalism and the agrarian feature of the country help to explain the rationale that would underpin police operations in Brazil.

This section provides an overview of the processes that led to the institutionalisation of a police force in the country. The perspective adopted, however, is the one that sees it as a response to socio-economic and political issues informed by the need to control a new and recently free population of former slaves who were fleeing to urban areas of Brazil in search of jobs, and by the fact that slavery had been the main mode of production until quite recently. In the rural part of the country, which was the majority, a political machine known as *coronelismo* centralised political dominance in the hands of local oligarchs personified as colonels.

In this same historical period, the police started to investigate and survey social movements, anarchists and 'dangerous foreigners'. The first important change to the police as an institution was the creation of the Political Police in 1907. At the time, the Investigative Body for Public Security[1] was created with the aim of preventing, investigating, and introducing mechanisms of surveillance.[2] The regulation that created it also reformulated the Civil Police.[3] In 1920 it was substituted by the Public Security and Investigation Inspection,[4] which was turned into the 4th Political Police Station in 1922,[5] a few months after a military rebellion against the government. The 4th Police Station, the first in the country dedicated to crimes against the state, used to have a special unit for political and social order, which included the suppression of social movements. This unit focused on the internal security of the republic, to apply preventive measures to the maintenance of the order, to assure the exercise of individual rights and to develop surveillance to the demonstrations or anarchic desires and pre-emptively act to expel dangerous foreigners.

(Bretas 1997: 30)

The creation of the 4th Political Police Station also helped to bring about the concept of technical police, who were divided into three different areas: the Chamber for Identification and Statistics, Forensic Services (which was in fact a morgue), and the Investigation and Arrests Unit; all three subordinated to the Ministry of Justice. These initiatives also saw the promulgation of a career plan for police officers and a Police School. The changes promoted in 1922 modified a previous presidential determination that only those who had a degree in law could take on the Chief of Police role. As a consequence, the Marshal, Manoel Lopes Carneiro Fontoura – a member of the armed forces – took on the position, gaining a reputation for being the greatest persecutor of military rebels in the 1920s.

In the process of consolidating a police force, it is important to acknowledge their historical role in racial oppression at a time when the urban areas were receiving a great influx of former slaves who were in search of work. At that moment, the police reinterpreted its role as manager of inequality, a crucial aspect of social control. The Penal Code, reformulated in 1890, legitimised the police's new role by regulating 'dangerous' practices, such as vagabondage, prostitution, drunkenness, and capoeira. Holloway (1997) concluded that the new Penal Code allowed better control over what was considered dangerous groups by criminalising their *mode-de-vie*. Da Costa (1998) advocated that a repressive apparatus was used against a flourishing proletarian movement, revealing the concern that such civil behaviour could gain European dimensions and become an organised social class movement.

In interpreting the treatment of the police towards criminalised populations, Maria Helena Souza Patto (1999) in her article about the link between the state, science, and politics during the First Republic challenged what she called an uncritical adaptation of Foucault's disciplinary power framework to analyse the context of the First Republic in Brazil. She argued that practices such as subtle repressive violence or the predominance of a non-corporal penalty fashioned as a disciplinary form of power, identified by Foucault in European countries at the turn of the eighteenth century, did not correlate Brazil. On the contrary, a disciplinary form of power had no place when physical violence impinged against those who were considered dangerous to the new political establishment. Patto (1999: 172) observed that institutions such as psychiatric hospitals, schools, or prisons used the repressive apparatus with brutality.

One example is the use of psychiatric institutions in Patto's (1999) detailed research on the articulation between psychiatric hospitals and the police. She showed that the Juquery Psychiatric Hospital located in São Paulo was by all accounts part of the police apparatus given that patients were often incarcerated without receiving mental health treatment, as argued by Maria Clementina

Pereira Cunha (1988, in Patto 1999) in her research into hospital archives. Mortality among patients was enormous. Most of them were children or elderly, and from black communities. According to Patto, what people experienced there was a terror, 'at that time, as now, impoverished people do not need to fit under the Penal Code to be targeted by the police' (1999: 190). The hospital did not follow any disciplinary duty. On the contrary, once inside, most of the patients would never return to society. Patto (1999: 190) argued that what used to break their resistance was not the disciplinary power oriented by medical knowledge, but the repression by the police, which resulted in reclusion and ruined self-image through a negative social representation.

The same type of overlapping between psychiatric institutions and the state can also be seen in the case of the Barbacena Mental Health Hospital, during the 1960s and 1970s – during the dictatorship. At this hospital, 60,000 people were admitted without a medical diagnosis or mental health disease to then be tortured and killed. Daniela Arbex (2013), who researched the hospital, stated that its population was of alcoholics, prostitutes, pregnant women, and other people who were considered outcasts.

The emergence of the police in Brazil is marked by a few different features of the social relations present at that time, such as slavery, colonialism, and the control of an emerging industrial working class. Daryle Williams (2001) argued that a selective appropriation of European bourgeois values reinforced the oligarchs' self-perception of governing over a largely poor and mixed-race society. In that context, labour radicalism, the pressing 'social question', rural delinquency, disquiet among junior military officers, and the emergent middle-class continued to test the notion of 'Order and Progress'. Alex S. Vitale (2017), reflecting on the creation and developing of U.S. policing activities, remarked that these elements are strongly impacting police activities and mindset in the United States. According to him, the police are supposed to be a tool for managing inequality and maintaining the status quo. This tool, as he calls, is in place by suppressing social movements and tightly managing the behaviours of poor and non-white people: those on the losing end of economic and political arrangements. Vitale (2017) claimed that a policed society had its roots in the eighteenth century when a point of contact between the coercive apparatus of the state and the lives of the citizens was forged to deal with demands for social justice. To Vitale (2017), when social order is at risk, whether from slave revolts, general strikes, or crime and rioting in the streets, the elites rely on the police to control such upheavals.

> Therefore, while the specific forms of policing have changed as the nature of inequality and the forms of resistance to it have shifted over time, the basic function of managing the poor, foreign and non-white on behalf of a system of economic and political inequality remains.
> (Vitale 2017: 34)

In the following section, I will address the politicisation of the police. In this period, the police take on new duties related to political dissidents and the suppression of social movements, especially those related to labour rights.

The Vargas Era and 'The New State': organising a nation-state through authoritarian rule

The disappearances in the military dictatorship have their roots in the general national narrative. The state security apparatus, in place during the last dictatorship, was created during another authoritarian regime in Brazil – the New State. Getúlio Vargas first took office as Chief of the Provisional Government (1930–1934), then as President (1934–1937), and as Dictator (1937–1945), inaugurating the 'New State', and again as a democratically elected President (1951–1954). Vargas gave his name to this historical period – the Vargas Era.

The historiography of the Vargas Era (1930–1945) focused on its advances when Vargas consolidated labour rights and regulated labour unions. Boris Fausto, who wrote Vargas's biography, defined the New State as 'authoritarian and *moderniser*' (2006: 91). In economic terms, Vargas protected the coffee market, and he is believed to have led the country's industrialism. Given that this was an authoritarian regime, it is not surprising that Brazil started to build up its security apparatus during that period, with features that remain to this day.

Brazil's shift to a nation-state is largely associated, in historiographical terms, to the moment of its independence and the first Constitution of 1824 (Derani 2002). According to this interpretation, the Independence crystallises the idea of Brazilian people – and their desire for an independent country. At the time, most of the population consisted of nobles, usually those who held people in slavery, the enslaved people themselves, and a few small business owners. The independence also saw the beginning of bureaucratisation in the country, and the Constitution of 1824 was the juridical milestone of the new nation-state (Derani 2002: 90). Other readings highlight different landmarks for the Brazilian nation-state, such as taxes (WP Costa 2003); law and rule (Lopes 2003), or the emergence of local elites (Dolhnikoff 2003). However, I argue that it was during the Vargas Era that important notions, such as nationalism and homogenisation inside borders, as well as a claim for the country's 'modernisation', gained force. Vargas focused on bureaucracy, homogenisation, and securitisation, mirroring the European process of nation-state consolidation (Carneiro 1994).

Regarding the role and development of the police, there is a lack of research, especially regarding the 1930s, as noted in the literature review elaborated by Marcos Luiz Bretas and Andre Rosemberg (2013) on this very topic. It was only after the National Truth Commission (2012–2014) permitted the investigation of archives that research on the topic was made possible. Aware of the roots of the state violence, the National Truth Commission had 1937 violations of human rights to investigate as a starting point. This section first presents the emergence of the 'modern' state apparatus in Brazil. I use the term *modern* here because I will argue that by using the perspective of state apparatus, it is during the Vargas Era that Brazil consolidates itself as a nation-state.

The disruption of the political agreement between the two most powerful oligarchies in Brazil marked the transition from a mostly rural country to its new urban phase, leading to a *coup d'état* conventionally called 'The 1930s

Revolution'. As a dictator, Vargas inaugurated what he called the 'New State' in Brazil, marked by the general belief that the authoritarian way was the only way to put Brazil in the right direction; in other words, on the path to industrialisation. Vargas advocated that a technical government, not involved with 'political games' played by political parties, was the solution to develop the country (Romani 2011).

The motto 'order and progress' inspired by positivist ideas[6] during the First Republic was still an inspiration. The desire of a *developed* country attached to the idea of 'modernisation' legitimised most of Vargas's policies. While positivism affected every Latin American country in the nineteenth century, its influence was nowhere as profound or widespread as in Brazil. It gained support by criticising the monarchy, slavery, and the Church, portraying these three institutions as the constraints of the natural progress of the nation. Positivism marks the doctrinal history of the National Army since the imperial period, including in the period of the proclamation of the republic and during the First Republic when military training began to be professionalised (Bellintani 2009). The most heterodox version of positivism advocates that order is the police state and progress is a society technically developed through industrialism (Bellintani 2009). The movement left its mark on the national flag, where it is possible to read 'Order and Progress'. The motto evokes the need to follow the government rules, and social demonstrations were considered against the national progress, a very popular idea during the Vargas government. The importance of the motto in the national flag would be renewed during the military dictatorship (1964–1985), when the state kept the internal order at any price, including the violent repression of political dissidents.

Williams (2001: 5) highlighted that the Vargas regime initially justified itself as a necessary measure to manage the economic crisis and to reform political institutions, inaugurating a political culture in the country that revolved around interventionism. Carneiro (2015) highlighted that the state-building process during the Vargas Era followed two prescriptions: the protection of the Brazilian citizen and the material and moral progression of the country. The second resulted in the deepening of the restriction to immigration. As an example, there was a prohibition of Jewish citizens to enter the country (Carneiro 2015). Ideologically aligned with the Gestapo, the persecution of Jewish communities in Brazil had its apex a few years later when Olga Benario, married to the leader of the Communist Party in Brazil, was extradited to Germany, after being handed to the Gestapo in 1936 (Carneiro 2012, 2015; Gaspari 2003).

With all the attention given to the military dictatorship in Brazil (1964–1985), less attention is generally given to the *dispositif* established during the authoritarian Vargas Era. Although Vargas had the support of the armed forces during his government, the police were the institution that assumed a prominent role under his rule. Marcos Tarcision Florindo, who researched the political police archives (DEOPS/SP in Portuguese), was able to demonstrate the changes that the 4th Political Police Station went through during the Vargas Era.

88 The police apparatus

Getúlio Vargas took power, for the first time, after a disruption of the electoral system. The electoral system was organised through regional oligarchies personified by the elites from São Paulo and coffee producers, and Minas Gerais dairy producers shared political power using a political arrangement known as *pax republican*. According to it, the country's presidents should alternate, favouring one of the two political oligarchies at each election. The agreement was put in check when President Washington Luiz from São Paulo supported a candidate from the same region. Getúlio Vargas, the candidate from the opposition who was not supported by the president, lost the elections but organised a coup with the help of a military junta in 1930. The coalition sent Washington Luiz into exile, suspended the federalist constitution of 1981, and put extra-constitutional measures into place as a means to solve the political crisis among the elites. Shortly after, the Vargas coalition turned the coup of 1930 into a Revolution by considering it a purifying force (Florindo 2011, 2015)

Once in power, Vargas strengthened federal agencies and expanded their powers to establish control measures on agricultural production, with impact on the coffee market. He also created new agencies to coordinate policies in education, health, labour relations, industrial policy, and commerce, and he founded a number of state companies. Most of Vargas's policies are still active in the country (Williams 2001: 4–5). Florindo (2011: 124) claimed that Vargas's reforms, especially labour-related ones, strengthened the control over social relations by the state.

Getúlio Vargas was celebrated as a messianic figure that protected the new state against the communist threat, especially after a frustrated attempt by the communists to take power during the Communist Revolt in 1935. The coup in 1937, legitimised by the communist threat, which was reinforced by the Communist Revolt, closed the National Congress, extinguished political parties and elections, and criminalised political dissidents. A new constitution was written. Authoritarianism was considered the only way to contain 'new forces' represented by the new urban-industrial population and communism (Schwarcz and Starling 2015). The 'New State' was inaugurated in 1937.

Although Vargas governed with the support of military forces, his authoritarian rule was not a military one. This variation is important because later, although armed forces were in power during the dictatorship, the police did not take a secondary role. On the contrary, the police acted in parallel with the armed forces, even though their actions are not perceived as political. During the 1930s, Vargas reinforced the role of the Special Unit for Social and Political Security (DEOPS, in Portuguese), created in 1924 as the 4th Political Police Station to foresee and restrain political dissidence. At this point, the unit started to change its institutional role (Florindo 2011: 125). Among its attributions, it had to analyse national and international publications and survey all public organisations and suspected individuals. Florindo (2011: 125) also highlighted that the truculent manner in which the political police unit controlled the working class would characterise the way the police worked in Brazil for years to come. He also emphasised their arbitrary behaviour towards legal norms, changing them of their own accord.

The DEOPS was dismembered to give birth to two agencies, one focusing on the political and the other on the social. There was a special focus on the reconfiguration of what social and political deviance would mean. The agencies gave attention to the surveillance and repression of those who instigated class violence, inciting strikes or social revolution (Florindo 2011: 126). It was also during the 1930s that the police gained financial resources, hired and trained agents, organised its internal structure, assumed new duties, and started a process of bureaucratisation. The political police units gained resources from the federal state to expand their duties, and a new unit was created that was responsible for 'police inquest', making the process of police investigation more normative (Misse 2011).

Florindo (2011) argued that the new police division indicated a change in the way social issues were perceived during the Vargas period, which went from being seen as a police problem to being considered a state and political police problem. In order to address the issues caused by 'the dangerous classes' without causing a political contestation or resistance, it was necessary to distinguish social and political crimes from common crimes (Florindo 2011: 127). As a political mechanism, this is very important because it highlights the political need to create an exception, according to which certain crimes and related punishment should be separate from common crimes. This logic can be observed during the 'war on drugs', as I will explain later in this chapter.

The social regulation was so central to Vargas that the political police gradually expanded their duties from surveying the working class and political dissidents to incorporating other activities. The list encompasses the surveillance of the movement of foreigners in and out of the country, the transit of people at airports and train stations, the repression of crimes against the popular economy, the oversight of the production and distribution of guns, and the surveillance of hotels and their guests (Florindo 2011: 129). The division inside the police changed a lot through the 1930s, showing initiatives of cooperation with the police of Uruguay and the American Federal Bureau of Investigation. Regarding structural organisation, it followed the example of the Soviet Union Police, the British Secret Service, and the Nazi Gestapo (Florindo 2011: 132). Based in São Paulo, the system started to be expanded in 1936, first to Rio de Janeiro and then to the rest of the country. However, there was resistance at the state level to the administrative centrality of the police. Mechanisms of management were incorporated into the structure of the police from other states. Florindo (2011: 134) argued that although bureaucracy could bring legitimacy to police intervention, it should not constrain the activity of the police at the street level, where the arbitrary action was a requirement for effective intervention.

It is also the same police apparatus, created during the Vargas Era that later during the military dictatorship would regain importance in its role of political and social repression. Getúlio Vargas never denied his appreciation for the fascist government of Italy and the Gestapo police in Germany. It was also during this period that Jewish citizens were forbidden to enter the country, and migrant populations in the southern regions of Brazil were not allowed to speak their native language (Carneiro 2012).

90 *The police apparatus*

Traditional historiography of Brazil establishes the departure of the Portuguese Crown as the start of the nation-state, an event that brought an end to the empire and initiated the First Republic. I will argue the contrary, that the state-building process in Brazil started only later. In discussing the security and police apparatuses in Brazil, it is crucial to discuss the Vargas Era because it is through authoritarian measures, as highlighted by Heather Rae (2002) regarding the European process, that Brazil consolidates itself as a nation-state. What is important to observe, however, is how the idea of modernity plays a crucial role in the national imaginary, as a need to assert itself as a nation-state and a player in the international system. This section discussed how the police, as a status apparatus, evolved to enforce the authoritarian rule, which is seen as beneficial to the country to constrain disruptive new urban populations. As Bretas and Rosemberg (2013: 172) highlighted, research on the police from the 1930s onwards is still lacking. The police units archive was only recently opened by the National Truth Commission.

The military dictatorship (1964–1985)

The wave of *coup d'états* led by the military, which started in 1964 in Paraguay, spread throughout Latin America and was marked by authoritarianism, violence, and the presence of military groups in the political realm. In Brazil, there was, at least in the beginning, no intention that such a scenario would become permanent, nor that deep institutional reforms would take place (Aquino 1999; Paixão 2006). The Army used the legislative to bring legitimacy to the state of exception. From 1964 to 1969, 17 norms and decrees were created by the Army, endorsed by the President who was a member of the armed forces, and approved by the National Security Council. The first Institutional Act (AI-1, in Portuguese) changed the Brazilian Constitution of 1946 concerning the presidential elections. From this moment onwards, the armed forces had the power to cease all political rights, including legislative ones. The second Institutional Act (AI-2, In Portuguese) from 1965 established indirect elections and reduced the number of political parties to only two – the ARENA, representing the government, and the MDB, representing the opposition but also controlled by the government. All the Institutional Acts ruled above all other laws and contributed towards bringing legitimacy to the regime. The country gained a new constitution in 1967 enforced by the fourth Institutional Act, AI-4. The new constitution institutionalised and legitimised the military regime while establishing the power of the Executive over the Legislative and the Judiciary.

The idea of the internal enemy, widespread by the Superior School of War, which was responsible for training Army officers, was the reason given for the *coup d'état*, affirming the need for a transition from democracy to dictatorship. Similarly to the First Republic and the Vargas Era, the armed forces were in charge of 'cleaning' and 'fixing' the country against corruption, putting the country back into the 'right' direction and defeating the revolutionary communist war (Leandro de Araujo 2011; de Araujo 2013). As will be discussed later, the idea of an internal enemy is recaptured in the context of the military intervention in favelas (Carvalho 2006; Martins 2013). The National Security Police, which set the guidelines for national goals, encompassed different realms, such as the political, economic, and social realms, as well as the military. The political sphere was marked by the removal of all individuals who could be against the new regime. The first measure taken by the Army, expressed in the AI-1, was the suspension of political rights of all citizens considered to be against the regime.

Regarding society, there was an ideological debate, which de-legitimised claims for social justice with respect to workers, students, peasants, or low-ranking soldiers by associating them with communists or anarchists. The military sphere was at the core of this new regime. With huge investments, the military realm was deeply marked by the creation of the National Intelligence Service (SNI, in Portuguese). The agency, created in 1964, was the backbone of the regime, focusing on identifying and articulating with anti-communist actions (Comissão de Familiares de Mortos e Desaparecidos Políticos 1995; Passetti 2013). The National Defence Policy was permeated by the idea of an enemy inside the borders, driven by an ideological goal of making the population suspicious. Understanding the concept of national defence as a protection of the borders against foreign attacks, the defence forces focused their attention on enemies inside the national borders. Informed by the international bipolarity of the Cold War, with the United States representing democracy versus the Soviet Union representing communism, the term communist-subversive characterised those who should be eliminated (Bueno 1985; Bauer 2011). Alves (2005) concluded that, in creating this kind of enemy, the government developed two types of defensive structure based on the creation of a repressive apparatus backed by the armed control to coerce the population, and on an information network to identify the enemy, mostly relying on torture. The present section will first examine the structure of the armed forces, which articulated with the police and private companies in the fight against communism. This analysis highlights how the idea of citizenship, which started during the Vargas Era, continued during the military regime.

According to the recent work of the National Truth Commission Report (2014), political killings and disappearances made 434 victims in Brazil over the Military Regime (1964–1985). The NTC examined how the security state apparatus was disseminated with the notions of 'to make die' and 'make disappear', working in collusion with public and private institutions, such as the morgue, cemeteries, public notary, and private companies (2014: 320). Focusing on the armed forces as the main perpetrators of such violations, the NTC was able to trace the alliance between the armed forces and the police at the time (2014: 729). Amongst the wide-ranging techniques of violence deployed by the state, with torture being the most widespread, enforced disappearances became the symbol of the regime. In numerical terms, Brazil was not the most dramatic scenario regarding the disappearance of leftists groups during the military dictatorship by comparison to other countries in the Southern Cone. The official number of *political disappearances* in Brazil,

92 The police apparatus

according to the National Truth Commission Report (2014), was 243 cases, which accounts for more than half of the overall 434 fatal victims. However, even if the numbers in Brazil are not too dramatic, the figures deserve more attention. For example, indigenous populations and rural workers have not included in the 'political disappearance' figures by the National Truth Commission, or by other similar initiatives for that matter. By classing some victims as enforced disappeared, the truth commission process politicised enforced disappearances fixing it regarding the particular historical time, the dictatorship, where the victims are the leftist groups, and the perpetrators the Army. Everything else outside this frame is de-politicised. I argue this is crucial to understand the way disappearances and police killings are de-politicised in contemporary Brazil.

The armed forces and the police: the security apparatus against leftist groups: torture, killings, and 'political disappearances'

The cooperation between the police and the armed forces had different configurations over time. The Department of Social and Political Order (DOPS), created in 1924 during the Estado Novo (1937–1946), suffered many changes in its hierarchy and structure until it reached an established model during the dictatorship. Before the dictatorship, under the administration of the police, the department was responsible for investigating social movements and strikes, inspecting unions, and producing reports about political activities outside urban centres. During the 1960s, it also started to investigate student unions and guerrilla groups, to censor the media, and to provide documents for job seekers to certify potential employers that the person had never been listed in the department's records (NTC Report 2014 162 v1). With the end of the dictatorship, the DOPS was replaced by the Civil Police, the structure of which will be explained.

The cooperation between the armed forces and the police was first conceived with the *Bandeirantes Operation* (Oban) created in 1969. The joint action brought together a number of agencies and different levels of the security apparatus. The idea was to centralise the work of the intelligence unit against subversive groups. The operation that had its headquarters in São Paulo was coordinated by the Department of Information Operations and the Centre for Internal Defence Operations, DOI-CODI. The centre for Investigation and Intelligence was created by the Army and financed by businessmen from the energy sector. The main aim of those organisations was to fight against the internal enemy that was threatening national security. The headquarters of OBAN and DOI-CODI in São Paulo was the place where the largest number of people were tortured and disappeared (NTC Report – volume 1, 2014). It involved a collaboration between the police and an Army task force; a model replicated in many units in the country (NTC Report 2014 112 v1).[7] Later, the work carried out by Oban was taken over by the DOI-CODI (NTC Report 2014 165 v1).

When the DOI-CODI took over the responsibilities from Oban, the DOPS/SP stopped being the main actor in the repressive police apparatus. In 1975, the Department of Social and Political Order of São Paulo (DOPS/SP in Portuguese) was re-housed under the State Department of Social and Political Order (DEOPS/SP in Portuguese), in operation until 1983. The information gathered by the NTC Working Group is that at least eight people disappeared at that place between June 1969 and October 1973 (NTC Report 2014). According to the NTC Report (2014), the DOPS/SP was still important because it coordinated other activities that were necessary to cover torture and disappearances, such as the Forensic Institute, the Public Notary, and an exclusive team under police commissioner Sergio Paranhos Fleury (NTC Report 2014 165 v1). The commissioner known as Fleury led a death squad during the dictatorship responsible for killing 'common criminals', i.e., criminals not connected to the *political* struggle (NTC Report 2014 166 v1).

The death squad led by Commissary Fleury shows that the violence perpetrated by police officials during the dictatorship was not only against political opponents. The cooperation between the armed forces and the police in the terms described earlier shows that the armed forces were directed to suppress the internal enemy, meaning communist groups that wanted to take over power. The police were not only in charge of institutional support but also of 'death squads', whose concern was those considered 'common criminals'.

The Brazilian Military Regime followed a similar rationale towards the repression of communist groups to that during the Vargas Era. Considered as a threat, the military dictatorship in Brazil used the idea of the internal enemy as ideological background, articulated by the National Intelligence Service. The armed forces gradually empowered themselves by applying methods such as torture and disappearances towards their opponents with the support of other institutions, such as the morgue, hospitals, and cemeteries, to erase the act of making someone disappear. This is important to establish commonalities and differences between the practices in place during the dictatorship and contemporary cases (1985–2015), which serve to illustrate how society and institutions are dealing with that type of violence.

The National Truth Commission (NTC) Report (2014) pointed out that enforced disappearances were both a systematic practice applied by the civil-military dictatorship to intimidate their opponents, and a strategy to cover state violations such as torture and killings perpetrated by state agents against communists. Robben (2005), who discussed the Argentinean dictatorship, highlighted that disappearance was a strategy to spread fear in society. By 1973, disappearances had become an end to those who were abducted and tortured by the Army. Besides being a way of hiding 'unwanted' persons by the regime, disappearances were also implemented as a means to conceal evidence of atrocities committed by the regime (Robben 2005).

In Brazil, disappearances were used to cover cases of torture followed by murder, perpetrated by state agents inside official bases or at unofficial camps. It is difficult to be precise about how many people were tortured during the military regime in Brazil. Seventy-five thousand requests were presented by the Amnesty Commission, created in 2002 by the Ministry of Justice. Torture was used to get information from and about those considered communist or

94 The police apparatus

subversives. Another way to identify those who were tortured is through testimonies by survivors (Fon 1979; Truth Commission–Sao Paulo 2014). The NTC Report stated that 191 people died as a consequence of torture from 1946 to 1988. From accounts of confrontation against the police to the staging of suicides inside the cells, many attempts were made to hide the violence taking place in Army cells. The NTC organised the reports of political killings and disappearances by year. The data presented by the NTC report informed that:

> The fake confrontation involving firearms was presented in 32% of statements presented by the Army to justify its opponents' deaths, which suggested a certain preference in staging it. This strategy changed from 1971 when there were 30 cases of enforced disappearance, a huge peak in comparison to the previous year when 14 people were disappeared by force. In 1972, the number of disappearances, 44, was higher than the number of deaths, 25. The trend continued in the following years. In 1973 there were 15 deaths and 54 political disappeared; in 1974 there were two deaths and 53 disappeared; in 1975, seven deaths and eight disappeared. These data indicate a change in the way the repressive apparatus hid their crimes. In 1976, there were 11 deaths and 11 disappearances. From 1977 onwards, the number of victims started to decrease. In this year, and in the next, there were two deaths and two disappearances. In 1979, there were six deaths and in 1980, five deaths and five disappearances. In 1981, no one was reported victim of political violence. From 1982 onwards, there was no information indicating cases of enforced disappearance. Up until 1985, there were four deaths. There are still eight occurrences lacking information.
> (National Truth Commission Report, volume 1, 2014: 443)

Narratives used to cover killings that happened as a consequence of torture were also used to cover enforced disappearances. Until 1973, torture and murder of regime opponents were often followed by the staging of fake suicides or accounts of confrontation with the police. While the regime was deemed legitimate, there was an increase in the number of people being tortured and killed – especially after the 5th Act (AI-5) in 1968. From this point onward, the military forces institutionalised enforced disappearances as a practice to cover their violations.

From that moment onwards, enforced disappearances involved bodies being buried under different names or classed as non-identified. The Army failed to give any information to the family about the fate of those who were missing. The Army often misled families by directing them to different military stations throughout Brazil. According to families' testimonies and many documents found by the NTC Working Group (NTC Report 2014), the repressive apparatus knew where the disappeared was because the information was registered in documents produced by the regime; however, they would deliberately give inaccurate information or fail to inform the family. The narrative given by the armed forces usually reinforced the culpability of the victim for his or her fate.

It was mainly from 1974 to 1976 that the military regime invested in eliminating communism from Brazil. During that period, the regime incarcerated almost 700 leftist members and killed more than 20 leaders of communist parties and associations (Gaspari 2003). From 1964 to 1985, the regime also killed and disappeared 434 guerrilla members. Following a political plan to organise a new election in Brazil, the military dictatorship in Brazil ended in 1985 with the first indirect elections. Direct elections would happen only in 1989.

Violence against communists for ideological reasons ceases with the end of the dictatorship. The state security apparatus created to work against the internal enemy – the supposed communist – which operated in an official regime of exception was disarticulated. However, another security apparatus, in place even before the exception posed by the communist threat, continues. This other security apparatus targets mostly racialised communities in favelas and peripheries of urban areas in Brazil. This is not to say that during the Vargas Era or the Military Regime, this other state apparatus was not operating. Nevertheless, from the perspective of national memory, rare are the occasions of killings and disappearances in communities not engaged with communism. The second volume of the National Truth Commission Report (2014) was dedicated to the violation of human rights among indigenous communities, homosexuals, workers, rural workers, etc. The report from the Truth Commission Local Group in Rio de Janeiro (2015) dedicated a chapter to violence in favelas, violence against homosexuals with a racialised bias, and death squads. The Recife Truth Commission Report (Comissão Estadual da Memoria e Verdade Don Helder Camara 2017) presents some chapters on the biography of 'political' disappearances of Peasant League members.

While the term *enforced disappearances* is used by the Truth Commission when referring to indigenous communities, for example, the term does not circulate broadly in the media. Closely related, but carrying a narrower meaning, the 'political disappeared' refers to those who, because of their political engagement with the communist ideology, were killed and disappeared by the military regime (1964–1985). The consequences of such an understanding of the term is twofold. Firstly, regarding the operationalisation of the security apparatus, it casts a shadow on the violence perpetrated against other groups, and it also depoliticises their struggles. Secondly, by making the term unchallengeable, 'political disappearance' becomes so tightly associated with the dictatorship that it is not possible to discuss this type of violence in other contexts. One example is how it was portrayed in the media immediately after the dictatorship.

Re-democratisation in Brazil: new actors and a *dispositif* in the governmentality of death

The 1960s and 1970s marked the emergence of new episodes of urban violence especially in Rio de Janeiro and São Paulo. The emergence of death squads and slaughters perpetrated by police officers against crimes not related to the communist threat were broadcast and widely circulated by the media

(Da Costa 1998). In this context, the state apparatus involved in the political violence against communism was also part of the violent urban struggle. A constant point of debate is the extent to which the military dictatorship penetrated social relations and everyday life. Among many recommendations, the Truth Commission of Rio de Janeiro, in its final report (Comissão Estadual da Verdade do Rio de Janeiro 2015), pointed out the need for external accountability in cases of violence perpetrated by the police and its de-militarisation.

Traditionally organised around the field of urban violence, the literature on public security in Brazil is strongly marked by concepts of citizenship, poverty, and development. Alba Zaluar (1999) who explored how this literature addressed the issue of violence in Brazil over the last 25 years, identified two major trends. On the one hand, following a Marxist tradition, Brazilian researchers commonly use a Foucauldian perspective in an attempt to explain the correlation between mechanisms of power and discipline evidenced in the police and prison systems (see Adorno de Abreu 1990; Carrara 1991; Kant de Lima 1989, 1997; Motta and Misse 1979). On the other hand, there are those who focus on the democratic *dispositif* and how it takes control of criminality (see Bretas 1997; Cavalcanti 1985; Fischer 1985; Velho and Alvito 1996). By the end of the military regime, researchers were more concerned with understanding the challenge in building a democratic society marked by military interventions (Zaluar 1999). In the 1980s, the debate of causalities of violence in Brazil was politicised and dichotomised (Zaluar 1999) between those who understood misery, capitalist exploitation, or lack of investments on education as the reasons for the increase in urban violence, and others who decided to investigate institutional issues as police practices of violence aiming to solve the problem by improving public policies.

The police apparatus at this point was marked by the emergence of militia groups, the action of death squads – in many occasions responsible for disappearances, and the continuity of a *dispositif* called *autos de resistência*, created during the dictatorship. This present section will focus on discussing the impact of militia groups and death squads, and the *dispositif* of *autos de resistência* which, I argue, is an important aspect of the governmentality of death. Those topics will be discussed in light of the 'war on drugs', which ultimately justifies, legitimises, and de-politicises resulting deaths.

Autos de resistência

The murders committed by police officers on duty, known as 'resistance killings' (*autos de resistência* in Portuguese), sanitise the killings committed in the name of law enforcement, included in the Criminal Code as a lawful homicide. The norm was first signed by the Security Secretary of Rio de Janeiro during the dictatorship in the country and later became an article in the National Criminal Code. According to it, there is no crime if the agent acted out of necessity, self-defence, in strict compliance with a statutory duty, or while exercising the law (Misse et al. 2013). Misse et al. (2013) highlighted that the different category granted to these crimes influences how related court procedures are conducted in the criminal justice system and explains why there is hardly ever a contestation of the versions presented by police officers. The problem is that resistance killings have been distorted by the police who can make crime scenes appear to be the result of a confrontation. Misse et al. (2013) compare this situation with what happens in the United States, where killings committed by police officers on duty are not classed under a different category, arguing, however, that while these investigations follow the same path as any other homicide, the outcome suggests that they are treated differently.

Figures for police violence in Brazil are astonishing. The six-day average number of killings by the police in Brazil is equivalent to the 25-year average number in Britain (Anistia Internacional 2015). The police in Rio alone killed more than 10,000 people from 2001 to 2011. Research conducted by Misse et al. (2013) discussing the criteria, discourses, and relations that play out in the period between the registration of a 'resistance killing' to the final court decision, concluded that extrajudicial killings are being carried out under the pretence of 'resistance killings'. Furthermore, the connivance of courtroom members suggests that the issue may be deeper than just police deceit.

The decision over *autos de resistência* is not only made by police officers but is supported by other public spheres – also embodying sovereign decision. Research led by Ignacio Cano (1998) on the procedures adopted by military justice in the investigation of *autos de resistência* showed that in Rio de Janeiro, 295 cases were dropped, out of a total of 301, following a request by the Attorney's Office (Cano 1998).

Autos de resistência has been problematised in multiple aspects, such as the way it is reported, the way it is investigated, and the way it is used to cover summary executions, as I will discuss further. Michel Misse (2011) explained that the first step following death by a police agent during operation is to register the occurrence at the police station. However, once the incident is classified under 'Homicide due to *Auto de Resistência*' a report is written describing the events that led to that homicide. As advised by the Secretary of State for Public Security during the dictatorship, the murdered person is described in two contrasting ways: as a 'victim', since he or she was murdered, and as 'the author' of a crime that originated the confrontation, such as robbery, resisting arrest, or attempted murder against the police officers. Misse (2011: 10) claimed that a formalisation of guilt whereby people are criminalised through 'a narrative that justifies their death' is almost systemic. All homicide investigations in Brazil, whether voluntary or involuntary, will trigger a police inquiry because of the undeniable materiality represented by the body.

The discussion on how *autos de resistência* is reported and investigated reflects the concern that this *dispositif* is being used to cover summary executions. A public persecutor stated that almost all the cases he examined that were classed as *autos de resistência* were, in fact, fake (Human Rights Watch 2009: 30). Souza (2010: 171) pointed out that in many cases, evidence indicates that the murder happened after the confrontation between the police and drug dealers. In other cases, evidence pointed out that there was no confrontation – as in the example of Juan, which will be discussed in Chapter 5. Police officers from the Military Police and Civil Police often state that 'criminals deserve to die', justifying police lethality in situations where the person murdered was involved with crime at some point in his or her life (Misse 2011: 40). Souza (2010: 173), who compared police killing in São Paulo to figures in other countries, concluded that in São Paulo, the police killed 0.97 people per 100,000 inhabitants, compared to South Africa, 0.96/100,000, and the United States, 0.12/100,000 (Human Rights Watch 2009: 35).

The need for militarised forces and the use of *autos de resistência* has changed over different governments. The ascension of militias in Rio de Janeiro followed implicit, and at times explicit, support from state governments (Cano 2008; Souza 2010; Gaffney 2012). During the re-democratisation period (1987–1991), police officers used the 'missing person' category to tackle police killings (Souza 2010: 158). Later, during Marcelo Alencar's government (1995–1999), police officers were granted a 'Bravery Bonus' for best performance. A series of denunciations accused police officers of falsifying evidence to make summary executions look like *autos de resistência*. In other cases, the police were accused of killing those who tried to escape (Carvalho Filho 2004). According to Farias, police officers were told 'to shoot first and ask later' (Farias 2014: 34).

In 2012, the National Secretariat of Human Rights recommended the abandonment of *autos de resistência*, and Rio de Janeiro and São Paulo stopped using the expression. In 2016, the Higher Council of Police, the Federal Police Agency, and the National Council of Civil Chiefs of Police abolished the term. However, the term was replaced by 'corporal injury resulting from opposition to police intervention' or 'homicide resulting from opposition to police action' – which, according to Cano (in Lemgruber et al. 2017), still indicates that there was resistance and, consequently, a presumption of the victim's guilt.

Analytically speaking, by registering a death at the police station and producing a legal document, the police officer remains inside the law; but he is also outside the law given that his act is by definition an 'unlawful homicide'. Furthermore, the term *auto de resistência* can be analysed within a similar framing to that used by Agamben when addressing a lacuna in law. As discussed in the previous chapter, when there is no definition that clarifies the difference between drug consumers and traffickers, a lacuna in the law is created leaving room for the police officer to make a decision – that is the first sovereign decision from an authority that will be legitimised, or not, by other actors in position of authority, as is the case of an attorney.

When discussing the intersection between law, lacuna, killings, and the narrative of the 'war on drugs', which targets a specific parcel of the population, it is important to bring to the fore the relationship between law and sovereign decision. To Agamben 'the sovereign, having the legal power to suspend the validity of the law, legally places himself outside the law' (1995: 17).

Indeed, the condition of exception occurs once the sovereign has the power to enforce the law, to create new laws, or even to bypass them. Agamben (1995) explains that a relation of inclusion and a regime of exclusion/exception are constituted when the sovereign creates an exception.

Militia groups and death squads: summary executions, mass slaughter, and disappearances

Over the last few decades, the image of the disappeared and their families start to appear in the public scene, but they are not framed as such. During the 1990s, for example, the kind of violence that was more visible was the so-called 'slaughters' (*chacina* in Portuguese) associated with 'death squads'. Later, the increase in a number of *autos de resistência*, which reached a peak in 2008 with 2,232 victims in Rio de Janeiro (Misse 2011),[8] attracted a great deal of attention from the general public, media, and social movements, who focused on the killings perpetrated by the police. Such dramatic figures enhanced the tension between the police and drug dealers and often made favela dwellers victims in the resulting confrontation. The fact is that killings have more visibility than disappearances given that the latter is much more complex both in terms of investigation and accountability.

Since there is a general sense that disappearances are caused by militia groups, it is noteworthy that militia members are often off-duty or retired police officers. Over the years those groups have taken control of more than half of Rio's favelas (Cano 2008; Gaffney 2012; Oosterbaan and van Wijk 2015). The main aim of these groups is to 'clean the area' and 'maintain the peace' (Ribeiro and Oliveira 2010). Their activities are usually related to the fight against the dominance of drug cartels, and their action is legitimised through the understanding that 'those who kill outlaws are not outlaws themselves' (Monteiro 2007). More recently, militia members are taking part in the by-elections. Whereas drug dealers stick to the trade of drugs and guns, militia groups have offered all sort of services to favela residents, such as cable television, cooking gas, and private security to shop owners (Ribeiro and Oliveira 2010; Gaffney 2012). It is important to notice that militias are more present in Rio de Janeiro than in São Paulo.

In the 1990s the increase in violence was associated with unprecedented urban growth – favelas and peripheral areas in particular – and with the emergence of drug cartel activities. At that time, militias were taking over some territories and forcing out drug cartels from the area. It was only after 2006 that these groups expanded – supported, tacitly or explicitly, by police units in those areas – rapidly taking over territories that had been controlled by drug dealers (Cano 2008). In some cases, their control over a new area was through the killing of local drug lords. Militias have also reportedly kidnapped drug lords and intimidated and executed public officers, judges, and journalists (Cano 2008; Gaffney 2012). In a more recent trend, after occupying favelas and other peripheries, militias have guaranteed the vote for specific politicians – by coercion, collusion, or corruption. As a consequence, those groups have consolidated their power by increasingly taking over higher positions in public administration at the city and state levels (Zaluar and Conceição 2007; Cano 2008; Gaffney 2012).

During the 1990s there was an increase in massacres and slaughters by 'death squads' associated with the police and militias. Although the focus here is not on cases of police killings and disappearances related to agrarian disputes, such as Corumbiara (1995), Eldorado dos Carajás (1996), and Felizburo (2004), the Eldorado do Carajás marked a change in the investigation of related cases. Fernando Henrique Cardoso, then president of Brazil, decided to transfer the investigation of police killings, in cases where there was clear intention to kill, to the non-military judicial system (Misse 2011: 30). In the agrarian areas, a massacre is seen as a way to solve disputes between peasants and farming-related corporations. In those cases, the police have systematically opened fire against rural workers.

Cases of disappearances in the urban context, which involves police and militias, are usually classed in the media as slaughter. One example is the Acari Slaughter (1990) in Rio de Janeiro when 11 young people, including seven minors, were disappeared. Some teenagers from the Acari favela were having a day off in a house in Mage – another periphery, when a group who identified themselves as police officers came to the house asking for money and jewels. The 71-year-old resident and her 12-year-old grandson managed to escape, but none of the others was ever seen again, and their bodies were never found. The mothers of the teenagers organised themselves as the Acari Mothers to fight for justice, but in 1993, one of the mothers was murdered while investigating the case. In 2010, the file was closed by the Homicide Division due to lack of evidence. The investigation of the case acknowledged that an extermination group known as *Cavalos Corredores*, or Running Horses, composed of police officers, caught the group of 11 youngsters. Their disappearance is seen as a result of the action of death squads. However, the question about the disappearance as a modality of extermination did not attract attention. For now, it is important to highlight that the understanding of disappearances in Brazil is directly related to the dictatorship. In the case of disappearances after the military regime, we find the use of the term massacre, associated with the action by 'death squads'.

Another case of extermination was the *May Crimes* in May 2006, a succession of attacks led by the First Command of the Capital (PCC), considered one of the main criminal organisations in Brazil, based in São Paulo. The reason for the violence is still debatable. For some, it started when the Public Security Secretary, Saulo de Castro Abreu Filho moved one of the PCC leaders to a high-security prison (G1 2016). However, there are also versions that point to the kidnapping of one of the PCC leaders by police officers (IHRC 2011; Guerra 2016). As a response, rebellions were organised in 73 prisons in the state, and PCC members attacked post offices, banks, and a police officer's house, and also set fire to 43 buses.

To deal with the wave of violence, the Public Security Secretary summoned the police force to the streets (BBC News 2006). In that occasion, the secretary declared that the population did not have to worry because, according to him, the police action was very successful: 'the police had already killed more than 100 people' (2006). There are no official numbers stating how many people were killed. The report of the Special Commission for 'May Crimes' by the Ministry of Human Rights estimated that in the following nine days, the police of São Paulo killed 564 civilians; 110 were injured, and three civilians disappeared. Fifty-nine police agents were killed in the same period. The report also highlighted that more than 96 per cent of the victims were males, more than 80 per cent of the victims were under 35 years old, and more than half of the victims were black. Also important, 94 per cent of the victims did not have any criminal record (CPPDH 2010: 4).

It was still difficult to trace how many people were killed in the context of May Crimes even ten years later. The Police Ombudsman Service acknowledged 493 victims, but the case has no official figures. Among those victims who were accountable, more than 96 per cent were males, more than 80 per cent were younger than 35 years old, and more than half were non-white (CPPDH 2010: 3). Some people are missing.

The report written by the Human Rights Bureau Special Committee regarding the May Crimes acknowledged at least 124 cases with consistent traces of execution, such as shots being directed to the most vulnerable parts of the body, fired at very close range and vertically aimed – from above to the victim below (CPPDH 2010: 5). The report also shows that the official narrative for the killings was the same; police officers shot only those who attacked them first (as a description of *autos de resistência*). In contrast, the narrative presented by some witnesses was of open fire by police from inside their vehicles, and random search of people in the street by police officers who then contacted the information centre to check their criminal record – 94 per cent of the victims had no criminal record (CPPDH 2010).

Cases of massacres or slaughters resulting from the action of death squads show important features on the politics of death and how they regulate the way and circumstances in which some people die. In both examples, there was the participation of police officers, either organised as a militia group or acting as members of death squads. In the example of May Crimes, the police used the framework of *autos de resistência* to justify or legitimise their actions.

Conclusion: governing death

This chapter has addressed the development of the police apparatus in Brazil. The way the police understands its role is endorsed and legitimised by how society sees the police. Its role is crucial when analysing police killings and disappearances in the country. As showed in this chapter, the feature of those killings and disappearances has changed a lot following different political contexts. During the re-democratisation, there was a complete change regarding who the victims were and how both killings and disappearances were de-politicised in the context of the 'war on drugs'.

Following a historical account, this chapter discussed the emergence and development of the security apparatus in Brazil, focusing on practices and policies, which encouraged the police to act in the name of public order. One may argue that the sovereign apparatus is not restricted to the police; however, the police have a central role in implementing what is understood as a sovereign decision. The first and second sections focused on the emergence of the security apparatus, especially in Rio de Janeiro, where the Portuguese Crown escaped to after fleeing the Napoleonic troops. In the colony, they found a society based on slavery, having the plantation structuring not only economic but also social relations. The police at that time were in charge of public safety, which translated into defending the aristocracy and aggregates, but was also responsible for managing the city – building watercourses and roads and controlling enslaved populations.

The following section focused on the *Era Vargas* (1930–1945) and signalled a disruption regarding the role of the police. The communist threat, politically manipulated by Getúlio Vargas to justify a *coup d'état* that allowed him to remain in power for 15 years, also enlarged and deeply changed the police role. With Vargas, the police became *political*. Vargas gave the police power to torture those who were considered communists and to interfere in the everyday lives of the Brazilian population. The police repressed anarchists and communists at the same time that Vargas regulated working activities and unions.

In the period between the authoritarian regimes in Brazil, social movements pressed the government for agrarian reforms. It did not last. A new communist threat that began following the Cold War led to a military coup in the country. At that time, the police decreased its influence in the *political* aspect of the guerrilla repression, and the armed forces took over that role. At that point, not only the police had an expressive role in the fight against communism but also institutions such as cemeteries, notary's offices, and hospitals, which also played a role in 'political disappearances'.

Following the end of the military regime, actions by 'death squads' and militias, and the institutionalisation of *autos de resistência* stood as new versions of a *dispositif*. In the section on contemporary police killings and disappearances, I discussed the urban violence that followed the 'war on drugs' and its logic of confrontation. That section also addressed the collusion between the police and militias, the use of *autos de resistência* to potentially cover summary executions, and the way disappearances were played down following a large number of police killings.

The focus on killings, however, demands a multi-layered analysis. One of them is about identifying the perpetrators. In crimes such as slaughters followed by the action of death squads, it is difficult to prove whether there are police officers involved and to make them accountable for those acts. In the example of May Crimes, 505 people were killed, but the four disappearances are hardly mentioned. Although in this particular case the explanation can be the scale of the deaths compared to a considerably smaller number of disappearances, in the example of the Acari Slaughter, all 11 victims involved were disappeared. In that case, the word *slaughter* is used instead of 'enforced disappearance' or 'disappearances'.

In short, the present chapter paves the way for the emergence of the security apparatus in Brazil, showing how the apparatus operated through different political contexts. However, if we examine the security apparatus by focusing on the war on communism and the 'war on drugs', an important element is lost: the fact that most of the victims during the military regime (1964–1985) and the re-democratisation (1985–2015) process were from racialised communities. In the following chapter, I will address how notions of race have informed police action since the country's slave-based past, up to the present day.

Notes

1 Decree n 3.610, from 14 April 1900.
2 Decree 6.440 from 30 March 1907.
3 The Civil Police in Brazil stands for the Judicial Police whose main duty is to investigate crime. It is subordinated to the states' governors and it is under the Public Security umbrella.
4 Legislative Decree n 4003 from 7 January 1920, after regulated by decree n 14079, in 25 February 1920.
5 Decree 5.848.
6 Positivism is a philosophical system based on the view that in the social and natural sciences, sensory experiences and their logical and mathematical treatment are the exclusive source of all worthwhile information (Bellintani 2009).
7 The Army divided the country in areas such as São Paulo, Rio de Janeiro, Recife, Belo Horizonte, Porto Alegre, Salvador, and Curitiba; the Department of Information and Operation followed the division proposed by the national Army having operational centres in each of those cities.
8 In 2014, the police in Brazil killed more than 2,500 people (G1 2015).

4 Black bodies

The meat of lowest value in the market

Introduction

> Since he [Mateus Alves dos Santos] disappeared, we were looking for him everywhere. We registered his disappearance at the police station; we went to hospitals, we spread the word around our community, and we asked for help on social media. We would have never imagined that we would find his body at Sumaré.
>
> (Aline do Nascimento, Mateus's aunt, in *Revista Forum*, online edition, 10 July 2014)

It was 11 June 2014, the day before the start of the World Cup. On that day, two military police officers in Rio de Janeiro took three teenagers into custody in the city centre area. The youngsters were suspect of committing petty theft in the region. The two police officers drove the three lads around, stopping at three different police stations. One of the stations was a special force unit that dealt with young offenders. But the police officers decided to take the group to Sumaré – a hill in the downtown area. On the way there, the police released one of them. At Sumaré, one of the two adolescents was shot in his back and knees and pretended he had been killed; he sensed when his friend's body fell over him after the police officers had shot Mateus in the head. The camera located inside the police vehicle, an outcome of social demand for more accountability by the police, recorded most of the action. The teenager who pretended to be dead walked away after the police left and asked for help. Mateus had been missing a few days when his family was contacted. The Public Prosecutor's Office convicted both police officers of murder and concealment of the corpse. The case was investigated, and both police officers were temporarily in jail in 2015. In 2016 they were judged at a Military Justice trial.

The example that opens this chapter sheds light and shadow over the topic. It is clear that the camera in the car should guarantee some degree of surveillance over police misconduct. That said, police officers arrested three young males and killed one of them. The police officers were driving an official vehicle and using state resources provided to make the streets safer for the

DOI: 10.4324/9781003032519-5

population, which prompts the question: for whom do the streets need to be safe, and from whom? The police answered the latter question when they arrested the teenagers. What remains unknown is whether the killing and disappearance of Mateus was indeed the result of an *auto de resistência*. The police officers were patrolling the streets on an ordinary day. There was no confrontation with any drug cartel members – something that is highly visible in urban Brazil. Apart from the World Cup that was about to start, there was nothing special on that day, nothing exceptional.

The previous chapter on the emergence of the security apparatus in Brazil focused on the armed and police forces. It followed historical accounts of political regimes in Brazil giving special attention to the period when Getúlio Vargas was head of the nation (1930–1945) and later to the military dictatorship (1964–1985). The chapter showed the evolvement of the state apparatus, which dealt with the communist threat over these two different periods. This apparatus was responsible for torture, killings, and disappearances of those identified as communists or suspected of conspiring to establish a communist regime in the country. It was also argued that both regimes framed their strategies around a de facto state of exception. In the case of the dictatorship in particular, those implicated with communist guerrillas framed their struggle as a fight for democracy. As a consequence, their fight is celebrated, their deaths are remembered, and their existence has been incorporated into the national memory.

The re-democratisation process also shows a deepening of militarised relations between the police and drug cartels. This military apparatus is not targeting a communist threat. As figures show, black communities are the most victimised despite its high percentage among the population. In 2014, 68 per cent of violent deaths were of black individuals even though this community represents 53 per cent of the population (Fórum Brasileiro de Segurança Pública 2014). Over the last 15 years, almost 500 blacks died violently in Brazil (2002–2017). Such high numbers mean that their deaths have become part of the everyday.

The present chapter accounts for the existence of an apparatus, which makes use of violence to apply exceptional measures towards black bodies. This apparatus does not follow a political regime or the suspension of law. This chapter focuses on policing practices in Brazil to explore how by embodying a sovereign decision, the police plays a role in structuring the politics of life and death. It also addresses the question of how disappearances represent a *dispositif* as it establishes connections between forms of violence in urban spaces Rio de Janeiro and São Paulo. I argue that as part of the security apparatus, the police decide whose lives are disposable by killing and disappearing bodies from specific and marginalised populations. While killings and disappearances are usually considered part of an exceptional framework, the high number of victims of police violence in Brazil[1] suggests that decisions over life and death are made on an everyday basis. This connects with the discussion about the 'state of exception' in the way those killings and disappearances are legitimised by the 'war on drugs' against the poor and black favela dwellers who allegedly opted for a life in criminality.

106 Black bodies

The military police that is under the umbrella of public security is not a branch of the armed forces, as in other contexts. Instead, it is responsible for both pre-emptive action and social control. At the moment, there is a debate in the country regarding the de-militarisation of the police, endorsed by officers who also want the end of a strict military hierarchy. The movement, mostly led by human rights organisations, also defends the end of the military rationale that bases the strategy used by the police at urban areas in Brazil. However, in the context of the 'war on drugs', the need for military forces in the Brazilian police is reified, as I will discuss later in this chapter.

The chapter engages with historical moments in Brazil regarding issues concerning race, such as the colonisation process, the implementation and development of the slave system, the 'whitening' of the population, and the erasure of race as a category of analysis. Those moments are important because they address the process of shaping national understandings of race and racism. Also important are the impact of those racialised notions on actions by the police apparatus and the criminalisation of the behaviour of racialised communities. When discussing the racialisation of the state apparatus in Brazil and the politics of death towards black communities, it is essential to look at the historical process towards race and to discuss it in relation to a broader context such as the colonisation process and its impacts on Brazilian society. In the following chapter, I will show how this perverse nexus gains spatial dimension by following the context of the 'war on drugs', when violence against black communities is normalised.

Race in Brazil

The present section will discuss the colonisation process in Brazil when race was first conceived regarding hierarchy by the Church to justify domination in the colonies, and later by the Portuguese Crown as a mechanism of social control and political power. At this point, it is important to clarify how race is understood in Brazil and how I am using different racialised categories to refer to different subjects. This section shows the fundamental conditions that enabled certain bodies to be subject to violence based on the idea of different skin colours. The following section will bring a few examples of how the suppression of racialised groups, such as indigenous peoples and black communities, was based on exceptional measures not applied to 'white' groups in Brazil.

The Brazilian Institute of Geography and Statistics (IBGE in Portuguese) started to apply a survey in 1967 to evaluate the socio-economic development of the Brazilian population. In 1987, the IBGE included in the survey a category for people's skin colour with five racialised options: white, black, yellow, brown, and indigenous. In the survey, yellow stands for eastern ethnic features and brown for four different mixed-race categories.[2] But for convention's sake, 'black stands for black and brown populations' (IBGE 1999; Htun 2004).

Racialized notions change a lot from one context to another. In Europe and the United States, *white* tends to refer to European communities who have not mixed with any other racial group. In the United States, specifically, the one-drop rule determines that any person with even a single ancestor from Sub-Saharan Africa is *black* (see Hickman 1997; Khanna 2010). To make everything more complex, racism is not only about visual perceptions of skin colour.

In Brazil, racialised categories do not follow the same rationale, and the one-drop rule does not exist or make sense. Instead, perceptions of race focus on visual markers and socio-economic conditions; *white* are those with a clear complexion; *brown* are those with darker skin, usually mixed-race, and not to be confused with Middle Eastern groups who would probably be considered to be *white*. A debate provoked by a television advert broadcasted in 2011 revealed how class influences perceptions of race in Brazil. The video showed Machado de Assis, one of the most famous novelists in Brazil, as a white man. Civil rights activists immediately reacted by stating that the writer was not white, but black. The son of a white woman and a mixed-race father, Machado de Assis was a mixed-race male and part of the intellectual elite in nineteenth-century Rio, but he was not perceived as such. In 1908, Joaquim Nabuco sent a letter to Jose Verissimo who had written an obituary celebrating the life of Machado de Assis in a newspaper, saying:

> Your article in the newspaper is excellent, but the following sentence caused some distress: '*A mulatto* [mixed-race], he was in fact, a Greek from the golden days'. I wouldn't have called him [Machado de Assis] a *mulatto*, and I think that he would have been extremely offended. ... The word is not literary, and it is derogatory. Machado was for me a white man, and I think he saw himself as such; even if there was strange blood [in his veins], it did not affect his perfect Caucasian features. I, at least, could only see him as a Greek.
>
> (1908, in Silva 2014)

At the time of Machado de Assis, and as part of a French literary style called Parnassianism, it was common for novelists to refer to Greece and its gods as the locus of erudition. Although Machado referred to Greece by using satire, being mixed-race was a sign of decay, and Machado de Assis was resentful of his black origins (Silva 2014). Many were the efforts to whiten the writer's image. One was his death certificate, where it stated *white* for race and his pictures in school textbooks which depicted him as a white man. Silva (2014) highlighted that the use of chemicals in photography to whiten the person's complexion was common during the time of Brazil as an empire.

To clarify how these terms will be used in this book, *black* will refer to mixed-race individuals and members of African Diasporas. *White* refers to those who are perceived as such in Brazil, even if mixed-race, and who belong to the privileged background. It is important to say that because of the context of socio-economic inequality in the country, white people are mostly members of the elite. As part of the same context, and probably because the history of slavery was not addressed in socio-economic terms, except for an affirmative action policy created in 2012 to give black communities more chances to access university,[3] blacks are usually associated with poverty.

Mignolo (2000: 51) analysed the narratives about 'the discovery' of America to explain the myth of Latin America as an extension of Europe rather than its foil (2000: 51). According to him, the new financial circuits created an imaginary link between the Mediterranean and the 'new lands' tying together Europe and Latin America. I would argue here that this rationale persisted among the white elites in Latin America and can be noticed, as I will explain later, in the perception of Amerindians as naïve subjects in need of (white/European) protection, and in the idea of the 'new lands' as an empty space. Both attributions, naïveté and emptiness, are still fundamental to explaining local processes that articulate these two concepts to intervene in areas populated not only by indigenous peoples but also by black communities. The difference is that in the latter, intervention is often based on the idea of degeneration rather than naïveté.

A hierarchic system based on race

Alexander Anievas, Nivi Manchanda, and Robbie Shilliam (2014) revisited the work by W.E.B. Du Bois, an African American sociologist who published a book in 1915 on the imperial determinants of the First World War and an article in 1925 claiming that the problem of the twentieth century 'is the problem of the colour-line – the relations of the darker to the lighter races of men' (1961: 23). According to Du Bois, race is a crucial organising principle in international politics. According to him, the colour-line was constituted by multiple dimensions – geographical political, economic, psychological, spiritual, and social.

The experience of drawing lines in Latin America started during the colonisation process and followed notions of skin colour first articulated by the Church. It is crucial to locate 'the discovery' of the Americas in the period where sovereign power was shared between monarchies and the Church; the beginning of the nation-state as we know it. Also, as argued by Mignolo (2000: 49), race was only 'invented' as a concept in nineteenth-century Europe, and the idea of skin colour only later in the twentieth century. However, in the examples that we will look at in this section, members of the Church were already explaining differences regarding skin colour during the colonisation of Brazil. Here, I go along with the argument proposed by Anievas, Manchanda, and Shilliam (2015: 10) that the emergence of the nation-state as a project, which inextricably tapped into a racial logic, and its maintenance were informed by that racial rationale.

Following a theoretical debate on sovereignty, I will first discuss the idea of 'purity of blood' and degeneration of race, both deeply rooted not only in socio-economic relations but, more importantly, in an arrangement that ultimately establishes which lives matter and which can be killed without being considered homicide.

In Europe, the Iberian region had Catholic monarchs expelling other religious groups, such as Jews and Muslims, placing religious identity at the centre of the foundation of those nation-states. This process, described by Heather Rae (2002) as pathological homogenisation, appears in contrast to actions by Christian representatives, such as the Jesuits, who were protective towards Amerindians. Anibal Quijano (2000), Tzvetan Todorov (2003), Immanuell Wallerstein (2007), and Walter Mignolo (2012), among others, have departed from the conquest and discovery of America and subsequent re-articulation of the hierarchical racial imaginary to establish a global order based on difference. The difference between people of different skin colour from different regions would be the determinant in the creation of a global hierarchy according to which violence and death would be justified. In international relations little is said about how this process impacted the local, or more specifically, how this global project shaped local realities. Regarding race, the theory of 'purity of blood' and later the degeneration of race were both fundamental in shaping racial relations in the Americas.

Focusing on the Spanish colonisation of Latin America, Mignolo discussed 'purity of blood' as constituting the bridge between 'race' and 'skin colour' (2000: 49), which marked the beginning of the modern/colonial world system imaginary. According to him, the crucial moment is the historical process in which the expulsion of the Jews and Moors from Spain, as well as the 'discovery' of America, became part of the same phenomenon (2000: 49).

> The 'purity of blood' principle was formalized at the beginning of the sixteenth century, in Spain, and established the final 'cut' between Christians, Jews and Moors (Sicroff 1960; Netanyahu 1995: 975–80, 1041–47; Harvey 1990: 307–40; Constable 1997) ... While the expulsion of the Moors demarcated the exterior of what would be a new commercial circuit and the Mediterranean became that frontier, the expulsion of the Jews determined one of the inner borders of the emerging system.
> (Mignolo 2000: 30)

However, research on race does not usually question why the principle of 'purity of blood' acknowledges only Christians, Jews and Moors, failing to account for African populations who later suffered a critical shift in the imaginary of the modern/colonial world system. To Mignolo (2000), if the sixteenth and seventeenth centuries were dominated by the Christian imaginary, the end of the nineteenth century witnessed a radical change. 'Purity of blood' was no longer measured in terms of religion but by the colour of people's skin. It started to be used to distinguish the Aryan 'race' from other 'races' and, more and more, to justify the superiority of the Anglo-Saxon 'race' above all the rest (Gobineau 1967; Arendt 1968: 173–80, in Mignolo 2000: 31).

Another significant principle adopted to organise life in the colonies was the 'rights of the people'. Mignolo (2000: 30) contrasted 'purity of blood', which he considered a punitive principle, with the 'rights of the people', which he considered as the first legal (and theological) attempt to write down a canon of international law. The 'rights of the people' emerged from the Valladolid debate between Gines de Sepúlveda and Bartolomé de Las Casas on the humanity of the Amerindians and was followed up by further debates in the School of Salamanca on cosmopolitanism and international relations

(Mignolo 2000: 30, Wallerstein 2007: 31–40). Mignolo (2000: 30) highlighted that the 'rights of the people' was a discussion about Amerindians rather than about African slaves: while Amerindians were considered vassals of the king and servants of God, which meant that in theory they should not be enslaved, enslaved African were not in the same category, being considered part of the Atlantic trade (Manning 1990: 23–37, in Mignolo 2000: 31). An important consequence of applying these tenets was the regulation and interpretation of the rights of those who later would be considered mixed-race.

It is important to observe that, in contrast to Mignolo's time frame, discussions on skin colour were already present among Jesuit priests. The conversion of Amerindians to Christianity became the Church's main goal during the sixteenth and seventeenth centuries (Duviols 1971; MacCormack 2021). During the colonial process, priests were concerned with answering the question about difference in skin colour among peoples. I argue that the first sovereign power in Brazil to structure society around racialised notions was the Church, which gave ideological grounds for the abolition of slavery of indigenous populations; a motivation not extended to African populations.

The priest Simão Vasconcelos explained that the change of skin colour was caused by the weather, which could lead to changes in the behaviour also noticeable among white men. The priest gave the example of white people who, after living in tropical areas, would start to act differently and to give less importance to clothing, thus losing their whiteness. Among non-priests, the answer was quite often based on the Catholic Bible (Raminelli 2012: 704). Francisco de Brito Freire (1625–1692) a Portuguese colonial governor, puzzled by the difference of skin colour among Amerindians and Africans who were living within the same distance from the sun, indicated two possible explanations. One was that the warm tropical weather changed the nature of men, turning their skin darker. For example, because Ethiopia is warmer, the result is black skin, and because America is relatively cooler, the skin colour was red (Mignolo 2000; Raminelli 2012). In short, both skin colours, black and red, represented an alteration of original white skin as a climatic consequence. Note that the sun changes not only the colour of the skin, but the *nature* of men.

Alfredo Bosi (2015) notes how Antonio Vieira, the Jesuit priest and advisor to kings and diplomats in the courts of Europe, referred to the contradictions of the colonial system. Deeply involved with politics, Vieira made use of sermons to address the issues that he considered important, having written 207 sermons, exegetical texts, prophecies, letters, and political reports (Bosi 2015). Vieira vociferously opposed Amerindian slavery. In his Sermon for Epiphany, the priest addressed race following two main arguments. The first was based on the *reasons from nature*, using the metaphor of proximity to the sun; and the other followed *reasons from the scripture*, rooted in the Christian story of 'one of the Three Kings, Melchior was black while the other two were white. All three were saved by God from Herod's fury, since men of all colours are equal by nature, and even more so through faith' (Bosi 2015: 111). Bosi identified double movement regarding internal coherence in Vieira's sermon. On the one hand, there is the star of Bethlehem and the unit through faith, which can be associated with the conversion of all indigenous peoples; and then there is the mention of Herod, which could be read as a possible liberation of the Amerindians from the colonialists. From the examples by Father Vieira, Father Simão Vasconcelos, and Francisco de Brito Freire, it is possible to affirm that while the colour of the skin was acknowledged, the recognition of people as subjects depending on the onlooker's affiliation regarding religion rather than race.

Vieira was supported by the Church, which at that time was in favour of the liberation of the Amerindians. That said, there was some tension when Father Vieira started to advocate the end of Amerindian slavery. Vieira ultimately opposed the Crown, who had granted permission for him to stay in Brazil. To deal with this tension, Father Vieira divided the Amerindian population into three different categories that seem to follow the status quo at the time. There were those who were already enslaved in cities and worked for the colonisers, those who lived in the king's villages as free people, and finally, those living in the wilderness. This last group was the main target of colonialists but, according to Father Vieira, the only ones who could be enslaved were those who had already been captured by an enemy tribe or who were in imminent danger of death.

The supposed freedom involved a change in belief systems using catechisation. The first regulation about indigenous peoples dates from 1549, granting power to the Jesuits to make decisions regarding these populations (Wojtalewicz 1993). In 1680, a Royal Charter recognised the right of Native Peoples to their traditional territory (Araújo 2003; Melo 2009), which meant that in the process of land concessions, the rights of indigenous peoples should be observed. However, the Charter applied only to the regions where Pará and Maranhão are located nowadays, in the North of the country, and failed to stop the occupation of indigenous lands (Branco and Rosa 2008).

Many are the narratives over the centuries that used the idea of purity of blood in the American continent. Hebe Mattos (2006) discussed how miscegenation between Europeans and Africans in the Portuguese empire led to hierarchical categories for racial gradations during the seventeenth century. She also highlighted that it was in this period that the categories of 'mulatto' and 'pardo' were included in the regulations for 'purity of blood'. These categories determined who could have access to the honours and privileges normally reserved to the Christian Portuguese. From the seventeenth century onwards, 'these regulations stipulated that no one of the race of Jew, Moor or Mulatto was eligible to receive honours and privileges from the crown' (Carneiro 1983; Lahon 2001, in Mattos 2006: 43).

Another example that illustrates a later consequence of these ideas was discussed by Luciana da Cruz Brito (2016), who remarked on how the principle of 'purity of blood' that guided the United States national project was in contrast to the Brazilian national project, which promoted racial mixing. Brito (2016) claimed that Brazil was portrayed as an example of backwardness and degeneration, reinforcing the need for the United States to maintain segregation policies based on old slaveholding ideologies well into the twentieth century. In opposition to the treatment given to Amerindians, African communities were enslaved and seen as 'assets'.

Contextualizing slavery in Latin America

In this section, I introduce a few examples of violence against enslaved Africans in the colonial past, such as the death penalty in Bahia, and later against the recently freed urban populations, which served to criminalise their behaviour. The most relevant event during the empire concerning the security apparatus was the end of the slavery system in 1888. However, in Brazil, the end of slavery did not happen immediately after the Golden Law (Lei Aurea). Instead, many were the laws that gradually set free specifically parts of African populations. As a consequence, especially in pre-urban areas such as Rio de Janeiro, skin colour did not equate with being enslaved. The police, on the other hand, constantly harassed black communities, accusing them of being fugitives from slavery.

It is estimated that 10.7 million African peoples were shipped from Africa across the Atlantic Ocean to Brazil from the late fifteenth century up until the late nineteenth century. Among them, 4.8 million is estimated to have landed in Brazil after surviving the crossing (Klein and Luna 2009: 151). In late 1750, more than three-quarters of the emigrants to the Americas were African natives shipped as part of the transatlantic slave trade (Klein and Luna 2009: 16; Marquese 2006). The intensity of forced migration and slavery is highly correlated with the growth of Brazilian export and expansion of the local economy, based first on sugar plantations and later on coffee plantations and mining. While in the sixteenth and seventeenth centuries, the arriving port was in the Northeast, more specifically Salvador and Recife, by the eighteenth century Rio de Janeiro had become the single most important arrival port for Africans in Brazil, accounting for 43 per cent of all immigration of African enslaved populations (Klein and Luna 2009: 152–153).

Before the fifteenth century, slavery as a system of production was a limited phenomenon, (Klein and Luna 2009: 4) at least in scale. Most accounts describe western societies in the century before the Christian era as being based on the Greek city-state system and the emerging Roman Empire. Portuguese trade relations with the Kingdom of Congo after the 1500s substantially changed the nature of the Atlantic slave trade. The shift in scale happened after the introduction of sugar production in the Eastern Atlantic Islands and the European conquest of the Western Hemisphere (Klein and Luna 2009: 4).

To start with, the exploitation of Brazil was marginal in the grand scheme of the Portuguese imperial expansion over the fifteenth and sixteenth centuries. To Portugal, the most important colonies were those in the Mediterranean Sea, which enabled trading with Africa and Asia, and in parts of Central America, where sugar plantations were profitable (Marquese 2006; Klein and Luna 2009: 19). Brazil would gain relevance only when French and British merchants began to send their ships into Brazilian waters to collect dyewood themselves. England and France started to set up logging camps in the Amazon region and on Guanabara Bay in the South. The Dutch did the same in Recife (Klein and Luna 2009: 19). Only then did Portugal realise they needed to occupy the land and exploit their American colony.

The beginning of the Portuguese slave trade system involving Africans mainly focused on household activities in the Iberian Peninsula (Marquese 2006; Klein and Luna 2009: 10). According to Klein and Luna (2009: 15) the use of African populations as a workforce in the Americas followed the increase in cost of Eastern European slaves; a declining cost of African slaves; and the high wages of European workers that at the moment were more interested in exploring Africa and Asia – attracted by a profitable trade of gold, ivory, and spices. In addition, Amerindian enslaved populations, although also involved, posed some difficulties because of epidemics and religious contentions over the right to enslave them (Klein and Luna 2009: 17).

In contrast to Central American empires where native populations were largely integrated into complex social systems, in Brazil, indigenous communities were not used for major agricultural activities. By 1540 Amerindians started to be replaced by Africans as enslaved populations (Klein and Luna 2009: 21), given that Portugal had already experience with African enslavement on the Atlantic Islands where sugar plantations were booming (Klein and Luna 2009: 21). The Brazilian slave plantation model became the norm in many parts of the British, French, and Dutch colonies in the Americas. The experience of the Portuguese American colonial development set up a precedent, and related modes of production were directly transferred from the Caribbean region, in the mid-seventeenth century, to other parts of the world, and South America in particular (Klein and Luna 2009: 24).

Overall, there were three main regions where African populations were shipped to Brazil. Not coincidently, they were the regions where Portugal was also exercising colonial power, such as Angola-Loanda (Central Africa), the Bight of Benin (Western Africa), and Mozambique (Eastern Africa region). It is estimated that 94 per cent of all Africans shipped to Brazil came from these regions (Klein and Luna 2009: 153). Interestingly, North America captured slaves in different regions: Western Africa and the Senegambia region (Klein and Luna 2009: 153). A complex system emerged from the Portuguese exploitation, linking the economies of Asia, the Americas, Europe and Africa (Klein and Luna 2009: 151).

It is not surprising that a different range of laws would be applied to enslaved populations given that they were perceived as an asset bought and sold in markets. In the following paragraphs, I will bring a few examples that corroborate my argument that a different body of norms and rules translated into an apparatus that applied exceptional treatment to black communities in Brazil – as it probably did in other former colonies. It is important to investigate the body of laws that were applied to black bodies, whose lives were regulated regarding reproduction and death by private and public spheres during colonial and imperial Brazil. Also, Brazil needed to occupy and work the land. Death was regulated by the apparatus – a different one, which perpetuated even after the end of slavery in Brazil, as we shall see.

The Constitution of 1824 banned the use of 'whips, torture, branding, and all other cruel punishments' for all citizens, but citizenship was restricted to those born in Brazil, excluding those born in Africa (Brown 2000: 103).

Algranti highlighted that in the first half of the nineteenth century, two-thirds of the enslaved population in Brazil were African-born (Algranti 1988a: 40). In this section, I will bring some examples of how the law was applied to the enslaved population in Brazil as an exceptional measure. A few laws were created following some attempts to end slavery in Brazil. In 1831, a law was written to prohibit the international trade of slaves. However, the law was not very efficient as trade continued, mostly with governmental approval (Conrad 1972). The process to end enslavement was proceeding, albeit at a very slow pace. The first significant outcome was the Rio Branco Law, better known as the free-womb law, from 1871, which granted freedom to every child born in slavery from that day onwards. The child was free, but he or she was either taken under custody by the government or allowed to remain on the enslaver's land until they turned 21 (Abreu 1996). The critique of this law was that 'freed' individuals would still be subjected to the master's whim during the most productive part of their lives. Another law from 1885, known as the Sexagenarian Law, granted freedom to slaves who turned 65. Its downside was that many slaves did not reach that age because of their life conditions (Conrad 1972). The Golden Law (Lei Aurea) from 1888 is considered the legal mark for the abolition of slavery in Brazil (Fiola 1990).

The manner through which Brazilian society dealt with the enslaved populations is revealing. It is possible to observe, for example, the importance of social control. To make a huge population work against their will required enforced violence against them. Still, there was tension between the public and private spheres regarding how slaves should be managed. While landowners needed slaves 'in good condition' to work, the public power had the role of protecting the elites against the danger posed by enslaved populations. In urban areas, slavery-related activities went beyond the private realm of plantation lands, but in rural areas, the fear of a revolution following the one in Haiti in 1791 haunted enslavers and public authorities. It is important to note, as I will discuss over the next paragraphs, that a whole body of laws, norms, and security apparatuses were specifically drafted to deal with those who were enslaved. The need for 'social control' permeated the discussion on changes in the law, investments in the police force, and the extent to which the legal system should mediate and regulate how much corporeal punishment was adequate to keep a *humanitarian slave system*. In many occasions, the discussion clashed with the aspiration of an emerging Brazilian society eager to get integrated into a civilised and modern ethos associated with Europe. At this point, it is important to bear in mind that Brazil was the last western country in the world to abolish slavery, and that in 2017 the country was condemned by the Inter-American Court for slavery and human trafficking.

The rebellion of those people under slavery that occurred in Haiti in 1791 made the elites afraid of a similar movement in Brazil. As a consequence, punishment had to be exemplary. Many were the revolts organised at Bahia; 12 such revolts took place between 1807 and 1831, and this activity culminated with the great urban uprising of 1835 (Reis 1988). The Malê Revolt in Bahia in 1835 expanded the scope of capital punishment in Brazil. Before that, the 1831 criminal code limited the death penalty to those convicted of only two crimes: insurrection, defined as 20 or more slaves who gathered together 'to obtain their liberty using force'; or homicide under certain aggravating conditions, such as by conspiracy or for profit. In March 1835, an executive decree sentenced to death all the African enslaved individuals involved in the rebellion. In June of that same year, the exceptional death penalty was incorporated into the national law, with the exceptional measure applied only to those who were enslaved. The 1835 law was also extraordinary because it permitted the death penalty to be applied to enslaved people even in the absence of aggravating circumstances. Furthermore, all ordinary avenues of appeal were denied to enslaved people (Brown 2000: 102). In contrast to the United States, Brazilian courts imposed the death penalty relatively sparsely (Brown 2000: 101). The new law in Brazil translated into a greater police control over slave surveillance and less use of the death penalty per se.

Alleging an increase in the number of enslaved and freed black people, Bahia's local authorities demanded greater investment in policing, such as additional guards, and more social regulations, such as the prohibition of enslaved people wandering the streets at night (Brown 2000: 97). To Francisco Goncalves Martins, the local chief of police and later president of the province, the Muslim revolt of 1835 demonstrated that enslavers were negligent who failed to exercise adequate control over those who they claimed as property (Brown 2000: 95). The police were called to take on the responsibility of punishing enslaved persons and ended up punishing enslavers as well by denying them their workforce after sending enslaved persons to jail or whipping them. Algranti (1988a: 43) argued that the severe punishments inflicted on the enslaved acted as an extended penalty for the negligent master, who did not pay attention to public laws, such as curfews.

As we will see, the managing of the enslaved populations by government officers brought tension to the social relations between the enslaved, the landowners, and state representatives. Still, it is important to highlight that the tension between enslavers and the state apparatus did not mean that enslavers were more concerned about the well-being of people they held in slavery, as exemplified by Thomas Holloway (1989) in the opening of his article 'A Healthy Terror: Police Repression of Capoeiras in Nineteenth-Century Rio de Janeiro' (1989). In his article, Graciano, an enslaved person who attempted to escape after being caught by the police of Rio de Janeiro and returned to his enslaver, was whipped by the latter in a cruel way. Graciano was 'bound so tightly that his hands and forearms were deeply injured by the cords' (Holloway 1989: 638). The following day, Graciano was 'able to lie only on his side, unable to stand or walk' (Holloway 1989: 638). Although Diogo Antonio Feijo, the regent of the empire who exercised executive authority in the name of Pedro II, insisted that the state must intervene to regulate disciplinary punishment and rule over criminal activities by enslaved persons, he decided not to bring formal charges against Graciano's enslaver (Holloway 1989: 638), indicating that the tension was more a result of regulations over private property then any genuine concern for the enslaved.

The general demand for order also required absolute obedience to overseers at plantations, but the implementation of a law that imposed death on enslaved persons convicted of killing overseers proved to be more problematic. Bryan McCann (in Brown 2000: 106) has shown that in Paraiba Valley, a rich coffee plantation area between Rio de Janeiro and São Paulo, some enslavers refused to cooperate with courts that prescribed death to enslaved persons for murdering overseers. When the police arrested an enslaved person claimed by the Baron of Massambara, the Vassouras aristocrat insisted that he would do everything in his power to defend his property rights and ignored two subpoenas before finally appearing in court (Brown 2000: 90). As they were considered human property, enslaved persons had a higher value than overseers, whose replacement could be easily found among the large numbers of poor whites inhabiting the region (Brown 2000: 106).

The emergence of new police forces enabled daily supervision of enslaved persons whose claimants were not always attentive. Thus, police authorities started to act as 'urban overseers', exerting vigilance over enslaved persons and the free African population to ensure that they would work assiduously, and arresting them for any wrongdoing according to the limits set down by Brazilian law (Brown 2000: 95). With the increasing importance of centralised administrative structures during the nineteenth century, state agencies sometimes took actions that violated the interests of enslavers (Brown 2000: 95). In Rio, as in Salvador, the state's interest in maintaining public order had begun to supersede the enslaver's private right to wield unbridled power over his human property.

In semi-urban areas, enslaved persons and the recent freed population were sharing the same space (1818), and it is estimated that three-quarters of the population in Rio de Janeiro was black (Abel, in Algranti 1988a). While freed populations were generally mixed-race and born in Brazil, enslaved persons were African migrants. The nature of the work carried out by urban enslaved persons meant that they were less tied to their masters and more involved with diverse social networks, by comparison with their counterparts in the plantations. Many of them worked as artisans and were required to bring a sum of money to their masters. Freed populations were forced into precarious and temporary work without a fixed wage (Algranti 1988a: 30). The easy transit of black populations and concerns with insurrection were perceived as a significant danger to social and political stability.

Social mobility was almost impossible, and most of the recently freed population became enslavers known as '*capitão do mato*', working as agents in a system that had previously oppressed them (Algranti 1988b: 122). To Brown (2000: 105), because they were excluded from citizenship, enslaved persons could never undergo the internal transformation necessary to qualify as productive members of civil society. Physical violence remained the basis of punishment for the enslaved, though it was now cloaked in the legal rationale.

Algranti highlighted that it is probably not coincidental that Rio de Janeiro's police force was created and organised as the population started to increase dramatically (1988a: 28). When examining the police arrest records from 1810 to 1821, Algranti (1988a) claimed that a large number of laws and decrees were passed to control and intimidate these urban groups. The police were particularly concerned with gatherings of black people, such as social events or *capoeira*. Holloway (1989: 637) defined *capoeira* as

> beyond the gymnastic fighting technique still associated with the term in Brazil today, in the nineteenth century it was used to denote groups or gangs that police authorities in Rio de Janeiro considered a scourge of the city, an activity notorious among young male slaves and the free lower classes.

Black vagrants were also taken to jail as a matter of course, and it was quite common for a black male who happened to be outside a tavern to be arrested. Most of the arrests recorded at the beginning of the nineteenth century were for petty crimes, such as small theft. Algranti did not find sentences for murder in the documents that she analysed. Also, the majority of crimes were committed by a single person, indicating the absence of organised criminal groups. In Rio de Janeiro, recently freed individuals received the same treatment given to enslaved populations. They were under a law enforcement system based on ethnic precincts that frequently failed to distinguish the formerly enslaved from the actual enslaved.

Regarding sentences and punishments, Algranti (1988a: 42) identified a few patterns, but the most common penalty given to enslaved persons who were convicted was forced labour and corporal punishment. If they were caught participating in capoeira, three common punishments were flogging, incarceration, and forced labour. The use of convicted slaves in public work was common in Rio due to a shortage of urban workers. The government even kept slaves in jail longer than necessary to fill the quota of workers needed.

Alexandra Brown (2000: 96) argued that violence became intertwined with the process of state formation because it was codified in the laws sentencing death and the corporeal penalty for the enslaved. Thus, violence towards enslaved persons and state formation were inseparable. It is possible, then, to conclude that a way to consolidate the state apparatus at the time was through the consolidation of power over the enslaved in a dynamic relation between enslaved persons' rebelliousness, daily crime, and efforts by the elite to contain a population that was seen as threatening.

Concerns with establishing social control were evident at the highest levels of the Brazilian government, as in Dom Pedro II's speech at the opening of the legislative session in 1841, the year of the criminal code reform. The Emperor of Brazil instructed the national senate to focus on the 'improvement in criminal legislation and procedure' to promote political and social stability. 'The consolidation of order', Pedro II added, 'is essential to elevate the Empire to the level of prosperity and greatness that I desire' (in Brown 2000: 98). According to Brown (2000: 98), by the early 1840s, elites had come to realise that Brazil could not survive economically without adequate law enforcement, and it was necessary to create a police apparatus and a judicial system capable of exercising effective punishment to consolidate order.

While there was a tightening of the social control regulations towards enslaved populations, there was also an awareness of the tension between civilisation and barbarism as a foundation of a slavery-based society. The expansion of public power that lawmakers saw as essential to protecting 'civilisation' meant that enslavers faced limits regarding their private authority. Changes in law and policing enacted in the early 1840s signalled efforts by legislators to use the power of the state to control the enslaved, but also to control the level of surveillance of their enslavers through a regulatory framework. The Brazilian nation legislators aspired for during the nineteenth century centred on a 'civilised' society, free from the 'barbarism' of crime and social disorder, racially oriented terms often used by political leaders and other influential elites. Brown (2000: 100) pointed out that in 'the early part of the century, upholding civilisation meant controlling what elites saw as a dangerous and culturally foreign African population'.

National laws regulating the behaviour and punishment of enslaved persons, such as capital punishment or the regulation of how many lashes were appropriated, are central to analyse the formation of the Brazilian state. When focusing on the security apparatus, the exceptional measures applied towards black communities are undeniable. As defended by Brown (2000: 112) 'from the alleged establishment as an independent nation in 1822 to the final years of the Empire, the issue of violence against slaves wrapped itself around the state-building process'. The constant fear that there could be an insurrection by enslaved persons and Africans provided the foundation for the creation of a judicial and police apparatus capable of exerting the kind of control over the enslaved that was essential for the development of the economy. In the 1830s, laws supporting violence against enslaved persons with the extreme use of the death penalty had been crucial for the survival of the socio-economic system. The elites who sought to establish Brazil's presence among the 'civilised' nations of the world felt uncomfortable with the high levels of violence at public floggings, while the death penalty law signalled a 'barbarism' inappropriate to the level of greatness that Brazil aspired for. Brown (2000: 112) claimed that lawmakers engaged with eliminating the most brutal elements from slavery not out of humane motivations but due to a class-based vision of portraying the Brazilian nation as 'civilised', rational, and just. Her view is that the abolition of the death penalty in 1889 did not end killings by the military forces or the police, given that the enslaved continued to suffer violence at the hands of their enslavers and even illegal beatings by police, even in the final years of the empire. By taking the issue of castigation to public debate, elites helped convince themselves that their kind of slavery was not so cruel after all. The more the elites tried to convince themselves that their labour system operated within limits of civilisation and humanity, the more they questioned the continued existence of that system. Slavery and civilised society were at their essence opposed. Banning state-imposed whipping of enslaved persons and challenging the justification for a death penalty law made salient the level of violence enslavers relied upon to force people to work against their will. A decade earlier, state-mandated violence against enslaved persons had ensured the survival of the newly emerging Brazilian nation; however, by the 1880s, attacks on the principles underpinning that violence signalled the end of the institution of slavery and of the state structures that had developed around it (Brown 2000: 112). That said, the legislative debates did not end the violence against black communities.

Making Brazil a 'racial democracy' as part of the nation-building process

In the 1930s, Brazil started a process of erasing race as a category and locus of analysis. As part of the same process, there was the attempt to erase black bodies. The erase of race has deeply marked the nation-building project in the country and its different components, such as schooling, culture, and migration, as well as the subsequent abandonment of racialised communities to social and economic precariousness. One of the consequences is that little was written about racialised communities, especially during the Vargas Era, when the national myth of racial democracy was forged and class became the legitimate locus of analyses for some issues, such as inequality and police violence. Uncountable are the consequences, and the action of the police apparatus towards racialised populations more specifically remains mostly invisible.

This problem was addressed by Reiter and Mitchell (2010) in the book *Brazil's New Racial Politics*. They open the book by discussing the process of unveiling race among scholars in the country. According to them, during the 1950s and 1960s, when inequalities in Brazil could not be explained by class alone, there were attempts to dismantle the ideological construct of the Brazilian version of 'cosmic race', which dates back to the 1930s under the Vargas regime. The forging of this ideology included the use of propaganda as well as a widespread production of 'historically correct' textbooks to be used in the growing number of state primary schools (Mitchell and Reiter 2010: 2; Dávila 2003).

When the effort to bring race to the national debate was at a point of impacting the broader society and government, the military regime took over the country. One of the consequences of the new regime was to suffocate any attempt to produce the kind of knowledge that could have been used to mobilize parts of society to demand greater justice and participation in politics (Mitchell and Reiter 2010: 2). In 1985, when the military regime finally ended, the social sciences in Brazil had to start from where they were cut off 20 years earlier. Brazil then reintroduced skin colour categories in its censuses and surveys (Mitchell and Reiter 2010: 2).

To Mitchell and Reiter (2010) only ethnicity can explain Brazil's extreme inequalities in central spheres of life such as education, labour market, job mobility inside firms, marriage, and even life expectancy. Mitchell and Reiter (2010) reiterated that the research produced more recently, and after the dictatorship in Brazil, could prove without a doubt that Brazilian blacks were worse off than their white countrymen and women. Furthermore, this inequality could not be explained by educational backgrounds or unequal income and wealth alone. Brazilian whites (and Asians) fared much better than Brazilian blacks and browns with similar educational backgrounds, who suffered from discrimination even if they had access to middle-class incomes. Money did not *whiten* after all.

(Mitchell and Reiter 2010: 3)

As discussed by Andrews (1988), in the historiography of the working class in Brazil, the assumption that former slaves did not contribute to working-class consciousness is common. According to mainstream historiographical accounts, working-class consciousness would have being brought by European immigrants in the 1930s. However, as pointed out by Andrews (1988), Europeans who migrated to Brazil were peasants and not yet engaged with ideas of class or anarchy. A consequence of this view is also to strip out the agency of black populations from the working-class movements. Many were the attempts of black communities to mobilise themselves. Notwithstanding, they were silenced by the different manifestations of Brazilian authoritarianism in the 1930s and 1950s.

A special case was the Brazilian Black Front created in São Paulo in 1931, which boasted 200,000 members concentrated mostly in the industrialised south (Davis 1999: 187; Mitchell and Reiter 2010: 3). The Brazilian Black Front was the first Afro-Brazilian organisation demanding full rights of participation in society. Spread around the country, its complex structure included an institutional newspaper, *A Voz da Raça* (*The Voice of Race*) created in March 1933. Also during the 1930s, other newspapers were created to make black communities voices heard, *Clarim d'Alvorada* (*Clarion of Dawn*). For the first time, a large number of Afro-Brazilians were organised politically, seeking to redefine their identity, take pride in their heritage, and fight racial prejudice (Mitchell and Reiter 2010: 2; Htun 2004). The Brazilian Black Front pioneered an agenda many years before other civil rights movements in the country.

As explained in the previous chapter on the consolidation of a police apparatus in Brazil, Getúlio Vargas, President from 1930 to 1945, felt threatened by the dissatisfaction expressed both by the right and left parties, and decided to initiate the *Estado Novo* with a coup (the New State, 1937–1945). Seeking to engender a new model of development based on industry, Vargas courted the urban middle and working classes to the detriment of rural landowners. Thus, Afro-Brazilian city dwellers indirectly benefited from Vargas's approach. In 1936, however, the authoritarian government of Vargas outlawed the Black Front, together with all other oppositional political parties (Mitchell and Reiter 2010: 3). The Vargas government sought to discourage any association that had the potential of endangering his project of national unity. Much later, when the military regime started to crumble, and a new intellectual wave started to look at race, the Unified Black Movement (MNU) was created (Mitchell and Reiter 2010: 3). The movement, which started in 1978, provided a national framework for black activism.

The present section addresses the whitening process of Brazilian populations and looks at other policies that aimed at erasing race from the national lexicon. The third subsection will address the notion of citizenship that developed at the same time. As we will see, the whitening process had a deep impact on the marginalisation of racialised communities by making them responsible for their own fate. It also impacted what is known as the criminalisation of poverty, which will later contribute to the association between poverty, favelas, and drug cartels without, however, addressing the issue of race. As I will discuss in the following section, the policies implemented to make race invisible lead to distortions that associate for example, *autos de resistência* with criminality and drug cartel activities, but never with the structural racism of institutions such as the police, even though figures show that 77 per cent of the victims of such *dispositif* are black populations (Folha de Sao Paulo 2016b).

Rendering race invisible by whitening the population

In 1888, enslavement was officially abolished in Brazil with the Lei Aurea, or Golden Law. Facing severe restrictions regarding constitutional rights, impeded access to literacy skills, and constant persecution by the police under the accusation of being fugitives from slavery, the newly freed population had sparse resources to be included in the emerging capitalist system (Chalhoub 2011: 406). Enslavers and other members of the Brazilian elite reasoned that the institution of slavery combined with racial prejudice destroyed the potential for Afro-Brazilians to work in the new capitalist society as free men, despite having the know-how to do the work (Oliveira and Kimberly 2003: 103). European migrants were then considered a new source of labour, especially by coffee growers in the Southeast (Oliveira and Kimberly 2003: 103). Struggling with the resistance of former enslavers as political elites, former enslaved persons were not incorporated into the political project, social systems, or economic workforce (Oliveira and Kimberly 2003: 103). Post-abolitionist policies in Brazil worked to promote a country with European roots, consequently marginalising black communities.

In the mid-nineteenth century, many theories about race had achieved scientific status in both Europe and the United States. Racist ideologies greatly influenced Brazilian intellectuals, as well as medical practitioners, as discussed by Patto (1999). Oliveira and Kimberly (2003: 104) suggested that because the Brazilian population had already experienced significant racial miscegenation, intellectuals adapted foreign theories to elaborate local policies based on the ideology of 'whitening', or *branqueamento*. In short, the intellectual community and members of the elite believed that the combination of an increasing number of European migrants and the low reproduction rate of the black population – resulting from poor access to education, healthcare, and jobs – would gradually dilute non-European influence in the country (Oliveira and Kimberly 2003: 104) and help Brazil overcome its racial predicament.

European migration became essential to Brazil's goal of becoming a white and progressive capitalist country. Bueno (2013: 36) highlighted how the national project aimed at specific nationalities. The proximity of language, skin colour, religious background, and culture stood for the civilisation ideal, making Spanish, Portuguese, and Italian communities the most welcomed in the country (see also Oliveira 2001 and Htun 2004). From the perspective of Brazilian elites, those similarities would make the process of assimilation and blending easier (Oliveira 2001: 10). Populations from the Far East, such as the Chinese and Japanese who also migrated to Brazil, faced greater resistance to establish themselves in the country because they did not match these criteria (Bueno 2013: 36 and Geraldo 2012). This early hindrance was alleviated later, however, with the onset of World War I and subsequent interruption of European migration (Bueno 2013: 36).

To Ianni (2004: 156), Brazilian elites decided to prioritise the immigration of 'white-western-Europeans', members of the Christian western civilisation, and to exclude Asian, African, and indigenous populations. According to her, this migration policy resonated with 'the Arian doctrine and social-Darwinism' (Ianni 2004: 156). Bearing in mind that at that time, notions of race also related to cultural aspects such as language, religion, traditions, and behaviour, the whitening project in Brazil encompassed both skin colour and values. Bueno highlighted (2013: 1) that in the nineteenth century and first decades of the twentieth century in Brazil, the motivation to bring immigrants was twofold. In economic terms, immigrants were seen as a working force needed for the development of the country; and in racial terms, part of the elites wanted to make sure the whitening process of the Brazilian population was successful (see also Skidmore 1976: 81–96; Seyferth 1990: 18).

A highly successful endeavour that supported this cause was the book *Casa Grande e Senzala* (Big House – as in Master's House – and the Slave Quarters)[4] by the sociologist Gilberto Freyre, published in 1933. The book, a landmark in modern Brazilian sociology, discusses a supposed Brazilian national character and exalts the importance of miscegenation (Melo 2009). Freyre (1933) argued against hegemonic social theories from the 1920s that blamed the country's racial mix for the resulting economic arrested development (2018: 175). Lissovsky and De Matos (2018) discussed the image of the slave quarters as part of a racial trope, in which the Master's House and the Senzala, or Slaves' Quarters, were a fundamental duality of Brazil, visible not only in the private sphere but also in the political culture of the country (Freyre 1933, in Lissovsky and De Matos 2018: 176).

The Vargas regime did everything possible to disseminate this ideology. It envisaged Brazil as a racial paradise inhabited by one race, the Brazilian version of a 'cosmic race'—a tropical mulatto republic. The concept of racial paradise promised a solution to finally catch up with the developed world, even if – and especially because – Brazil had such a large mixed population (Mitchell and Reiter 2010: 4). In the 1930s, under Vargas, the concept of race was removed from textbooks, censuses, and the official discourse about Brazil. The state produced the main official representation of the country, and any Brazilian –

black, white, mixed or indigenous – had no other choice but to accept it. The core of the doctrine disseminated under Vargas was that, no matter what one's ethnic background was, Brazilians were all mixed and hence one (Reiter and Mitchell 2010: 4). The risk of factionalism and even secession was so great during the 1930s that Vargas undertook extraordinary measures to forge a sense of nationality, national pride, and even a sense of what it meant to be Brazilian (Reiter and Mitchell 2010). Vargas's term in office severely delegitimised any attempt to forge a sense of racial solidarity among excluded blacks.

Vargas gained a national and lasting reputation for creating the Ministry of Work, which regulated the minimum wage, and for a series of decrees to protect workers, such as the eight-hour working day, restrictions to women and children labour, as well as a regulatory framework for vacations, pensions, and union activities (Pandolfi 2006). Vargas was also known for addressing 'the workers of Brazil' in his speeches (Lago 2015). When analysing the symbolic dimension of Vargas's idea of citizenship and workers, Lago (2015) claimed that Vargas invested in the idea of creating a modern and industrialised country. Lago analysed the public propaganda from the Vargas period and concluded that, at the individual level, citizenship started to be defined by the idea of an order-abiding worker (see the positivist ideas outlined in Chapter 3) who respected the family (Schwartzman 1980 and Gomes 1994) and consumed certain goods (Lago 2015: 93). To pursue this ideal, Vargas used samba, a musical form typical of Rio de Janeiro that exalted street savviness or *malandragem* (Lago 2015: 93), as the opposite of his worker ideal. Gomes (1994: 231) highlighted the morality implied in Vargas's vision of worker and citizen, which excluded the unemployed, outlaws, and anyone who did not subscribe to that ideal.

As black-power movements regrouped during the 1950s and early 1960s, the state stepped in again, this time to avoid a potentially explosive articulation between labour and racialised groups. During the military regime, black-power activism became subversive and was subject to prosecution and state-sponsored persecution, imprisonment, torture, and even death. The military regime also ensured that the category race was absent from the census, seeking to curtail even the prospect of racial solidarity amongst all those affected by the forces of racism and racialised exclusion (Rio de Janeiro [Estado] 2015). Without numbers, mobilisation was much harder (Reiter and Mitchell 2010).

Following efforts to erase racial categories in Brazil, social mobility was simplified as a matter of overcoming poverty. At the individual level, this was translated into the need to work hard based on meritocracy, and at the national level, into the need to fight inequality disregarding the role played by racism. Robbie Shilliam (2018), when analysing the interface between race and class in the context of Britain, argued that the idea of the working class is a constituency, and not a neutral category, produced and reproduced through struggles that have subsequently shaped the contours of British postcolonial society. According to him, elite actors have racialised and re-racialised the historical division between deserving and undeserving poor through terms that encompass the idea of 'working class', colonial 'natives', and nationalities (2018: 6). As a consequence, native Africans – and blacks in general – have been continuously racialised to reinforce distinctions between those considered 'deserving' or 'undeserving' of social security and welfare.

Dictatorship and the violence against indigenous communities

Thirty years after the (re-)democratisation of Brazil, historiographic research allows us to explore in greater depth the existence of two security apparatuses: one that targets communist groups, and the other that targets racialised groups. The fact that the National Truth Commission (2014) dedicated a chapter to the genocide of indigenous populations does not invalidate the overall argument of two security apparatuses acting differently towards different subjects. The genocide of indigenous populations although addressed is still depoliticised. The death of more than 20,000 indigenous people (National Truth Commission 2014: v2) is not remembered as part of the political struggle – limited to those who were involved in political associations and engaged with the fight for democracy. Furthermore, the way Brazil relates to indigenous populations has changed a lot over time.

The dictatorial regime in Brazil used forced disappearance to target leftist groups which were mainly from a well-educated background. The same regime also enforced the disappearance of other groups such as peasants (National Truth Commission 2014: v1) and indigenous populations (National Truth Commission 2014: v2). However, their disappearance is not classed as political disappearances whether in reports or public talks by the National Truth Commission. The NTC (National Truth Commission 2014) alleged that indigenous communities did not participate in the political struggle for the establishment of a democratic regime in the country.

The experience of indigenous populations during the colonisation in Brazil was marked by genocide and 'conversion' to Christianity. The difference, articulated first as religion, and later as race, placed indigenous populations outside the white European and Christian experience. During the dictatorship, the land inhabited by indigenous populations was coveted by private interests due to its abundant resources. A new wave of violence targeted these populations, such as forced displacement and forced disappearances. Still, their 'disappearance' is somehow perceived as a 'historical contingency' (FUNAI 2016),[5] following the idea that they belong to 'another time'.

A Law for Indigenous people drafted in 1755 repressed indigenous traditions, obliging them to wear clothes, use the Portuguese language, and live in villages. The government was in charge of providing schools that were free to attend where students were separated by gender. Flexor (2006) observed that the settlements for indigenous people followed two motivations. First, to reclaim control over a population that had been in the hands of Jesuit priests who were subsequently expelled from Brazil, and secondly, to prevent the Spanish advance into Portuguese territory. Another policy at the time was to promote interracial marriage by offering rewards to white males and giving citizen status to their offspring (Freyre 1933).

Indigenous populations were not mentioned in the 1824 Constitution text since they were considered legally unqualified and not classed as civilised (Gomes 2000). With regards to other aspects, their right to land was written off following the claim that indigenous peoples were part of the Brazilian population and consequently did not need any special treatment (Gomes 2000). In 1850, however, there was a national regulation for private property, which guaranteed indigenous peoples the right to ancestral lands. That said, other laws were put in place allowing other people the right to work on land that was deemed unproductive (Araujo et al. 2006: 1). In practical terms, it meant that if the land was not being used for farming, which was not a practice that indigenous peoples commonly used, other people could take over that land (Ibid).

In 1910, the National Service of Indigenous Protection was created to advocate on behalf of those populations and integrate them into the nation. For the first time, the government had to create and administer policies concerning indigenous populations. However, in 1916, the Civil Code once again declared indigenous peoples as legally unqualified and in need of tutelage, a policy that would cease to apply only if they were seen as having adapted to civilisation (Ibid). It was not until the 1934 Constitution that indigenous peoples were given the right to the land where they lived. At this time, the indigenous population was around 120,000 (Ibid). In 1961, the first National Park of Xingu was created.

In the 1930s, during Vargas's government, there was another peak in the conquest of indigenous lands. It was during his term in office that the 'March to the West' started, a body of governmental actions that included the creation of new agricultural settlements, and the construction of new national roads and hospitals. Schallenberger and Schneider (2010) described the advance towards the national borders as being driven by two motivations. From a political and military perspective, it would answer the need of occupying the territory and guaranteeing national sovereignty. Secondly, from a socio-economic perspective, it would offer more land to agriculture and minimise conflicts for land while expanding the labour market and stimulating food production. The way that this policy dealt with indigenous communities meant that invasion and the violation of legal rights on their land went unpunished, favouring private interests. Invasions by private entities that were later legalised by the government was a common practice. The National Truth Commission report pointed out that this kind of policy was already in use before, but local governments received federal endorsement during the Vargas Era.

The National Truth Commission (2014) found documents containing recommendations for land occupation with the purpose of fostering 'acculturation and assimilation' of indigenous peoples, approved by the First Brazilian Conference of Immigration and Colonization in 1949. There were also killings of indigenous populations through food poisoning by private companies and other groups, as well as the kidnapping of indigenous children. Since the expedition into the Xingu area in 1946 carried out by the Villas-Boas brothers, the general public had become aware that indigenous peoples had no immunity against common diseases. Many indigenous peoples were killed by the intentional and unintentional spread of diseases, namely chickenpox, smallpox, and mumps, among others. The immunisation of indigenous populations that had started during the 1950s was interrupted precisely when the military regime started making changes to related policies.

Considered enemies of national development in the 1930s, indigenous peoples were re-interpreted as an issue of national security during the dictatorship. The National Truth Commission report claimed that there was an inversion of the traditional view of indigenous people who during the colony, empire, and the First Republic 'were given the task of defending Brazilian territory to then being perceived as a risk to national security and nationalism' (National Truth Commission 2014: 205). Although the suggested friendly relationship with indigenous communities can be questioned, given the accounts of violence and unhindered occupation of their land throughout Brazilian history, during the dictatorship, indigenous communities were actually targeted.

According to the NTC report, the year 1968 marked the brutality of the regime not only against leftists in urban areas but also against indigenous peoples. Huge construction projects for the development of the country were set in motion. One of them was the Trans-Amazonian Highway that covered 4,000 kilometres over land previously occupied by 29 communities which had to be displaced forcibly. To put the program in place, FUNAI worked with the Superintendence for Amazonia Development to pacify rebellious indigenous groups. Another project was the Itaipu, a huge hydroelectric dam on the Parana River between Brazil and Paraguay, a country also under a military regime at the time. The hydroelectric dam flooded an area of 1,300 square kilometres, invading the last territory conceded to the Guarani ethnic group, after having moved them on different occasions in previous years. Nowadays, there is a Museum of the Guarani Lands on the Paraguayan side.

Military officers also engaged in violent acts against indigenous peoples. The report suggests that it was through the AI-5 that the repression of indigenous peoples became part of the state's repressive apparatus. One of the practices during processes of illegal detentions, some of them in place for 30 years, was the reallocation of individuals to areas far from their original community. Other practices included incarceration, forced labour, and torture – sometimes extended to their entire family, including minors. Some indigenous communities were turned into 'prison camps' (National Truth Commission 2014: 240).

The NTC report pointed out a few measures applied by the military forces aimed at evicting indigenous communities from their land and eliminating these populations. Among them was the creation of an Indigenous Rural Guard, which hired indigenous people from communities at Araguaia, Tocantins, and Minas Gerais to act as a police force in other communities. A specific prison was built as an illegal structure designed for incarceration, but which also included practices of torture and disappearance. During this period, indigenous populations were reduced to one-third of its former number.

The NTC team heard accounts by former prisoners who reported that some people were taken to an island and never returned; in other words, they were disappeared. Also, in certain prisons when someone was killed, military officers would throw the body into the river and tell relatives that the missing person had travelled. When someone was suffering a lot due to torture, relatives would be told that they went to hospitals, but they never met anyone who returned from hospital.

The systematic kidnapping of children in indigenous communities started to happen during the 1950s. After being kidnapped, those children were given to non-indigenous families who changed their names and adopted them. In other cases, some ethnic groups were displaced to live with rival groups leading to, in some cases, more killings. At times, those who survived were condemned to live in a state of constant marginalisation by the fostering groups.

The disappearance of indigenous bodies mirrors the erasing of their existence as a community. In 1969, the federal government established a requirement for the concession of financial resources to private investors in Amazonia called 'Negative Evidence of the Existence of Indigenous Communities'. According to this norm, the industry interested in exploring the land should provide information claiming that the land in question was not inhabited by indigenous communities. The problem was, as the president of FUNAI later admitted, that FUNAI did not know where all the indigenous communities were living. For that reason, they were not able to contest claims made by investors.

The same normative provision was used in different situations. One such example is the construction of Itaipu, the first initiative for the settlement of non-indigenous populations in indigenous lands. Following a report claiming that there was no evidence of indigenous communities living in the region, a Guarani community was reallocated to another piece of land, violating the indigenous legislation. After the displacement, most of the population died, having been infected by malaria and pesticides used by non-indigenous communities who had settled nearby. The emission of negative certificates of indigenous presence was one of the legal provisions largely applied by the state to expropriate their land while veiling the direct responsibility of the state for violating indigenous rights.

Conclusion: making difference invisible

When looking at the police, and more broadly, at the security apparatus in Brazil, the communist threat during the Vargas Era and the military dictatorship, and more recently the discourses on the 'war on drugs', become salient as major targets. But what those highly visible events make invisible is how there is an underlying approach towards racialised communities. In that sense, this chapter complements the previous one, 'The Police Apparatus', which highlighted the embodiment of sovereign power by the police towards racialised communities. The root of this approach is deeply entangled with the slave-based socio-economic system that marked the country's colonial past.

Regarding the development of the security apparatus in Brazil, I argue that it is possible to observe two main strands. One of them targeted leftist groups in the context of the communist threat during the Vargas Era and the military dictatorship. Another security apparatus presents continuity through history and is marked by violence against racialised communities. As argued before, if the 'war on drugs' can offer an explanation on how a state of exception is articulated, it does not explain why, for example, a black person has a 25 per cent greater chance of being a victim of a gunshot,[6] nor does it explain why those deaths have become part of the everyday, and somehow naturalised.

In Brazil, as in Latin America, the Church has deeply impinged upon the country's notions of race. Slavery at the time not only impacted social and economic relations but also characterised the role of the police. The first section addressed the body of norms and laws and how the police performed their role as 'slave patrols', in many cases overstepping private interests since black populations were considered valuable assets. Brazilian elites moved slowly in the process of freeing Africans and black native populations, being divided by the need to assert the young nation's humanitarian values to European countries, and economic demands that relied on slavery. The police acted arbitrarily when a semi-urban population became mixed with recently freed persons in the burgeoning city of Rio de Janeiro where most of the population were Africans. When blacks were finally freed from working on the plantations, their work was not considered good enough or sufficiently specialised to boost the economic development needed in the country. By denying those populations the economic conditions to succeed, poverty and criminality continued to be equated with skin colour, enhancing the negative discourse against black subjectivities.

Combined with the need to bring specialised labour from Europe was the desire to whiten the population. Vargas, however, was not only committed to whitening the Brazilian population but also to erasing racialised categories from research, school books or data in order to achieve the myth of 'racial democracy'. Citizenship was then re-forged in such a way that race was erased and *class* became the appropriate epistemological category to understand Brazil. As a result, black populations historically deprived of work conditions became associated with laziness and could only blame themselves for their economic failure.

Later, the military dictatorship marked racialised communities, such as indigenous and black communities in favelas, as the other, doubly excluding them: first, by killings and enforced disappearances; later, by erasing them from the national memory. More recently, as explained in the previous chapter, the killings of black communities are naturalised because they are associated with drug cartels in favelas. The following chapter addresses the space of favelas as the space of abjection, where the police embody a colonial logic.

Although the focus here is the role of race rather than that of class, the way the latter was used to disguise race is crucial in understanding, for example, why analyses of police violence in Brazil tend to dismiss the racialised bias in police actions. The focus on the 'poor' as a reason for criminality makes the state apparatus appear blameless for the violence that kills black people. Another consequence of the focus on class rather than race is that it gives legitimacy to the narrative of the 'war on drugs' that links criminality to poverty. This chapter paves the way to the next one, where I will discuss the operationalisation of a security apparatus that follows a colonial logic characterised by its lethality.

Notes

1 In absolute numbers, a survey conducted by the Ipea showed that the police killed 3,320 people only in 2015. The survey also highlighted that for the first time, the police are killing more than criminals, when numbers of police killings are compared to numbers of robbery followed by death perpetrated by criminals (Atlas da Violência 2017).
2 In Portuguese: mulato, caboclo, cafuzo, mameluco or mestiço. (IBGE 1999).
3 Created during the Lula government in 2012.
4 Published in English as '*The Masters and the Slaves: A Study in the Development of Brazilian Civilization*'.
5 As described at http://antigo.funai.gov.br/index.php/indios-no-brasil/quem-sao#
6 The Map of Violence (2015) indicated the most targeted age in firearm deaths: out of a total of 42,416 firearm deaths in 2012, 24,882 were between the ages of 15 and 29. The number is equivalent to 59 per cent of the total, with people in this age group representing only 27 per cent of the Brazilian population. While the 30-year-old mortality rate is 38.7 per 100,000, a 19-year-old has almost twice the chance of being killed: 62.9 per 100,000. Between 1980 and 2015 the Brazilian population grew by almost 61 per cent, but the deaths by firearm increased by 387 per cent. Among young people, this increase was even higher: 460 per cent. Men made up 94.2% of homicide victims in the country in 2012.

5 Hidden in plain sight
Liminal spatiality in Brazil

Introduction

To properly engage with police killings and disappearances in Brazil, it is crucial to consider that most police violence happens in favelas and other peripheries of contemporary urban Brazil, where death is an expected outcome. Favelas are considered the poorest areas in urban Brazil. They are also considered home for militias and drug cartels – a dangerous and abject place. Under the framework of the war on drugs, militarised interventions at favelas are perceived as positive. Costa Vargas (2013), when analysing *O Globo*'s coverage of the pacifying operations, identified some socially shared sentiments, including primordial fear and abjection, felt among self-identified white and respectable citizens towards black bodies and their communities. These feelings underpin the need to demarcate unambiguous boundaries between favelas and non-favela areas, between 'them' and 'us'.

Following the conceptualisation formulated by Agamben (2005), the camp is a permanent spatial arrangement that remains continually outside the normal state of law, intrinsically related to a state of exception. For Mbembe (2003), however, camps are not limited to an exception related to war but can encompass more permanent and orientalist arrangements such as colonial spaces. As Jessica Auchter (2014) argued, modern politics rests on the distinction between life and death. According to her, the process of literally constructing life and death is nothing less than the project of modern statecraft: the construction of subjectivity itself.

The last strand of analysis in the book is related to spatiality and its role in the decision that excludes some people and makes their life unworthy. This last strand, as does the previous two, follows Agamben's conceptualisations of camp, apparatus, and bare life, and Achille Mbembe's critique of necropolitics. Chapter 3 focused on state apparatus as an expression of the sovereign decision, and Chapter 4 explored racialised notions embodied by the state apparatus creating a hierarchic classification whereby some lives are unworthy. Finally, but no less importantly, I discuss how spatiality is deeply connected to a distribution of death.

In the context of the war on drugs, the police adopted 'operations' as a combat strategy. Police operations are organised and unforeseeable incursions in places dominated by drug cartels, namely favelas and peripheries. As discussed in previous chapters, killings that occur during operations in

DOI: 10.4324/9781003032519-6

Hidden in plain sight 131

favelas[1] under the label of *autos de resistência* are unproblematised because those killed or caught in the crossfire are perceived as culpable (Souza 2010: 157). Misse (2011: 4) highlighted that favela dwellers not only live under the rule of drug cartels but also have to deal with a constant interruption of their everyday by police operations, placing them in the crossfire.

I start this chapter by outlining some of the dominant trends in Agamben's accounts of the camp to present a few examples that illustrate some implications associated with camp, apparatus, and life. To do so, I focus on some discussions undertaken in the field of migration studies about the camp. I argue that each of these areas of work has made important contributions by providing a nuanced reading of the distinction between inclusion and exclusion. Considering more contemporary forms of camp, Rygiel (2012) argued that camps reproduce an orientalist mapping of the world that considers some people incapable or unworthy of citizenship. By bringing spatiality to the fore, as well as concepts used in migration studies, such as abject spaces, I will show how favelas and peripheries in Brazil are constituted as a particular field for sovereign decisions that include the death of specific populations. Part of my argument here is that although those populations might be acting politically, for example in the struggle for civil rights, violent events involving populations attached to specific spatial contexts are not politicised, and this was also the case during the dictatorship.

In this chapter, I anchor my analysis in the historical accounts of Brazil, mainly in the colonisation process, elaborating on how the process of land occupation resulted in the deaths of indigenous populations. Also, I engage with the socio-economic process that later displaced undesired populations, moving them to the first favelas in Rio de Janeiro and São Paulo. The present chapter addresses how particular spaces are understood as the place of the abject. Sometimes this abjection is informed by the concept of 'void', as in the examples of indigenous communities or rural areas; at other times it is interpreted as 'excess', as in the cases of favelas and peripheral areas. I argue that to analyse the action of the security apparatus, it is necessary to engage with a colonial logic permeated by race and space.

The present chapter reflects on the disappearances of Patricia Amieiro in 2008 and Juan Moraes in 2011 in Rio de Janeiro, and the killing and disappearance of five youngsters in São Paulo as revenge against the death of a municipal police officer. These examples show how notions of space and race are interplayed in the embodiment of sovereign decisions over death. I argue not only that space plays an important role in the geographical distribution of death, but also that modern camps are not necessarily a place where people are confined by official boundaries. Modern camps are places where death can happen in a normalised way.

Conceptualisation of camp in Agamben's work: development and critiques

An important element in the killings followed by disappearances perpetrated by the police in Brazil is the role of the favela, as well as of other peripheral urban areas, in the broader scenario. Symbolically, the favela is a space associated with poverty, criminality, and drug trafficking. This perception can be observed in a quote by Sergio Cabral, Rio de Janeiro's governor between 2007 and 2014, who defended women's right to abortion as a way to curb violence, given that the fertility rates of female favela dwellers turned that space into 'a criminal-making factory' (my translation, Folha de Sao Paulo 2007). In this section, I will first introduce the concept of camp as theorised by Agamben (1995) and its interpretations in IR. By considering the camp in its spatial-ontological dimension (Minca 2015), it is possible to explore how racialised notions of life and notions of criminalised space, informed by the colonial rationale, corroborate to legitimise the politics of death.

Agamben's theorisation on the camp follows the Jewish experience in concentration camps and draws on the materialisation of exception in territorial terms (1995). To Agamben, the camp is another feature of the state of exception. As a spatial arrangement, the camp is located outside the normal order, but inside its suspension. Agamben points out that 'whoever entered the camp moves in a zone of indistinction between outside and inside, exception and rule, licit and illicit, in which the very concept of rights and juridical protection no longer make any sense' (1995: 97). Thus, those who are outside the normal order are not excluded from the sovereign power. Instead, they are interacting with the sovereign power, even if excluded. The camp is a space where the exceptional and the abnormal stand outside the juridical rule but inside the sovereign logic and under its domain. Individuals in custody in the camp become bare life, between fact and law, rule and exception.

The zone of indistinction in Agamben's work refers to a *logic of the field*, necessary to account for the imprecisions created by the state of exception. According to him, a zone of indistinction is marked by an indecidable decision between law and fact, giving the camp a symbolic meaning. Agamben associates the *logic of the field* to the Möbius strip, a surface with only one side whereby the inside and the outside enter a zone of irreducible indistinction (Vaughan-Williams 2009: 101; Bigo 2014). Vaughan-Williams contested the idea that a zone of indistinction could have led to a lack of clarity in Agamben's theory, suggesting that 'the alternative topology in Agamben's work provides a spatial theory that informs his analysis of the exercise and limits of sovereign power, subjectivity and political space' (2009: 102). Rather than focusing on borders, which perpetuate the modern geopolitical imaginary informed by binary understandings, we should be concerned about the production of indistinctions that result from the sovereign decision.

To Bigo, the Möbius strip suggests a topology that stops the continuous line of a circle. It does not divide sacred from profane, internal from external, as an intelligible border inscribed in time and space. From this new understanding, the border depends on the position of the observer. It is different from a simple relation of spatial interdiction which fabricates an outside by enclosing it in a circle. The Möbius strip can be related to the discussion here on *zoe/bios* – as a life that is deemed *un*worthy, or as public versus private – where the boundaries of sovereignty power are being disputed.

Hidden in plain sight 133

To Vaughan-Williams (2009: 104), the camp holds the ambivalences between *zoe* and *bios*. When the boundaries between the normal and the abnormal become blurred following sovereign logic, according to Agamben, 'we are all virtually homines sacri' (1995: 111). In IR, many scholars have drawn on Agamben's concept of the camp to discuss Guantanamo Bay. There, detainees are classified by the United States as 'unlawful criminal combatants' – a term not recognised by the United Nations or by any other international institution (Vaughan-Williams 2009: 739).

It is important to highlight that by including Guantanamo detainees under a category that is outside the Geneva Convention, those detainees are placed outside juridical norms. Under the juridical-political framework of war on terror, those subjects are altogether outside any type of agreement. Still, as detainees, their existence is established in relation to the norms by being excluded from them. Vaughan-Williams (2009) highlighted that conventional logic and frameworks reflect dominant notions about a juridical-political culture in which some people are de-humanised. Referred to as 'pure killing machines' (2009: 739), detainees in Guantanamo are seen as life that does not deserve to be fully accounted for regarding rights. The symbolic dimension of the camp as a zone of indistinction relates to practices according to which discursive frameworks sustain the power structures.

Migration studies often provide interesting insights into how camps constitute subjectivities. More specifically, the work of Isin and Rygiel (2007a, 2007b) and Rygiel (2012, 2016) argued that Agamben's interpretation of the camp is not helpful to understand frontiers, zones, and camps in contemporary times. Isin and Rygiel (2007a) drew on Arendt's view of the functioning of the camp to build up their critique of Agamben, claiming that contemporary camps represent a space where undesirable individuals are eliminated, following denationalisation and denaturalisation, or 'processed', referring to the process whereby migrants are considered non-citizens as they wait for their rights.

By following this reasoning, Isin and Rygiel (2007a) seemed to want to (re-)politicise those marginal spaces. What seems to trouble Isin and Rygiel (2007a, 2007b, Rygiel 2012) is the impossibility of political life, in Agamben's terms, for those located in contemporary camps. Vaughan-Williams (2009) addressed the differentiation between *zoe* and *bios* by emphasising the constant tension between them, instead of reaffirming a relation of exclusion. As explained in the previous section, bare life is not simply excluded from the political community; instead, it is permanently sustained in relation to the sovereign power, an existence marked by ambivalence. Brassett and Vaughan-Williams highlight that 'bare life is not merely an accidental by-product of liberal biopolitics, but rather a necessary component of the continuation of that rationality of governance in the face of its inherent instabilities and limits' (2012: 22). In that sense, the lives that inhabit the camp are bare lives, caught in a zone of indistinction between *zoe* and *bios*, and produced by sovereign practices.

Those ambivalences allow us to theorise on the importance of those lives through the lenses of the logic of exception. The consideration of life as *bios* – in its totalised manner – means that it could be completely exterminated.

134 Hidden in plain sight

However, its existence is vital to the sovereign logic. Although, as pointed by Edkins (2007: 76), sovereign power is happy to constantly (re)negotiate the boundaries of the distinction that leads to bare life, if only to keep the logic alive. The state of exception, though, is linked to the sovereign power and can be extended to an entire civil population; yet lines of difference are created.

Agamben's work (1995) on biopolitics is entangled with the materialisation of exception in territorial terms, or, as Carlos Minca (2007) argued in his article 'Agamben's Geographies of Modernity', with a spatial theory of power. According to Minca, the spatial aspects of Agamben's work would allow us to describe the 'constitution of sovereign power and the inscription of homo sacer within modern politics, based upon the eminently spatial concept of the camp and the ban' (2007: 80). Minca also claimed that 'the hidden matrix of politics' (Agamben 1995) is inevitable and needs to be elaborated in spatial terms. Carlos Minca (2006, 2007) highlighted the need to account for a spatial aspect that can ground political decisions. Life is happening some-*where*, and this *where* is important.

The spatial arrangement of the camp is located outside the normal order, but inside the suspension, a feature in the state of exception. Nick Vaughan-Williams (2009) identified a tension between intensity and structure in Agamben's work. This tension results from seeing the state of exception as a process, gradually emerging in the West since World War I through fascism. On the other hand, Agamben also argues that the state of exception is not a modern innovation but a constitutive paradigm in the juridical-political order. When exploring how bare life is constituted in relation to the state of exception, Vaughan-Williams also identified two different aspects of this process: method and location. Method is related to apparatus, and location to camp. It is important to highlight that these two processes are interrelated. These tensions allow a more nuanced analysis that opens up the possibility of identifying where exceptionalities are being constructed following political claims, such as the 'war on drugs'.

When discussing space and life in the context of war on drugs, it is important to observe what Campbell (1992: 169) has called the 'geography of evil' (in relation to the 'cold war'). Campbell explained that containment is a strategy associated with the logic of identity used to segregate and transform some subjects into enemies. He claims that discourses of danger have been highly effective in aligning social identity with the politics of space. Although discussing the 'cold war', Campbell identifies new discourses of danger, such as terrorism and drugs.

Agamben conceptualised the camp as space where the sovereign locates those in custody through the ban. Indeed, the ban is the element that carries a spatial dimension that later helps Agamben in the conceptualisation of camp,[2] while also bringing the idea of inclusive exclusion, blurring the lines between inside and outside (Minca 2006; Vaughan-Williams 2009). If someone is banned from a community, this person is still related to the group even if, for example, he or she is identified as an *out*law. In other words, the outlaw category implies there is still a law from which one is out.

In that sense, the camp is the space where the abnormal is outside the space reserved to the normal. Nevertheless, by being outside, the abnormal is still inside the sovereign logic, under the norm constituted as an exception, in a way that preserves the difference between normal and abnormal. An important feature in Agamben's (1995) consideration of camp is how it is conceptualised as an undistinguished zone. This fluidity or porosity can be observed in the way apparatus, life, and decisions navigate from inside the camp towards the outside.

To Vaughan-Williams (2009), the 'zone of irreducible indistinction' is precisely where sovereign power locates itself to produce the order which sustains its operation, highlighting the impossibility of drawing a line that separates two substances, already noted in Agamben's 'logic of the field'. Vaughan-Williams added that this logic represented an alternative paradigm where the idea of the border does not make sense, noting how this logic demonstrates the tense relation between inside and outside, rather than a bi-polarity.

Modern camps, abject spaces

Agamben's notion of camp has received some attention in the interdisciplinary field often described as 'border thinking'. The border thinking debate has focused on the character and extent of globalisation and state borders either 'as a thing of the past or as an enduring feature of world politics post-1648' (Vaughan-Williams 2009: 729). There are some differences regarding the emphasis given by authors to the features present in Agamben's conceptualisation of the camp. Vaughan-Williams (2009) for example, argued in favour of new alternative border thinking. He has challenged the idea that borders limit sovereign action and emphasised the 'logic of the field' as a spatial description that sees a constant tension between the inside and the outside of the border, rather than a simple opposition. Bulent Diken and Carsten Bagge Laustsen (2002) observed how the camp is a logic that combines discipline, control, and terror. Didier Bigo (2008) reflected on the use of the ban *dispositif* to create a 'governmentality of unease' based on practices of exceptionalism, acts of profiling and containing foreigners, and a normative imperative of mobility. In those accounts, borders are not strictly geographic, but they also stand for a body of laws, norms, and practices that limit and constrain movements – not necessarily located at the border division between two, or more, sovereign states.

The notion of camp has also inspired and influenced analyses of migration and refugees. While it seems that there is a consensus that Agamben's concept is ahistorical, suppressing political agency (Isin and Rygiel 2007a; Huysmans 2008; Redclift 2013), the way authors usually approach this constraint can take different directions. Isin and Rygiel (2007a, 2007b) perceive the camps of 'our times' as social and political spaces. According to Redclift, camp 'may be abject and alienated but it is not inert', and for that reason, it needs to be analysed from below (2013a: 309). These contributions (Isin and Rygiel

136 *Hidden in plain sight*

2007a; Redclift 2013) focus on the possibility of agency and resistance in such spaces. Because there are many forms of 'encampment' in place nowadays, camps assume different forms. Some camps are delimited by their geographical borders, as in the case of detention centres (Rajaram and Grundy-Warr 2004), humanitarian refugee camps (Rajaram and Grundy-Warr 2004; Darling 2016), camp-cities (Darling 2016), camp-based populations (Redclift 2013), or zones of protection (Isin and Rygiel 2007b) including Guantanamo Bay (Isin and Rygiel 2007a; Aradau 2007; Huysmans 2008). In other cases, it can assume diffused contours such as the City of Sanctuary (Squire and Darling 2013; Darling 2016) where borders are not so well defined, or border zones, which encompass practices of encampment (Agier 2011) and national boundaries (Isin and Rygiel 2007b), as in the example of the USA–Mexico border (Isin and Rygiel 2007b). Other contributions explore notions of hospitality (Isin and Rygiel 2007a; Squire and Darling 2013; Darling 2016) and citizenship (Redclift 2013, 2015).

The accounts just discussed on the (im)materiality of borders and the possibilities to understand them in contexts not restricted to state borders, also tap into what is considered (un)worthy lives. Of relevance to this discussion is how those boundaries can account for places inside the cities. When discussing favelas and peripheries in Brazil, it is important to acknowledge borders as porous and to understand them not only regarding how they relate to populations in transit, as in the case of migrants. On the contrary, marginalised populations also concentrate in spaces like favelas, although they are not confined to that space– as they are free to come and go daily. Still, they are crucial to the function of the neoliberal economic system by being included as a cheap labour market.

Migration studies quite often provide interesting insights into the relation of space and subjectivities. The nature of the migrant subject, however, is opposed to the subject analysed in the present book. Whereas in migration studies people are in transit and their settlements are temporary, in the present research the subjects' settlements, albeit precarious, are not temporary. Still, some notions discussed in migration studies deserve a closer look, such as how camps constitute subjects (Rygiel 2012), the interstitial zone (Redclift 2013), and abject spaces (E. Isin and Rygiel 2007; E. F. Isin and Rygiel 2007).

By arguing that Agamben's interpretation of the camp is not helpful to understand frontiers, zones, and camps in the present day, Isin and Rygiel (2007a) reframed those spaces as 'abject spaces'. The term 'abject' makes reference to Julia Kristeva's work (1982) who considers the term as 'neither subject nor object' (1982: 1). Kristeva explains the abject as the uncanny, a non-definable object.

> What is abject is not my correlative, which provided me with someone or something else as support, would allow me to be detached and autonomous. The abject has the only quality of the object – that of being opposed to 'I' ... it draws me toward the place where meaning collapses. ... A massive and sudden emergence of uncanniness.
>
> (1982: 1)

Isin and Rygiel (2007) took into account how Arendt saw the functioning of the camp: space where undesirable individuals were eliminated after denationalisation and denaturalisation; a space of abjection where people are reduced to bare life. Isin and Rygiel (2007a) differentiated it from the notion of 'abject spaces'. Isin and Rygiel (2007a) oppose the space of abjection, as a space rendered to invisible and inaudible entities, to abject spaces, where the same invisible and inaudible entities are located but with room for political agency. Discussions on the meaning of this opposition are significant to address how the spatial division is translated into political terms.

Isin and Rygiel claimed that frontiers and zones are spaces where subjects are 'processed' and turned into noncitizens while they wait for their rights – constituting a space of politics. In doing so, Isin and Rygiel (2007a) wanted to (re)politicise those marginal spaces – abject spaces. By differentiating spaces of abjection from abject spaces and politicising the latter, the authors built their critique of Agamben, who they deem unable to imagine spaces of exception asserting against abjection, criticising Agamben's notion of the city as 'nebulous and enigmatic precisely because it is trapped in the camp' (Isin and Rygiel 2007: 184).

Isin and Rygiel (2007a, 2007b, Rygiel 2012) constantly refer to the need to politicise camps by detaching it from the idea of space of exception. However, they do not seem to acknowledge the notion of 'ban' in Agamben's work, as a *dispositif* through which those spaces of exception may occur. For Agamben (1995), the ban is a *dispositif* through which the technical administration of life occurs. Ignoring a ban can be problematic, since it would make the apparatus that led to people being trapped in camps invisible. Moreover, putting together shantytowns, detention centres, and refugee camps can make us lose sight of the specificity and dynamics that each place entails. In addition to understanding the camp as a space of exceptionality, outside of and separated from the space of the citizen, Rygiel investigates how camp is both political and a politicised space. According to her, extraterritoriality can be read as an imperial rule designed to protect the rights of European citizens living overseas from the 'barbarism' of the cultural other surrounding them.

Discussing the context of migrants in Europe and the different types of settlements (Isin and Rygiel 2007a, 2007b), migrants are in transition whereby they are protected under the claim of human rights, but they are not yet full citizens. However, the discussion in the present chapter is looking at another population. Residents in favelas and peripheries are not outsiders, even if they are marginalised. They are confined not to detained camps or border zones, but in a situation more similar to the 'interstitial zone' (Redclift 2013: 309), which accounts for a more permanent settlement where politics, power relations, and citizenship are negotiated.

Regularly built as emergency devices for displaced and undesirable populations, and justified as temporary necessities, camps often turn into durable socio-spatial formations whose operating logic and effects are articulated at the intersection of global, state, and urban scales. When relating camps to the colonial logic, Picker and Pasquetti (2015: 684) claimed that camps could reduce inhabitants to mere abstractions deprived of subjectivity, fixing them onto a chthonic socio-spatial order, sustained by exception, and according to which seclusion is a necessary response to a seemingly threatening global and urban disorder.

Analysing the aesthetics of the movie *City of God* (2002), Diken used Agamben to highlight how the favelas were represented on the one hand as liminal spaces, and on the other as part of a clear-cut opposition between 'the 'city' versus the 'liminal' favela (Diken 2005: 310); civilisation versus gang violence. Diken concluded that in the Brazilian popular imagination, the favela is home to 'marginal ... people who are not really from the city' (Caldeira 2000: 78–79 in Diken 2005), rather than to ordinary citizens.

As we will see in the development of this chapter, although Agamben's conceptualisation of camp provides a hidden matrix associated with the modern political *nomos*, further considerations are necessary to account for how local experiences can be linked to this concept of camp. In the case of Brazil, for example, it is important not to lose sight of the intrinsic relation between disappearances and death, and the country's colonial past. As we will see, the need to occupy the 'new land' with 'the right people' seems to underlie the rationale behind discourses and policies that bring territory and population together. As an attempt to translate Brazil's experience as a post-colonial society, and the rationale towards killings and disappearances, it is necessary to grasp the concept of camp through historical accounts of the colonisation process in Brazil. I will first bring accounts of the occupation process in Brazil and then address how specific areas of the country developed following the same rationale.

The conquest of Brazil: a mindset predicated on the notion of territory and population

As in any other nation-state, the territory has always been a key issue in Brazil. The Treaty of Tordesillas signed in 1449 divided the 'New World' between the Portuguese and the Spanish rulers. The Roman Catholic Church, by dividing the world in half, granted to Portugal the monopoly on trade in West Africa and to Spain, also the right to colonise and to have direct shipment of captive Africans for trade as human commodities in the Spanish colonies in Latin America.

The interesting aspect of this treaty is that it was signed during what is considered a pre-Westphalian order when political decisions were arbitrated by the Church, with the Pope standing as the sovereign ruler over all islands (Goes Filho 2015). As the 'New World' was considered an island at the time, the Pope ratified the agreement. The Treaty established an imaginary line that established a demarcation along a north-south meridian whereby land at 370 leagues (1,770 km) to the west of the Cape Verde Islands would belong to Portugal, and the remaining side would belong to Spain (Goes Filho 2015: 24).

There were many disputes between France, England, and Holland over who had rights to the 'New World'. These countries contested the agreement that gave the lands to Portugal and Spain, and Portugal managed only to secure the north-eastern portion of the territory after a conflict against the Dutch. As for the lands that were in the south, they were secured only after several disputes with Spain that culminated with the Paraguay War, which lasted from 1864 to 1870. The borders of what today is Brazil have changed a great deal over the years. What is important in this process, however, is the role played by the *Bandeirantes* – Portuguese settlers who pushed further the borders previously established by the Tordesillas Treaty, a useful action that was later combined with diplomatic endeavours.

According to Goes Filho (2015), knowledge about the *Bandeirantes* expeditions is not fully consolidated in Brazilian official history, and the first research done on documents from that time only occurred in the 1920s. Goes Filho (2015) also challenges the dichotomised representation of expeditions carried out in the interior of Brazil, suggesting instead that the lines that divided public and private interests were rather blurred. Goes Filho's research (2015) showed that some expeditions were constituted by 900 people, mostly from white background or of mixed European and Indigenous descent, and two thousand indigenous people. If Goes Filho (2015) highlighted the positive political consequences of their actions, Vianna (1965) called attention to the military aspect of the expeditions.

> *Bandeirantes* is the name given to the group of men who went to the central portion of what is now Brazil, in expeditions to enslave indigenous populations and search for gold and silver. Generally speaking, they departed from São Paulo and advanced beyond the Tordesillas line into the Spanish side. Many are the national tributes paid to their endeavours in the country, from festivals to monuments.[3] A huge monument, located in the biggest park of São Paulo is noteworthy in the way it conveys the mixed racial background of the members of the expedition while omitting the fact that one of its main purposes was to enslave indigenous populations. The inscription on the base of the monument reads 'Glory to the heroes who tied our destiny to the geography of the free world. Without them, Brazil would not be as great as it is'.

This quote seems to indicate that the independence movement, which turned the colony into an empire, was helped by the advance of those groups into the Spanish side, making Brazil a force to be reckoned with in the continent. But it also connotes the European rationale, as highlighted by Mignolo (2000), that 'geographical boundaries coincided with the boundaries of the humanity' (2000: 283). It was only after the unknown was translated into 'savage' that the colonial space began to be conceived as a New World. In that sense, the *Bandeirantes* did not only redefine spatial borders in Brazil, but they also placed Brazil in the geography of modernity by filling the 'void' of Brazil's interior with the 'right people'.

Depicting the colonial space as 'empty space' was a common trope in the imperial discourse and imaginary of the modern/colonial world system in

Latin America (Mignolo 2000), not unlike the way Europe referred to the Orient and Far East (Said 1978). For Mignolo (2000), at the time of colonisation, Christianity provided the framing that turned those who stood outside European borders into 'pagans'. According to him, 'civilisation' and a passionate defence of 'progress' were later motifs that emerged with Enlightenment.

The 'empty space' or tabula rasa trope in the colonial discourse is also present in the national discourse, as evoked by the monument to the *Bandeirantes*. The common perception was that this massive portion of land was a challenge that needed to be faced with occupation, and many were the policies in place to fill the land with 'the right type of population'. Considering that the colony's territory was equivalent to 92 times the size of Portugal (Folha-Uol 2000), occupying Brazilian lands was a concern for Portugal at the time and explains the different posture towards governmentality by comparison with other countries. For example, even if there were massive killing and slavery of native populations, there were also efforts to 'include' them in the new society with juridical provisions that kept indigenous peoples outside the slave system, as seen in a law from 1755.[4] Among these provisions, there were economic incentives and legal rights granted to the offspring of a union between white male colonisers and indigenous women.

The consolidation of Brazilian borders is a result of a diplomatic endeavour that started at the beginning of the first Republic, soon after independence (1822). Considered by many as the great architect of the Brazilian borders, Baron of Rio Branco[5] also gave his name to the school for diplomats in Brazil. His great achievement was to secure the new borders without the need for wars (Goes Filho 2015). The size of the country was seen as a symbol of power and strength, as evident in the 'giant by nature' line in the Brazilian national anthem.

As discussed in the previous chapter, populations of natives and Africans were always subject to death and precariousness, and there is no attempt here to make their ordeal less harsh. However, as already discussed, the way that each of these populations was victimised is different. On the one hand, they were clearly considered socially abject or disposable; on the other hand, they were seen as a necessary means to colonise and occupy the vast territory of Brazil.

From a place to tame to a camp to kill: urban peripheries as abject space following a colonial rationale

In the following sections, I will bring some examples of how Brazil as a former colony applied the same colonial logic of governmentality. To do so, I will focus on the constitution of spaces where forced disappearances were likely to happen during the dictatorship, albeit without ever achieving the status of *political disappearance*. In some cases, as we shall see, those disappearances are very hard to trace, and this feature makes them closer to contemporary cases in the sense that they are also non-politicised and non-memorialised. To illustrate cases of historical disappearances I will draw on the work of the recent Truth Commission of Rio de Janeiro and São Paulo to discuss the disappearance of people living in favelas and peripheral areas, as well as that of indigenous people. I also refer to those examples in the chapters on bare life and state apparatus.

Traditionally, those who have discussed space, i.e. geographers and urban researchers, explored how places provide context for political identities and political interests, organising and mobilising political activity (Jones et al. 2004). Subjects, movement of people, or governmentality can be related to biopolitics. In that sense, politics of life can be related to the contention between groups to control development or standards of living (Atkinson 2000). The strategy deployed by Italy to control the nomadic Bedouin population in its Libyan colony (Atkinson 2000) or the apartheid in South Africa, which created the Group Areas Act to spatially divide racial groups according to residence (Western 1996), or even the migration over the Mexico–US border (Herzog 1990), are examples of such instances.

Other researchers, however, have argued that certain spaces are not characterised by biopolitics – as politics over life – but by thanatopolitics – as politics of killings, a concept employed by some different authors. Agamben (1995), for example, explored how the state of coma refers to the moment where the boundaries between life and death become blurred. The threshold created brought the need for legal and medical regulation and its politicisation. Mbembe (2003), on the other hand, questioned the politics of killing not against a single subject, but against a number of them as in the case of settlements.

In the following subsections, I will demonstrate how specific places become abject spaces. First, we will look at how peripheral areas in Rio de Janeiro and São Paulo developed in parallel with the wealthy areas enhancing the concentration of inequalities. Because they have not been planned to receive so many displaced people, areas in the periphery do not have access to basic rights such as water or security. We will then look at a diametrically opposed space, indigenous communities. It is common to hear indigenous accounts of how they had not been aware of the military dictatorship in the 1960s. In 2007, FUNAI reported that at least 32 indigenous communities in Brazil wanted to live in isolation.

The inequalities found in peripheries and indigenous communities prompt a reflection with Foucault on issues of power and knowledge. It was during the 1940s and the 1960s that indigenous communities and favela dwellers first received the attention of researchers. In the case of indigenous communities, knowledge turned into violence and into other measures to kill these populations. During the military regime, the idea that indigenous peoples were occupying valuable lands 'hindering national development' (Ministry Rangel Reis, in National Truth Commission 2014), and that shantytowns were associated with criminality, legitimised the violence against them.

Rio de Janeiro's favelas as abject space

Peripheral areas in Rio de Janeiro and São Paulo are quite different in geographic terms. Whereas in São Paulo the city grew around a wealthy centre so

142 *Hidden in plain sight*

that the further one moves from the centre the more unequal it gets, in the case of Rio de Janeiro, favelas emerged in the hills that surround the wealthy areas of the city. Located within a landscape of sea and hills, the existence of favelas in middle- and upper-class neighbourhoods enhances the deep contrast between the poor and the rich. The apparent dividing lines were explored in the book *Cidade Partida*, fractured or divided city, by Zuenir Ventura (1994).

Notwithstanding the idea of a divided city, peripheries have served to supply low-skilled labour for decades. In Rio de Janeiro, the proximity between favelas and wealthy neighbourhoods is part of a spatial structure that sees one-third of female favela residents commuting to nearby 'family houses' where they work as servants or housemaids (O Dia 2015). The transit of people from inside favelas and peripheries to wealthy parts of the city makes the ban conceptualised by Agamben (1995) even more fluid. In those locations, although people's movement is not restricted between one space and another, or from inside to outside the camp, their mobility follows specific features that are worth observing.

To illustrate what shapes mobility in these areas, it will be useful to narrate a particular episode. During the summer of 2015, the police started a special pre-emptive operation to protect the population against 'swarming-type robberies' that sometimes happen on the beaches of Rio de Janeiro during summer. It is important to remark that the operations happen during the weekends when there are more people at the beaches and less commuting by workers residing in favelas. As part of one of these operations, the police held a road check in the city centre, which is quite far from the beach and works as a borderline between the South (wealthy) Zone and the North (poor) Zone of the city. The same police operation also happened in other parts of the city that provided access to the beach. During those road checks, youngsters, generally young black males, who had no money or documents, were taken out of the buses even if they had not committed any crime (G1 b 2015; *Jornal do Brazil* 2015). Human rights groups criticised the police operation, the Judiciary considered the operation illegal (Carta Capital 2015), and social movements organised by the mothers of former victims of police violence claimed the police were arresting the youngsters and taking them to detention centres.

As the former federal capital of Brazil, Rio de Janeiro was subject to many interventions to achieve its 'modernisation'. This process involved both urban regeneration and gentrification. The first big urban change enforced by the government took place at the beginning of the twentieth century. Meade gives the following account:

> Despite a temporary easing of the vaccination law, the government pressed ahead with the bulk of the health campaign, including the destruction of the unsanitary tenements in the Old City. Property values rose, allowing foreign investors and domestic property holders with sufficient reserves to meet the taxes to turn a healthy profit selling to a new crop of developers. With affordable houses gone, and no plans in sight to build any more, the poor began to move in droves to the outskirts of

the city, to the favelas which were beginning to dot the hillsides, and to the company-controlled towns encircling the factories. For the articulate and propertied classes who resided in the newly 'beautified' downtown, Rio de Janeiro was earning its name: a *cidade marvilhosa*, the marvellous city. More than simply facilitating trade, or improving Rio's position in the international market, the renovation followed the established design as well as the cultural and racial bias of European society. Downtown Rio became off-limits to people of colour except as workers; the popular tent theatres closed; cafes catered to bank employees, not to tenement dwellers. The Brazilian elite had defined 'civilisation' according to the standard of their trading partners. Secondly, the renovation had separated the city's social classes by geography and eliminated the cross-class alliances found in earlier demonstrations. The proximity of their living arrangements had meant that wealthy residents had shared the grievances of the poor and had even found themselves in the disquieting position of aligning with people many despised to obtain the services they all lacked.

(Teresa Meade 1989: 253 and 254)

This quote shows the process of urbanisation in Rio de Janeiro that started at the end of the 1880s. It is important to observe how the urbanisation process followed ideas of modernisation and civilisation that meant the expulsion of those considered poor or from the wrong racial background. A passing observer can perceive how Rio's city centre with its grand buildings and narrow streets emulates European cities, as in the example of the Municipal Theatre, a copy of the Opera Theatre in Paris.

The favela, as a specific space, emerged during a time when national and local intellectuals were concerned about the future of the new republic, including its policies towards health, sanitation, and urban reforms. The lack of housing in underprivileged communities only aggravated the problem by bringing those who were not able to afford houses in the centre of the city, where jobs were on offer. The same elite that wanted to expel those who did not fit in their ideal of 'marvellous city' needed their labour force. A more contemporary example, specifically in Rio de Janeiro, is the data indicating that one-third of housemaids and cleaners in the city reside in favelas (Agencia Brasil 2015).

The enforced displacement of people did not stop after the end of the First Republic and continued through the modernising endeavour in the country. In 1964, the year of the *coup d'état* in Brazil, Governor Carlos Lacerda oversaw the new Guanabara state, which later changed to Rio de Janeiro state. The governor was committed to proving that although Rio was not the federal capital anymore, it would nevertheless stand as an example of modernity. As part of this modernist project, some favelas started to be removed, and families were forcibly displaced to rural areas. Vila Kennedy and Vila Aliança were two new neighbourhoods named after John Kennedy, President of the United States and head of the program, *Aliança para o Progresso* from

USAID (United States Agency for International Development), which also helped to fund the project.

Valladares recounted (2005) her trajectory to become a researcher specialised in favelas. In 1966 a research centre at the Catholic University of Rio de Janeiro hired a few students to apply a questionnaire to residents in three favelas – Bras de Pina, Mata Machado, and Morro União. The research was commissioned by the Guanabara state. In 1967 another research project was carried out through a partnership between UNESCO and CNBB – the National Conference of Brazilian Bishops of Brazil. At the time, the Vatican was concerned about losing its congregation members.

As discussed in the previous chapter, following Mignolo's (2000) argument, postcolonial elites tend to reproduce imperial (global) imaginaries and project them onto local realities. Coincidently or not, as we will see later, the first organisation to be interested in meeting and getting to know residents of Rio de Janeiro favelas was the Church. Part of my argument in the present chapter is that the connection that local elites make between specific populations and specific spaces is highly influenced by the colonial mindset. In Brazil, its historical experience of coloniality has also informed the more contemporary experiences of dealing with what is considered abject populations.

The Truth Commission Team of Rio de Janeiro dedicated two chapters of its report (Rio de Janeiro [Estado] 2015) to acknowledge the violence in Rio's favelas during the dictatorship and 'adding colour' (Rio de Janeiro [Estado] 2015: 125) to the memory of the political struggle in that same period. By doing so, the NTC Team acknowledged the concentration of black populations in the favelas, who were historically underprivileged in a country built with their sweat and blood. The chapter on the dictatorship in favelas aims at addressing the specific features of violence during the dictatorial regime, rather than just having the regime as a backdrop of the analysis.

The report claimed that one of the most recurrent forms of human rights violation in favelas was enforced displacement. More than 100,000 people were displaced from 1964 to 1973 (Valladares 1976). At the time, former residents from the same favelas, sometimes separating whole families, were put into waste collection vehicles and driven to different areas breaking kinship networks (Rio de Janeiro [Estado] 2015). Accounts by displaced people commonly remark that the new areas designated to them by the government lacked the infrastructure for housing and any form of security. The report highlighted that although the incursion of military forces in favelas was not new; during the dictatorship, their presence was doubly justified. Firstly, they subscribed to the rationale that favela inhabitants were dangerous and prone to criminal acts, and secondly, they feared that favela inhabitants could be easily recruited in the event of a communist revolution, a concern disseminated after World War II. The researchers found that many official documents proved that there was monitoring of favela resident associations based on the assumption that they 'would not be able to establish political mobilisation of any kind unless if followed third-party manipulation' (Rio de Janeiro [Estado] 2015: 121).

A national survey from 2015 evaluated that 47 per cent of those who live outside favelas would not hire favela residents as workers (Agencia Brasil 2015). According to the survey, there are still misconceptions about favela dwellers. Most of the interviewees fear they may be exposed to theft if they hired someone who lives in a favela because of its association with drugs and crime. Therefore, both the place and the lives of those associated with it become an expression of abjection.

São Paulo's peripheries as abject space

B.P. Manso and C.N. Dias (2017) described the geography of São Paulo and the relationship between its urban development and the growth of marginal populations:

> The map of São Paulo resembles a distorted crucifix, with the right arm longer than the left. The east side of the city is larger than the west, and the southern part longer than the north. As a result of these physical and territorial features, the eastern and southern peripheries of the city encompass the districts that suffered more violence, especially starting in the 1980s. In the south and north extremes of São Paulo, environmental barriers slowed growth and urban development making settlement difficult. ... In the middle of the territory, in the region where the horizontal and vertical axes intersect, are the wealthier and more pacific areas of the city. Here is located the older urban centre, built before 1930, with a greater proportion of high-rise buildings, few favelas, and families with greater income and educational levels.
> (2010: 13)

Once again, there is an association between 'peace', 'wealth', and 'family' in opposition to the 'poor', 'criminality', and periphery. Teresa Caldeira (2000) described two different forms of social segregation permeating the transformations of São Paulo's urban space. The first type, from the late nineteenth century to the 1940s, produced a condensed city in which different social groups were packed into the small urban area and segregated by type of housing. The second one dominated the city's development from the 1940s to the 1980s and consisted of different social groups separated by great distances: the middle and upper classes concentrated in central and well-equipped neighbourhoods, and the poor were moved to the peripheries.

Manso and Dias (2017) follow an economic perspective to describe how the process of de-concentration of low-income housing operated in São Paulo from the 1940s until the end of the 1970s. According to him, this process occurred in contrast to the dense population growth of the 1930s, which was concentrated in the central areas of the capital. Rather than living in places with cheap rent or tenements located in neighbourhoods that surrounded older industrial centres, the new migrants spread out to the countless areas in the periphery of the capital, and later to various points in the Greater São Paulo metropolitan area.

While up to the 1970s middle and upper classes bought flats through mortgages backed by public funding (Caldeira 2000), population growth in the peripheral neighbourhoods occurred mainly as a result of irregular land developments (Manso and Dias 2017). The urban patterns of urbanisation in São Paulo followed the centre-periphery model, which has marked the city since the 1940s. Caldeira (2000) pointed out four main features that resulted in the irregular occupation of land: the population is dispersed rather than concentrated; middle and upper classes live in central and well-equipped neighbourhoods while the poor reside in precarious and informal houses in the periphery; homeownership has become the general rule for both rich and poor; and in terms of transportation, working classes tend to rely on buses while middle and upper classes use cars.

Caldeira (2000) argued the narratives that emerged as attempts to reorder the chaos created by feelings of vulnerability exacerbate violence, usually following simplistic and stereotypical explanations that legitimise illegal reactions, such as the support of death squads and vigilantism as a response to the failure by institutions that should be maintaining order. In that sense, the social transformation in São Paulo and political instability are central to the discussion of violence in the city's periphery.

The context of the military dictatorship gave the green light to the police to combat urban guerrillas and accelerated the process whereby it is considered morally acceptable for the police to kill. In São Paulo, the police started to kill primarily young men from the periphery (Pinheiro 1979, 1982, 1991; Caldeira 2000). Another feature of this new form of apparatus was the mechanisms by the dictatorship to guarantee the impunity of its agents (Godoi et al. 2020). If in Rio de Janeiro death squads emerged at the end of the 1950s to curb prostitution and drug trafficking, in São Paulo they appeared at the end of the 1960s in close association with the activities by the Department of Political and Social Order led by Sergio Paranhos Fleury (National Truth Commission 2014: 165).

Urban violence in Rio de Janeiro and São Paulo caused dozens of people to be killed and to disappear. Justifying those murders as a way to keep the city free of 'criminals', the police officers who were part of death squads, benefited from 'extra-legal powers'. An investigation conducted by the Truth Commission Team of São Paulo pointed out that many of the detainees at the Penitentiary Tiradentes were sent to be tortured and killed in the periphery of the city.

In my reading, the politics of death associated with the logic of coloniality enable us to apprehend a rationale still in place that has its roots in the occupation of the 'new' colonial land. Described as an empty space without any traces of civilisation, newcomers completely disregarded whole societies that have inhabited the land from time immemorial. The need to occupy the supposed empty space with the *right* people meant that millions were killed in the process, which is still ongoing. Later, as the African diaspora was enslaved and put to work at the plantations, a new form of destitute life populated the 'new' land. Following hierarchical notions of race, this life was unworthy and not meant to survive.

As discussed in the previous chapter, notions of race in Brazil were shaped by the need to feed the myth of 'racial democracy'. This framework added to the metaphor of the war on drugs minimises the role of race in the analysis by Ignacio Cano (2010) who sees no racial bias in lethal police action. Although the quantitative methodology applied showed a clear racial disparity among the fatal victims of police interventions when compared to the general population, Cano (2010: 41) concluded that this disparity did not mean that there is a racial bias on the part of the police. Cano (2010) based his conclusion on the limitations of available data, on the assumption that all racial groups engage in violent crime and armed confrontations with the police to the same degree, and on the fact that black populations are overrepresented in favelas, an area where police interventions tend to be more lethal.

Costa Vargas (2013), who presented an opposing argument, claimed that police lethality reveals a broader pattern of violence that victimises people according to identifiable urban geographies. Costa Vargas does not deny inequality as one important aspect of criminality but also considers that the unequal distribution of police lethality results from, and is intensified by, historical and contemporary social inequalities, including vulnerability to violence and homicide (2013: 281). According to him, racial belonging intersects with vulnerability to violence in general and with police lethality in particular:

> Data from the 2010 Brazilian Institute of Geography and Statistics (IBGE) census indicate that in Rio de Janeiro's ten poorer neighbourhoods, 63 per cent of their inhabitants classified themselves as either black (*preto*) or mixed/brown (*pardo*). This breakdown is significant for, in the municipality of Rio de Janeiro, blacks and browns comprise 46 per cent of its total population. Blacks and browns, thus, are over-represented in urban areas defined by economic deprivation. These numbers suggest a three-way correlation between race, social class (or income, an admittedly incomplete index of class), and territory: in given social geographies, while a higher proportion of blacks is associated to higher levels of poverty, a higher proportion of whites is associated to higher economic power. Thus, for example, in one of the most well-known favelas in Rio, Mangueira, where per capita income is less than R$ 500.00 per month, 28 percent of its population declared itself black (negra, excluding browns/pardos), in contrast to the city's 10 percent self-declared black population (excluding browns/pardos). In the Lagoa Rodrigo de Freitas area, on the other hand, the average per capita income is R$ 6,160.00,[6] and blacks (excluding browns/pardos) are 1.5 per cent of the population.
> (Costa Vargas 2013: 281)

Costa Vargas (2013) concluded that lethal violence tolerated or perpetrated by the state indicates the low value of black lives from the perspective of those who embody institutions, or as I have argued, the state apparatus. To him, patterns of black victimisation persist – and indeed, increase nationally – because the symbolic and political price of black death is ultimately irrelevant to the state and its dominant constituents.

The colonial logic of death in favelas and peripheries

The skull's revenge: at the threshold of bare life

I begin this section by focusing on an example that illustrates relations between the sovereign apparatus towards life in the context of peripheral areas in Greater São Paulo. This example reveals understandings of the sovereign decision of killing and disappearing people when the police allege to be the first to be attacked and the police response. The example will be discussed in light of the May Crimes, already discussed in the previous chapter. Police response seems to follow a rationale predicated on the odds of counting bodies, by which the lives of those who are performing sovereignty are more valuable than the lives of those who are challenging it.

Five young males disappeared in São Paulo in November 2016. Three of them were being investigated for robbery and the murder of a guard, Rodrigo Lopes Sabino, from the municipality of Santo André, São Paulo (G1 2016). Three young males – Cesar Augusto Gomes Silva, Jonathan Moreira Ferreira, and Caique Henrique Machado Silva – a physically disabled friend – Robson Fernando Donato de Paula – and a driver – Jonas Ferreira Januario – all inhabitants of Sapopemba, a peripheral area of São Paulo, were kidnapped and killed by three members of a police unit. The unit is known as 'skulls' because of a metal skull emblem on their uniforms (Ponte 2016). One of the officers created a fake profile on Facebook to attract the group to a fake party in Ribeirao Pires (G1 2016). The group's whereabouts were unknown for 16 days.

Relatives informed the disappearances to the Human Rights Commission, linked to the Public Security Bureau. They informed that after the homicide of Rodrigo Lopes Sabino, members of the Military Police were threatening one of the missing young males (Estadão 2016). After reporting the disappearance, relatives of all missing persons started to be threatened by members of the police force.

The Military Police were called a few times to the crime scene following a tip-off that directed them to a remote rural area in Mogi das Cruzes, but they did not find the corpses. The Security Secretary (G1 2016) affirmed that the crime scene had been tampered with before the Military Police team finally found the corpses (G1 2016; FolhaUol 2016). Because the corpses were at an advanced stage of decomposition, it was difficult to identify them. The disabled young male had his head severed from the body, and all of them presented signs of torture (O Dia 2016; Terra 2016). The boys' relatives were demanding further investigations. For example, the police did not release a statement as to when the group was killed and who the perpetrators were. The Security Public Bureau was pushing the family to go ahead with funeral arrangements alleging that they would be buried as unidentified bodies unless relatives presented an 'evidence of irregularity in the work carried by official examiners' (Veja 2016). Relatives say they were not allowed to conduct an independent forensic exam (UOL 2016).

The investigators suspected the perpetrators were guards from the Municipality of Santo André because they found some amount of ammunition next to the corpses commonly used by the Military Police, while the guns were of a type used by the Municipal Police (Estadão 2016; Carta Capital 2016). Other evidence also pointed to members of the police force as the responsible ones for the disappearance. For example, a police officer had searched one of the missing persons in a governmental data system a few hours before their disappearance (Carta Capital 2016), and before being kidnapped, the group had been stopped and mistreated by a police officer (Estadão 2016; Folha 2016; G1 2016). The investigators also wanted to know if the Military Police officers and guards from the municipality of Santo André had formed a group intending to seek revenge for the murder of Rodrigo Lopes Sabino. It is not uncommon for a group of police officers from different forces to vindicate the murder of a peer.

The example of the disappearance and homicide of a group of youngsters can be seen as an isolated case perpetrated by a small group of police officers with the purpose of vindicating the homicide of a friend, and this type of action is not an isolated case. As in the example of the May Crimes, both cases show that death squads act with the acknowledgement of the state. After the denunciation of a video showing a few police officers in São Paulo in 2015 killing two people who had been tied together with no chance of self-defence, the governor of São Paulo at the time, Geraldo Alckmin, stated that death squads are not an intrinsic part of the police. Instead, there are a few bad policemen (G1 2015).

If we look at the bigger picture, what we see are not bad habits by bad members of the police force. A report prepared by the University of São Carlos in 2014 analysed 734 death registrations of 939 victims. The report showed that between 2010 and 2011, 61 per cent of the police victims in São Paulo were black. While among black people there were 1.4 deaths for every 100,000 inhabitants, among white communities the number of deaths was of 0.5 for every 100,000 inhabitants. It is important to remark that 79 per cent of the police officers self-declared as white.

The examples are important to illustrate the police reaction as corporatism. When one member of the police force is killed, those responsible for the killing should be eliminated. The second example, however, shows that death squads are acting with the acknowledgement of the state. Although it seems to send the message that lives on 'the other side' are not equivalent to the life of a member of the police force, the ultimate decision is not about counting bodies, but about showing who is in control.

To frame perpetrators as bad cops renders invisibility to the fact that the security apparatus is an expression of sovereign power. While killings happen only in favelas or in peripheral areas, never targeting those who live in wealthy urban areas, disappearances seem to reinforce the borderline that separates those who are inside from those who are outside the sovereign norm or *ethos*. Disappearances seem to represent the complete abjection of some peoples' lives, especially in the example of massive killings in São Paulo.

One important aspect of Giorgio Agamben's theory is the production of bare life through sovereign decisions. As detailed in the previous section, this decision can also be articulated in spatial terms. Among many forms of apparatuses, the security one is usually related to violence. In Brazil, the sovereign decision in applying violence to forms of life attached to specific places gains special contours in situations where sovereign authorities feel threatened, and the security apparatus is prompted to *react*.

Patricia and Juan: at the threshold of the camp

In this section, I will discuss the examples of Patricia Amieiro and Juan Moraes to exemplify the importance of space in locating sovereign decisions and notions of bare life. In the examples of police violence described earlier, two aspects are noteworthy. Firstly, it is not that the police are acting against the law. On the contrary, laws and norms open the possibility for violent actions as the interpretation of specific cases with non-specific labels. The juridical-political structure, however, which has the prerogative of investigating and stopping excesses, endorses them. Secondly, someone who does not belong to a specific spatiality is not usually the subject of police excess. The way subjectivities overlap with spatiality is another important point in Agamben's consideration of camp. Agamben points out that whoever enters the camp moves into a 'zone of indistinction' between outside and inside, exception and rule, licit and illicit, where the very concepts of subjective rights and juridical protection no longer make any sense' (1995: 97). Once in the camp, individuals are constantly facing rule and exception that do not follow the same rule or juridical order present outside the camp.

Sovereign decision was made through the primary act of killing and making bodies disappear based on their location. However, later it was not possible to make them to fit into a profile that matches age, gender, and racial background that is commonly associated with participation in the drug cartels or favela dwellers. Notwithstanding, the killing and disappearance of two people who did not match the camp logic bring us to Agamben's idea that the camp nomos makes us (virtual) homo sacer. When camp is the nomos of our society, we are all in danger. At the same time, making those disappearances problematic implies an understanding that other disappearances are not. Bigo (2006) called attention to the example of an airport check as the attitude of a normalised population who is pleased to be monitored 'against danger' without realising that they are also subject to surveillance, an example of international politics influencing everyday life (Bigo 2006). In the two examples discussed in this chapter, the emphasis on the disappearance of the *wrong* people implies that there are *right* people to be disappeared.

Vaughan-Williams (2009) discussed in depth the 'seemingly hyperbolic claim that we are 'all (virtually) homines sacri' and questioned the limits of such a statement. He looked at Butler's criticism of Agamben to say that power operates differentially depending on the populations, who will be more or less likely to be produced as bare life. Certain populations, especially if we consider race, are more likely to be framed as 'bare life'. Patricia Amieiro and Juan Moraes subverted this assumption, showing the question is not necessarily about who is identified as bare life, but how the existence of life *as such* is potentially a threat to all of us.

The case of Patricia Amieiro, who disappeared in 2008, is an example of how boundaries and sovereign decision relate to public response. Patricia was an engineer from a new wealthy area in Rio de Janeiro, Barra da Tijuca. She was driving back from a party in the South Zone of the city late at night. To get home, she needed to pass by the entrance to Rocinha, the largest favela in South America. Although Rocinha is portrayed as a very dangerous place and a war zone, it is also known for being vibrant, and for hosting an inordinate number of NGOs. It is culturally diverse, attracting the interest of foreigners, a few of whom decided to call it home. Patricia supposedly did not stop at a police road check at the end of the tunnel. Witnesses say that this particular police check consisted of one official vehicle with its lights off. The reports by the Public Ministry stated that two members of the Military Police shot Patricia's car 17 times, which made her lose control of the vehicle and collide against the lamppost, causing her death. Because of the unexpected attack, she could not react. The report states:

> The two police officers who shot Patricia were intending to guarantee their impunity. Helped by another officer from the same Police Force, they obliterated the crime scene by taking the body out of the vehicle and moving the vehicle to a nearby lake, thus preventing the homicide from being discovered. Following that, the officers hid the body of the victim in an unknown location.
>
> (G1 2015)

What was made clear by the investigation report is that the police got rid of Patricia's body as a way to cover up her killing, thus perpetrating a crime to cover up another crime. In Brazil, as elsewhere, it is the presence of the body that gives materiality to someone's death and evidence of a crime. In Patricia's case, the absence of her body removed the certainty of her death. Although her body was never found, her death was recognised by the judicial system in Brazil. The police officers involved in her disappearance back in 2008 are still waiting to be prosecuted; however, Rio de Janeiro's authorities had to pay reparation[7] to her family (*Jornal Extra* 2015). The judge that determined the compensation affirmed that Patricia contributed to her own death by not stopping at the road check.

Another case that received a lot of public attention was the disappearance of a child called Juan Moraes in 2011. Juan, who was 11 years old, his 14-year-old brother Wesley, and a 19-year-old friend of theirs, Wanderson, were walking down the street near to where Juan Moraes used to live, in a very poor slum area in Baixada Fluminense, just outside of Rio de Janeiro municipality. The group was supposedly caught in the middle of a crossfire between police officers and drug dealers during a police operation. The two older boys were shot but survived, and Juan Moraes disappeared. However, Wanderson, who managed to escape with Wesley, saw Juan Moraes falling to the ground. Because two people were shot and one minor disappeared, the

152   Hidden in plain sight

case was registered as *auto de resistência*. The police declared that Wanderson was carrying a gun, a small bomb, and a walkie-talkie radio.

The case presented a number of flaws and incorrect information given by the police. A specialist in public security well known for taking part in the local TV news highlighted that eight days after Juan Moraes first disappeared, no measures had been taken by the police to solve the case. It took more than eight days to examine the crime scene and the police vehicles. The Carlos Eboli Institute – one of the forensic institutions in Rio – declared that the body of a child found ten days after Juan Moraes's disappearance was that of a girl, but one week later, the Chief of the Civil Police stated that the body was that of Juan Moraes. Wanderson's and Juan Moraes's families received protection from the Witness Protection Program. The police investigation concluded that there was no police operation during that day in the area, nor any confrontation between the police and drug cartel members.

The boundaries of belonging in both cases were related to the spatiality and the symbolic dimensions of the specific spaces. What I want to highlight with the examples of Patricia and Juan is the attempt to associate their lives with the space of the favelas by connecting them with drug consumption and trafficking. In the case of Patricia, there were attempts by the police to frame her as part of 'the camp'. The police defence lawyers insinuated that she was addicted to drugs and alcohol.[8] In 2008 a local homeless person declared that he knew Patricia from the area (Rocinha favela) and that she was killed by drug cartel members at the top of the favela (far from the entrance). Disseminating an alleged connection between Patricia and the area would reinforce the narrative that she was co-responsible for her death.

Despite attempts by the police to associate Juan Moraes's brother and friend with drug cartel activities, it was not possible to forge Juan Moraes's involvement with drugs. Because his body was found, the case got the much-needed materiality. In the end, it was proved that there was no police confrontation with drug cartel members on that day, leading to the conclusion that Juan Moraes's death had been an execution. In Juan Moraes's case, which took place in 2011, the police officers involved were condemned two years later to more than 30 years in prison, and the city's governor offered to pay compensation[9] for the boy's death.

Drawing on the court proceedings of the police officials accused of shooting Juan, Eilbaum and Medeiros (2016: 16) observed that regimes of truth and morality are crucial to make the police innocent. Their analyses unveil the association between space and representations of morality. Juan's mother was asked 'who Juan was', to which she replied 'a *normal* boy – he used to attend school, play futebol, and liked horses'. Juan's mother emphasised the fact that he was *normal*: 'A kid like any other' (2016: 16). Eilbaum and Medeiros (2016) described the contrasting narrative presented by the criminal defence counsel (the defence attorney) who was aiming at connecting Juan's morality and territoriality with the drug cartels by focusing on his presence at the location where he was shot, and on a possible relationship between Juan and his relatives with local drug dealers. Juan's and Patricia's disappearances are examples of how spatiality plays a role in police violence. In both examples, it was very difficult for the police to prove that both were involved with drug cartels.

Conclusion: on abjection and the logic of coloniality

Under the metaphor of the war on drugs, the killing of certain populations is expected to happen if they are associated with drug activities. But the rationale, through which these individuals are identified, is informed by race and space. Also, it is very important to highlight that the war on drugs is not spread and fought everywhere in the city. On the contrary, this is a localised war, fought at favelas with armoured vehicles and helicopters as a weapon of war and intimidation. The geographical distribution of death, as claimed by Vargas (2013), does not occur randomly: it targets favela dwellers.

As discussed by Mbembe (2003), sovereignty power and colonial occupation are tighter under a combination of tactics of medieval siege warfare adapted to the networked sprawl of urban camps. He added, 'In contrast to early-modern colonial occupation, these two weapons establish the superiority of high-tech tools of late-modern terror' (2003: 29). As a result, whole categories of people are spatially fixed to then be disaggregated into rebels, child soldiers, and refugees – or, following the example of Brazil, drug traffickers.

In this chapter, I developed the discussion of camp from Agamben using a postcolonial interpretation of Mbembe (2003), as well as considerations of the camp from migration studies. Expanding the notion of camp, and applying it to postcolonial societies, the colonial logic has constructed racialised bodies distributed through geographies of difference. The use of this logic has systematically destroyed racialised populations first through colonial occupation and enslavement, and later through dispossession and social inequality. The militarised production of 'war on drugs' certainly legitimises death demarcating a spatial terror in urban spaces through lenses that hide the political geographies of death. The perversity of this logic is that even when not placed at 'the camp', black individuals are still perceived as part of it, being always under suspension as a potential danger.

Therefore, the present work does not follow the epistemological boundaries in which space, sovereign power, and modern states are (mis-/dis-) placed. Instead, it relates to how sovereign power reproduces special notions following 'the West'. Note that 'the West' here is not referring to its territoriality but to the European model of homogenising subjects as global citizens using a cultural identity inside its boundaries. Thinkers from Latin America have focused on a more specific and local perspective. For example, Walter Mignolo (2000) discussed how the local design of Latin America is intimately linked to a global design of world politics. In that sense, the present work relates to what postcolonial thinkers have to say about the re-articulation of sovereign power that decides over life and death in the postcolonial space.

154 *Hidden in plain sight*

What this chapter explored, nevertheless, is the role of space in the sovereign rationale embodied by the police in the context of the war on drugs. By engaging with the literature on abjection, I aimed to demonstrate how some places are considered a place of disorder, a place for criminality, and of an uncivilised 'other' that is considered unworthy to the point that their disappearance is not problematised. Indeed, favelas follow the logic of coloniality in the sovereign rationale where life is unworthy. And secondly, police killings and disappearances not only mark a sovereign decision over death, but they also expose those whose life is unworthy.

One important consideration in Mbembe's work is that the politics of death translates into the right to kill (as in Foucault) and the right to make some lives exposed to death, as in the lives of favela dwellers. As discussed in the examples of Patricia and Juan, the justification of the right to kill is framed by an association with the context of the war on drugs. Because there was no confrontation – that would put them under the *autos de resistência*, their lives are then associated with the abjection of drug consumption, associated with the abject territoriality of the favelas. I would like to add to Mbembe's formulation of the politics of death a third element – the sovereign right to kill in a specific way. To die by the hands of the police reifies the condition of bare life or unworthiness and forges a link between those lives and drugs. The answer from their families is to say that their loved ones did not deserve death by sovereign hands – as they are just *normal* people.

Notes

1 While *favela* tends to be the term associated with Rio de Janeiro, periphery is more common to designate similar areas in São Paulo. The specificity of favelas in Rio is that they are located in between the wealthiest neighbourhoods in the city. The differences and similarities between these two spaces are discussed in this chapter.

2 Foucault also deals with 'territory' in his conceptualisation on biopolitics. However, in Foucault's work, territory seems to suffer action instead of being part of it. For Foucault, territory seems to be the space of discipline, meaning the space where the population's strengths are maximised in the sense that they grow and may reach a peak in terms of production and capability. A reading of punishment that could complement Agamben's consideration of ban is conceptualised in terms of punishment and observation as in the case of the panopticon.

3 "The Monument to the Flags, which stands next to Ibirapuera Park, portrays indigenous, black and white members of the Bandeiras movement that set off from São Paulo in the seventeenth century towards the interior of the Brazilian territory in search of riches. Idealized in 1920 by the sculptor Victor Brecheret, the monument was inaugurated more than thirty years later, in 1953. Part of the landscape of São Paulo, it has become one of its most iconic landmarks. ... Measuring 11 meters high by 43 meters wide, the work is positioned in the southeast-northwest axis, representing the starting place of the search for land in the interior of the country" (São Paulo City Hall website, visited on 08/03/2017).

4 The Directory of the Indians was elaborated in 1755 but became public only in 1757. It is a document that elaborates on important aspects of the indigenous politics during the historical period known as Pombalino.
5 Before being appointed Minister in 1902, he had been the victorious lawyer of Brazil in the arbitration of the 'Palmas Issue' against Argentina (1895), and negotiating the Amapá lands with France (1900). Also, he made the preliminary research on the 'Question of the Pirara', later negotiated with England (1904). After taking over the Itamaraty, Baron of Rio Branco also negotiated lands in Acre (1903) and during his ten years as Chancellor he signed border agreements with five neighbouring countries (Goes Filho 2015). 'Before his death in 1912, Baron of Rio Branco freed the country of the problems regarding limits that today plague other countries in the continent' (Goes Filho 2015: 29).
6 The currency as of this writing makes 500 Brazilian Reais equivalent to 120 U.S. dollars and less than 100 British pounds. Thus, 6,160.00 Brazilian Reais correspond to 1,500 U.S. dollars.
7 The justice demanded from the city authorities to pay a compensation of 330 US dollars (*Jornal Extra* 2015).
8 Patricia's family presented the results of a medical test, from a few months before when she was hired by a large oil company in Brazil, to prove that she was not addicted to any substances.
9 The governor offered 200 US dollars to the family.

Concluding thoughts

This book discussed different aspects of police killings and disappearances in Brazil during the re-democratisation period (1985–2015). By exploring contemporary disappearances in Brazil, I asked why they are not problematised. To answer this question, I have examined more specifically the 'war on drugs', racialised notions by the police apparatus, and how abject space is implicated in the action of the country's security apparatus reproducing a colonial logic. As described in the introduction to this book, the enforced disappearance of Amarildo brought attention to a violence that is usually associated with the military dictatorship. His death, however, prompted a number of questions regarding state violence and rationale, as well as who in the state apparatus nowadays carries out such violence. In that sense, Amarildo's enforced disappearance, brought back to the public realm the discussion on police brutality and the possibility of disappearances being carried out as part of a set of police practices, even if unofficially. The present research aimed to discuss the implications of locating disappearances outside the exception of past political struggles but inside as a rationale in which killings are legitimised and unproblematised.

As discussed in the first chapter, 'political disappearance' is an extremely powerful political claim that requires answers concerning human rights. However, the consequence of limiting disappearances to a specific political context of a dictatorship erases the epistemological possibility of analysing other cases that lack the elements required for a 'political disappearance'. One very important consequence of narrowing the meaning of disappearance to a historical context, as is the case with the National Truth Commission, is the de-politicisation of contemporary cases. In Chapter 1, I argued that by crystalising 'political disappearances' and considering only the political context of the Military Regime, the armed forces as perpetrators, and leftist guerrilla members as the victims, contemporary cases of disappearances are classed as non-political. I have shown that a strict association between disappearances, and state violence more broadly, rendered invisibility to specific groups that have suffered similar violence during the dictatorship, such as indigenous groups and peasants, and to recent cases classed as slaughter or massacre. A result of narrowing down what is understood as *political* is a lack of theoretical and epistemological tools to deal with questions that emerge

DOI: 10.4324/9781003032519-7

from cases that are outside a traditional understanding of 'political disappearance'. Another consequence is the absence of a specific body of laws to account for disappearance as a crime and lack of more detailed data.

To reinstate theoretical tools that can account for (de-)politicised cases of disappearances and police killings, I have used Giorgio Agamben work on state of exception, bare life, and camp. By engaging with previous IR work on the 'war on terror', I have shown that a similar discourse of exceptionality is in place in the case of the 'war on drugs' in Latin America more broadly, and in Brazil. By tracing a parallel between the 'war on terror' and the 'war on drugs', I have discussed similar consequences of a logic of exceptionality that legitimises killings and disappearances of populations considered dangerous as part of the war. The use of militarised forces in those contexts presents a militarisation of life. In the case of the 'war on terror', as Bigo (2006, 2014) claimed, the armed forces assume the role of the police, being involved with law enforcement activities. In the case of the 'war on drugs', I have shown that the police are becoming increasingly militarised. Although in Brazil urban policing is performed by the Military Police, there has been an intensification of militarised actions in operations and interventions in favelas. In that context, I have argued, the police embody sovereign decision in the repression of drug cartel activities and in operations in favelas.

Although much has been said about how the 'war on drugs' legitimises killings and disappearances, as discussed in Chapters 3 and 4, the framework of war alone does not explain the process that targets black communities in favelas, and the roots of the negative narratives towards the subjectivity of these populations. The 'war on drugs' is an exceptional measure that legitimises police violence; however, it does not alone explain why the killing of racialised populations remains unproblematised. In that sense, it was necessary to revisit the historical process in Brazil, the creation of the police force, and its relation to the broader social context of enslavement.

To be able to bring this mindset to the fore, I engaged with the decolonial thought of Walter Mignolo to account for the role of local elites in Latin America and Brazil, broadly constituted by people who perceive themselves as descendants of white Europeans. Also important was to unpack the project of homogenisation inside borders to build a nation that mirrored European values, reflecting a motivation to make Brazil white. This process was discussed in depth in Chapter 4, where I analysed policies aiming at the whitening of the population. It was also necessary to revisit early attempts at whitening the population by opening the border to the right white populations, and the authoritarian regime of Vargas, which invested in erasing race as a category of analysis. It is interesting to note how those processes are articulated as modernity. Finally, the military dictatorship was able to reify certain boundaries of (un)worthy life. While the killings and disappearances of guerrilla members became visible, the violence against indigenous populations, peasant workers, and favela dwellers, remained silent.

Commonly accused of being unprepared and having its excesses blamed as a result of bad cops' actions, the police is often dismissed as embodying sovereign decision. By engaging with a historical account of the development of the police in Brazil, I have demonstrated how they played a central role in managing racialised populations. The role of the police in relation to African communities started with the plantation system and was extended to the control of freed populations and their descendants, a role that lasted until the 1930s. From then on it is more difficult to trace how racialised notions played out because of the myth of 'racial democracy' and the endeavour to whiten the country. One recent impact is the preponderance of 'class' and 'inequality' to analyse the 'war on drugs'. These results, however, do not account for the fact that most of the population targeted in this war are from a racialised background.

By grounding my analysis in the historical development of Brazil, I have shown a colonial mindset based on the racialised hierarchisation of life and on a logic of occupying 'empty spaces'. As a postcolonial rationale, this mindset has almost annihilated indigenous populations in the past and is now still targeting racialised groups. As very often violence is situated in favelas and peripheries, spatiality is the third key in discussing police violence in Brazil. As the book demonstrated, through the examples of the disappearance of Patricia and Juan, a whole category of individuals is fixed to the abjection that favelas represent in order to legitimise violence, killings, and disappearances by state officials. The idea of abjection becomes crucial here because it shows that certain places are not a mere stage but follow an orientalised mapping of the world – a rationale whereby certain places have the rights of their residents suspended, normalising violence and death.

Another consequence of this war is to make favelas and peripheries like a death camp in plain sight. This book has explored how some spaces become a place for abject lives. It is likely that given the diversity of locations, the experiences as bare life are diverse. However, as I have discussed, favelas, peripheries, and indigenous communities share a similar gaze. They have populations that are not supposed to live there. Indigenous peoples are perceived in some narratives as hindering national development, and favela inhabitants as those who disturb the dream of progress that big cities such as Rio de Janeiro and São Paulo nurture in the national imaginary. Ultimately, indigenous peoples and favela inhabitants share episodes of violence that reveal how sovereign power considers their lives disposable.

Following that reasoning, it was fundamental to engage with the politics of death as discussed by Achille Mbembe in the sovereign 'right to kill'. For Mbembe, sovereign power is expressed with different nuances in postcolonial societies. One of those nuances is the exposure of racialised populations to death. I also made a point that the politics of death go beyond the exposure of and right to kill certain populations, also drawing the boundaries regarding how certain individuals are killed and determining whose lives are unworthy. The link between certain types of violence and political regimes also hinders discussions about how violence can be linked to other contexts such as postcolonial societies, as in the case of the 'war on drugs'. Mbembe (2003: 13) made a critique of normative and mainstream theories regarding democracy, defining politics as both a project of autonomy and a collective agreement. According to him, late-modern criticism forged a specific idea of what is political within the community, creating a tale where the latter (the community) is his/her own master and able to create his/her own life through institutions.

The discussion brought by this book is not located in this understanding of politics – in which one can master his/her own life through institutions. On the contrary, it calls for a framework closer to what Agamben identified as a feature of authoritarian regimes: exceptionalities, which are now also present in 'so-called democracies'. But while Agamben's discussion on life and space is fundamental to the debate on sovereign power and life, he overlooked how the death of racialised populations is marked by the logic of coloniality. The debate on the possibilities of life and death under sovereign power in postcolonial societies is extremely relevant here, and I have engaged with this debate through the postcolonial work of Achille Mbembe and the decolonial work of Walter Mignolo. In that sense, Mbembe enabled a reflection on sovereign power regarding its articulation with death, while Mignolo shed light on and made possible to look at how the imperial logic operates at the local level and is incorporated by local elites in Latin America and Brazil.

Where does it leave us? Possibilities for further research

Many are the avenues for further research on past and present disappearances to be pursued from here. In Recife, one of the places where I conducted fieldwork, further research is needed to account for the 10,000 peasants killed and disappeared during the dictatorship. As discussed before, although the killing of rural workers was not considered political (National Trade Commission 2014) following a widespread land conflict in Brazil, it would be interesting to analyse its (de-)politicisation.

Regarding recent cases in urban Recife, most of the people that I interviewed declared not to know anything about disappearances or police violence more broadly. With the help of an NGO, I was able to contact a mother whose son was killed and disappeared by the militia. According to her, members of the LGBT communities are likely targets of this type of violence, signalling that moralities are played differently outside the large cosmopolitan centres of Rio de Janeiro and São Paulo.

Outside the scope of my research, there are other possibilities that could bring important questions on sovereign decision and power as in the cases of the disappearance of inmates or unidentified corpses in public morgues. Regarding the prison population in Brazil, there were investigations on the disappearances of individuals under custody (UOL 2014). The morgue could also be productive for further investigation. São Paulo (R7 2014) has been under the radar for corpse trafficking and for burying persons as unidentified bodies when information was available on the deceased.

Although I was stricken by the enormous number of unidentified people buried at the Perus Cemetery in São Paulo, it was not possible to affirm if among the 'political disappeared' there were victims of death squads who were still considered missing by their families. During one of my interviews, I was told that there was a public call for families to identify potential family members, but that only one person attended. I suppose that this is one of those cases that get lost after some time; the criminalisation of those who are killed by death squads may impact the feeling of injustice by families if they claim a body. It is also true that DNA recognition in Brazil is still underdeveloped and that in many of the political cases, as in the May Crimes,[1] DNA identification is not available.

After coming back to Manchester, and in the process of writing up the manuscript, a new series of military interventions started in Rio de Janeiro. The intervention has been justified by the collapse of the Pacification Units at favelas. Due to the end of the Olympic Games in Rio de Janeiro, the governor declared a state of emergency because a general financial crisis in 2016 left the city broken. With the political and financial crises in Brazil and Rio de Janeiro, the military interventions at favelas through Pacification Units also started to collapse. The narrative of war was intensified when *Extra*, a newspaper that belongs to Globo Media Group, decided to create a section dedicated to covering the "war" in Rio de Janeiro. The newspaper announced on their Facebook page on 16 August 2017:

> From today, the reader will find in our pages an expression that our journalists avoided until now: the war at Rio. This is not simply a change in our way of writing, but in the way we look, interprets, and narrates what is happening around us. EXTRA will continue to report in its police pages the crimes that occur in other metropolis of the world: homicides, robberies, sexual crimes ... But everything that escapes the standard of civilised normality, and that we only see in Rio, will be in the pages of a section on war. ... The use of rifles in a robbery at a pharmacy cannot be recorded as a common occurrence. The death of a child inside the school or the execution of a police officer is news that no longer fit in the pages that deal with crimes of the day to day. The creation of the war section was the form we found to shout: 'This is not normal!' It is our choice not to let our journalistic gaze get used to barbarism. We are aware that the war discourse serves to cover up the truculence of the police firing first and asking later. But we defend a war based on intelligence, in the fight against police corruption, and one that does not target the civil population, but the economic power of the mafias and all their articulations. ... War presupposes victories, defeats, advances, setbacks, correctness, and errors. It takes patience and awareness that nothing will be resolved in the short term. But we hope to lose the title of being the only daily newspaper on the planet to have a war office in a country that refuses to acknowledge that it is at war.[2]
>
> (*Jornal o Extra*, 16 August 2017 – reproduced on their institutional Facebook page, accessed 19 July 2018)

Among the many things that can be highlighted in this statement is the claim that an unacknowledged war is taking place. In sum, the answer to the violence is to make it official. The statement 'the death of a child inside the school' is paired with 'the execution of a police officer', reinforcing the idea of a war that is fought between two equal parts, making equal victims on both sides. It is important to highlight that the schools where children were exposed to stray bullets are in favelas and other peripheries where there is crossfire between the police and drug traffickers, not in the wealthiest areas of the city. The war section in the newspaper was launched 15 days after the federal government decided to call a military intervention in Rio de Janeiro at the end of July 2017. The need for such intervention was reified after a series of violent crimes during the carnival season in February 2018. The online publication *O Globo* launched a documentary at the end of 2017 called 'The Brazilian War',[3] as well as a series of talks and special issues around the problem of violence in the country. Within a week, the documentary had 160,000 views.

However, this book is not about killings related to specific political contexts. On the contrary, it examines the general interpretation of disappearances located in an exceptional political frame, legitimised by the 'war on drugs', and part of a collective rationale that disregards certain lives. While all the attention was with the impeachment and other highly visible violent events, a 'war', as it was called by newspapers (*The Intercept* 2017), was happening in Cidade Alta, a favela in Rio de Janeiro, for five months without being noticed by the non-local population. The 'war' is being caused by two different drug cartels that are fighting to control the area, and according to the article, the non-local population becomes aware of the war only when traffic congestions stopped the city for a few hours. The unnoticed conflict that happens in favelas and peripheries reveals the contemporary entanglement between race, abjection, and sovereign decision in Brazil.

Notes

1 A project funded by the Newton Fund started in 2016 aiming to develop forensic techniques to identify the corpses of 'political disappeared' buried in São Paulo. The project had as a secondary objective the provision of further necropsies of those who were killed as a consequence of the May Crimes, also in São Paulo.
2 Facebook link: https://www.facebook.com/jornalextra/posts/a-partir-desta-edi%C3%A7%C3%A3o-o-leitor-passar%C3%A1-a-encontrar-em-nossas-p%C3%A1ginas-uma-express/1747301785302764/
3 The documentary was also broadcast in Spain, Mexico, Argentina, Uruguay, Chile, Peru, Colombia, El Salvador, Cuba, Turkey, and Greece (*O Globo* 2017).

Bibliography

Abreu, M., 1996. Slave mothers and freed children: Emancipation and female space in debates on the 'Free Womb' law, Rio de Janeiro, 1871. *Journal of Latin American Studies*, 28(3), pp. 567–580.
Adorno de Abreu, S.F., 1990. *Violência urbana, justiça criminal e organização social do crime*. São Paulo: Núcleo de Estudos da Violência – USP, mimeo.
Agamben, G., 1995. *Homo Sacer: Sovereign Power and Bare Life*. Stanford, CA: Stanford University Press.
Agamben, G., 2002. *Remnants of Auschwitz: The Witness and the Archive*. New York: Zone Books.
Agamben, G., 2005. *State of Exception*. Chicago: University of Chicago Press.
Agamben, G., 2009. *What Is an Apparatus?* Stanford, CA: Stanford University Press.
Agier, M., 2011. *Managing the Undesirables*. Cambridge: Polity.
Algranti, L.M., 1988a. Slave crimes: The use of police power to control the slave population of Rio de Janeiro. *Luso-Brazilian Review*, 25(1), pp. 27–48.
Algranti, L.M., 1988b. Os registros da Polícia e seu aproveitamento para a História do Rio de Janeiro: Escravos e Libertos. *Revista de historia*, 119, pp. 115–125.
Alves, J.A., 2014. From necropolis to blackpolis: Necropolitical governance and black spatial praxis in São Paulo, Brazil. *Antipode*, 46(2), pp. 323–339.
Alves, J.A., 2018. *The Anti-Black City: Police Terror and Black Urban Life in Brazil*. Minneapolis, MN: University of Minnesota Press.
Alves, J.A., 2019. Refusing to be governed: Urban policing, gang violence, and the politics of evilness in an Afro-Colombian shantytown. *PoLAR: Political and Legal Anthropology Review*, 42(1), pp. 21–36.
Alves, M.H.M., 2005. *Estado e oposição no Brasil (1964–1984)*. Bauru, SP: EDUSC, pp. 43–44.
Amar, P., 2013. Black-blocking Rio: Dislocating police and remapping race for Brazil's megaevents: A conversation with vargas' 'Taking back the land: Police operations and sports megaevents in Rio de Janeiro'. *Souls*, 15(4), pp. 304–311. doi: 10.1080/10999949.2013.884447.
Amnesty International, 2015. "Você matou meu filho!": Homicídios cometidos pela Polícia Militar na cidade do Rio de Janeiro. August 3. Index Number: AMR 19/2068/2015.
Amnesty International, 2017. *If You Are Poor You Are Killed: Extrajudicial Executions in the Philippines' War on Drugs*.
Amnesty International (AI) Brazil, 2006. "We have come to take your souls": The caveirão and policing in Rio de Janeiro. March 13, 2006. Index Number: AMR 19/007/2006. Available at: https://www.amnesty.org/en/documents/AMR19/007/2006/en/

Bibliography

Anderson, B.R.O., 1991. *Imagined Communities: Reflections on the Origin and Spread of Nationalism*. London: Verso.
Andrews, G.R., 1988. Black and white workers: São Paulo, Brazil, 1888–1928. *The Hispanic American Historical Review*, 68(3), pp. 491–524.
Anievas, A., Manchanda, N., and Shilliam, R. eds., 2014. *Race and Racism in International Relations: Confronting the Global Colour Line*. London: Routledge.
Anievas, A., Manchanda, N., and Shilliam, R., 2015. Confronting the global colour line: An introduction, in Anievas, A., Manchanda, N., and Shilliam, R. (eds.), *Race and Racism in International Relations: Confronting the Global Colour Line*, pp. 1–15.
Anistia Internacional, 2015. *Você matou meu filho!: Homicídios cometidos pela polícia militar na cidade do Rio de Janeiro*. Available at: https://www.amnesty.org/en/documents/amr19/2068/2015/bp/
Aquino, M.A., 1999. *Censura, Imprensa, Estado Autoritário (1968–1978)*. Bauru: EDUSC.
Aradau, C., 2007. Law transformed: Guantánamo and the 'other' exception. *Third World Quarterly*, 28(3), pp. 489–501.
Aradau, C., and Huysmans, J., 2017. Performing methods: Practice and politics, in Basaran, T., Bigo, D., Guittet, E.P., and Walker, R.B. (eds.), *International Political Sociology: Transversal Lines*. London: Routledge.
de Araujo, R.B., 2013. *A Brigada Militar e a Segurança Nacional: Inimigo Interno e Guerra Revolucionária na Academia de Polícia Militar do Rio Grande do Sul – 1980/1985*. p. 233.
Araujo, F.A., 2014. *Das técnicas de fazer desaparecer corpos*. Lamparina.
Araújo, A.V., de Carvalho, J.B., Oliveira, P.C., and Jófej, L.F., 2006. *Povos indígenas ea Lei dos' Brancos': o direito à diferença*. Ministério da Educação.
Araujo, C., Bonjean, C.A., Combes, J.L., Motel, P.C., and Reis, E.J., 2006. Land tenure insecurity and deforestation in the Brazilian Amazonia. *Correspondance*.
Araújo, F.A., 2014. *Das 'técnicas' de fazer desaparecer corpos: desaparecimentos, violência, sofrimento e político*. Lamparina.
Araújo, R.I.S., 2003. *'Como se fossem casados': mancebia e moralidade no Maranhão setecentista*. Monografia (Graduação) – Faculdade de História, Universidade Federal do Maranhão, São Luís.
Arbex, D., 2013. *Holocausto brasileiro*. Geração Editorial.
Arendt, H., 1968. *The Origins of Totalitarianism*. New York: Harcourt, Brace & World.
Article II OAS, 1994. Available at: https://www.oas.org/juridico/english/treaties/a-60.html
Atkinson, D., 2000. Nomadic strategies and colonial governance, in Paddison, R., Philo, C., Routledge, P., and Sharp, J. (eds.), *Entanglements of Power: Geographies of Domination/Resistance*. London: Routledge, pp. 93–121.
Atlas da Violência, 2017. Ipea/Forum Brasileiro de Seguranca Publica. Available at: https://www.ipea.gov.br/atlasviolencia/arquivos/artigos/2898-atlasdaviolencia-2017completo.pdf
Auchter, J., 2014. *The Politics of Haunting and Memory in International Relations*. Routledge.
Bauer, C.S., 2011. Um estudo comparativo das praticas de desaparecimento nas ditaduras civil-militares Argentina e Brasileira e a elaboracao de politicas de memoria em ambos os paises.
Bauer, C.S., 2017. *Como Será o Passado? Historia, Historiadores e a Comissao Nacional da Verdade* (1st edition). Jundiai, SP Paco Editorial.

Bibliography

Baum, D., 1996. *Smoke and Mirrors: The War on Drugs and the Politics of Failure*. New York: Little, Brown & Company.

BBC News, 2006. Sao Paulo residents under siege. Available at: http://news.bbc.co.uk/1/hi/world/americas/4774185.stm. Accessed October 2014.

Benjamin, W., 2018. *Critique de la violence*. Éditions Payot.

Bellintani, A.I., 2009. O Positivismo e o Exército Brasileiro, in *ANPUH – XXV Simpósio Nacional De História*. Fortaleza, pp. 1–9.

Bhambra, G.K., 2014. Postcolonial and decolonial dialogues. *Postcolonial Studies*, 17(2), pp. 115–121.

Bigo, D., 2002. Security and immigration: Toward a critique of the governmentality of unease. *Alternatives*, 27(1), pp. 63–92.

Bigo, D., 2006. Security, exception, ban and surveillance, in Lyon, D. (ed.), *Theorizing Surveillance – The Panopticon and Beyond*. London: Routledge, pp. 46–68. doi: 10.4324/9781843926818.

Bigo, D., 2008. Globalized (in)security: The field and the ban-opticon, in *Terror, Insecurity and Liberty*. London: Routledge, pp. 20–58.

Bigo, D., 2014. The (in)securitization practices of the three universes of EU border control: Military/Navy – border guards/police – database analysts. *Security Dialogue*, 45(3), pp. 209–225. doi: 10.1177/0967010614530459.

Bigo, D., and Guild, E. eds., 2005. *Controlling Frontiers: Free Movement into and within Europe*. London: Routledge.

Bigo, D., and Tsoukala, A., 2008. *Terror, Insecurity and Liberty: Illiberal Practices of Liberal Regimes after 9/11*. Routledge.

Bignall, S., and Svirsky, M.G., 2012. Introduction: Agamben and Colonialism.

Björnehed, E., 2004. Narco-terrorism: The merger of the war on drugs and the war on terror. *Global Crime*, 6(3–4), pp. 305–324.

Bosi, A., 2015. *Brazil and the Dialectic of Colonization*. Urbana, IL: University of Illinois Press.

Branco, T.C., and Rosa, H., 2008. Artigo publicado no site: conjur.com.br: 'A Constituição de 1988 não permite invasão de terras por índios'.

Brasil, Secretaria Especial de Direitos Humanos. Comissão Especial sobre Mortos e Desaparecidos Políticos, 2007. Direito à memória e à verdade. Brasilia.

Brassett, J., and Vaughan-Williams, N., 2012. Crisis is governance: Sub-prime, the traumatic event, and bare life. *Global Society*, 26(1), pp. 19–42.

Bretas, M.L., 1997. Observações sobre a falência dos modelos policiais. *Tempo Social*, 9(1), pp. 79–94.

Bretas, M.L., and Rosemberg, A., 2013. A história da polícia no Brasil: balanço e perspectivas. *Topoi (Rio de Janeiro)*, 14(26), pp.162–173.

Brito, L.D.C., 2016. O crime da miscigenação: A mistura de raças no Brasil escravista e a ameaça à pureza racial nos Estados Unidos pós-abolição. *Revista Brasileira de História*, 36, pp. 107–130.

Brown, A.K., 2000. 'A black mark on our legislation': Slavery, punishment, and the politics of death in nineteenth-century Brazil author(s): Alexandra K. Brown source. *Luso-Brazilian Review*, 37(2), pp. 95–121.

Brysk, A., 1994. The politics of measurement: The contested count of the disappeared in Argentina. *Human Rights Quarterly*, 16(4), pp. 676–692.

Bueno, A.M., 2013. *Língua, imigração e identidade nacional: análise de um discurso a respeito da imigração no Brasil da Era Vargas*. (1976).

Bueno, B.B., 1985. *Os Fundamentos da Doutrina de Segurança Nacional e seu Legado na Constituição do Estado Brasileiro Contemporâneo*. pp. 47–64.

Cabral, D., 2011. Intendente/Intendência de Polícia da Corte e do Estado do Brasil, in *Dicionário Online da Administração Pública Brasileira do Período Colonial (1500–1822)*. Disponível em: https://goo.gl/E8vT1t. Acesso em: 14 set. 2015.

Caldeira, J., 2011. O Processo Econômico, in Schwarcz, L.M. (dir.), *História do Brasil Nação: 1808–2010. Volume 1: Crise Colonial e Independência, 1808–1830*. Coordenação: Alberto da Costa e Silva. Rio de Janeiro: Objetiva; Madrid: Fundación MAPFRE, Parte 4, pp. 161–205.

Caldeira, T.P., 2000. *City of Walls: Crime, Segregation, and Citizenship in São Paulo*. Berkeley, CA: University of California Press. do Rio. Available at: https://ponte.org/gcm-preso-por-chacina-de-5-jovens-integra-grupo-chamado-caveiras/

CÂMARA DOS DEPUTADOS, 1980. *Anistia: legislação brasileira 1822/1979*. Brasília: Centro de Documentação e Informação.

Campbell, D., 1992. *Writing Security*.

Cano, I., 1998. Uso da força letal pela Polícia do Rio de Janeiro: os fatos e o debate. *Archè*, pp. 201–229.

Cano, I., 2008. Seis Por Meia Dúzia: um estudo exploratorio do fenomeno das chamadas milicias no Rio de Janeiro, in *Seguranca, trafico e milicias no Rio de Janeiro*, pp. 48–83.

Cano, I., 2010. Racial bias in police use of lethal force in Brazil. *Police Practice and Research*, 11(1), pp. 31–43.

Cano, I., and Duarte, T., 2012. *No Sapatinho: A Evolução das Milícias no Rio de Janeiro (2008–2011)*. No Sapatinho: A Evolução das Milícias no Rio de Janeiro.

Cao, B., 2011. Review essay: Race matters in Brazil. *Social Identities*, 17(5), pp. 709–717.

Carneiro, M.L.T., 1983. *Preconceito racial no Brasil-Colônia: os cristãos-novos*. Brasiliense.

Carneiro, M.L.T., 1994. República, identidade nacional e anti-semitismo (1930–1945). *Revista de História*, 129–131, pp. 153–163.

Carneiro, M.L.T., 2012. Rompendo o silêncio: A historiografia sobre o antissemitismo no Brasil. *Cadernos de História*, 13(18), pp. 79–97. Available at: http://periodicos.pucminas.br/index.php/cadernoshistoria/article/view/P.2237-8871.2012v13n18p79/3871

Carneiro, M.L.T., 2015. Sob a mascara do nacionalismo. Autoritarismo e anti-semitismo na Era Vargas (1930–1945). *Estudios interdisciplinarios de America Latina y el Caribe*, 1(1), pp. 23–40.

Carrara, S., 1991. O crime de um certo custódio e o surgimento do manicômio judiciário no Brasil. *Dados. Revista de Ciências Sociais*, 34(2), pp. 279–301.

Carta Capital, 2014 Desaparecidos e esquecidos. Available at: https://www.cartacapital.com.br/sociedade/desaparecidos-e-esquecidos-1402.html

Carta Capital, 2017, by Caroline Oliveira. Atlas da Violência 2017: Negros e jovens são as maiores vítimas. Available at: https://www.cartacapital.com.br/sociedade/atlas-da-violencia-2017-negros-e-jovens-sao-as-maiores-vitimas

Carvalho, S.D.E., 2006. Política de guerra às drogas na América Latina entre o direito penal do inimigo e o estado de exceção permanente. *Revista Crítica Jurídica*, 1(25), pp. 253–267.

Carvalho Filho, L.F., 2004. Impunidade no Brasil: Colônia e Império. *Estudos Avançados*, 18, pp. 181–194.

Cavalcanti, B., 1985. *A polícia e a nação: a necessidade de 'segurança interna e tranqüilidade pública'*. Rio de Janeiro: Revista OAB/RJ – A instituição policial, n. 22.

Cerqueira, D., 2012. Mortes violentas não esclarecidas e impunidade no Rio de Janeiro. *Economia Aplicada*, 16(2), pp. 201–235.

Bibliography

Chakravorty, G., 1999. *Spivak 'Can the Subaltern Speak?'*. Cambridge, MA: Harvard University Press.

Chalhoub, S., 2011. The precariousness of freedom in a slave society (Brazil in the nineteenth century). *International Review of Social History*, 56(3), pp. 405–439.

Comissão de Familiares de Mortos e Desaparecidos Políticos, I. de E. da V. do E.-I. G. T. N. M.-R. e P, 1995. *Dossie dos Mortos e Desaparecidos Politicos a partir de 1964*. Pernambuco.

Comissão Estadual da Memoria e Verdade Dol Helder Camara, 2017. Truth Commission Report. Recife, Pernambuco. Available at: https://www.comissao-daverdade.pe.gov.br/index.php/comissao-da-verdade

Comissão Estadual da Verdade do Rio de Janeiro, 2015. Available at: http://www.memoriasreveladas.gov.br/administrator/components/com_simplefilemanager/uploads/Rio/CEV-Rio-Relatorio-Final.pdf

Comparato, B.K., 2014. Memória e silêncio: A espoliação das lembranças. *Lua Nova*, 92(36), pp. 145–176.

Conrad, R.E., 1972. *The Destruction of Brazilian Slavery, 1850–1888 (No. 89)*. Berkeley, CA: University of California Press.

Constable, O.R. ed., 1997. *Medieval Iberia: Readings from Christian, Muslim and Jewish Sources*. Philadelphia: University of Pennsylvania Press.

Costa Vargas, J.H., 2013. Taking back the land: Police operations and sport megaevents in Rio de Janeiro. *Souls*, 15(4), pp. 275–303.

CPPDH (Conselho de defesa da Pessoa Humana), 2010. *Relatorio Sobre os "Crimes de Maio" – Resolucao n 16/2010*. Brasilia.

Da Costa, E.V., 1998. *Da Monarquia à República: Momentos Decisivos*. Unesp.

Dalby, S., 1997. Contesting an essential concept: Reading the dilemmas in contemporary security discourse. *Critical Security Studies: Concepts and Cases*, 3, p. 31.

Darling, J., 2016. Forced migration and the city: Irregularity, informality, and the politics of presence. *Progress in Human Geography*, 41(2), pp. 1–21.

Dávila, J., 2003. Building the 'Brazilian Man', in *Diploma of Whiteness* (Chapter 1). Durham, NC: Duke University Press, pp. 21–51.

Davis, D.J., 1999. *Afro-Brazilians: Time for Recognition*. London: Minority Rights Group

Debrix, F., and Barder, A.D., 2009. Nothing to fear but fear: Governmentality and the biopolitical production of terror. *International Political Sociology*, 3(4), pp. 398–413.

de Castro Gomes, A.M., 2005. *Gênero, família e trabalho no Brasil*. Rio de Janeiro: FGV Editora.

Denyer Willis, G., and Mota Prado, M., 2014. Process and pattern in institutional reforms: A case study of the police pacifying units (UPPs) in Brazil. *World Development*, 64, pp. 232–242.

de Paula, F.R., 2015. The decolonial thinking and the limits of geographical imagination, in *Colóquio Internacional Epistemologias do Sul: aprendizagens globais Sul-Sul, Sul-Norte e Norte-Sul*. Universidade de Coimbra, pp. 443–458.

de Paula, F.R., 2018. *The Emergence of Brazil to the Global Stage: Ascending and Falling in the International Order of Competition*. London: Routledge.

Derani, C., 2002. Brasil – Estado e Nação. *Revista Da Faculdade De Direito*, 97, pp. 85–103.

Diken, B., 2005. City of god. *City: Analysis of Urban Trends, Culture, Theory, Policy, Action*, 9(3), pp. 307–320.

Diken, B., and Laustsen, C.B., 2002. Zones of indistinction: Security, terror, and bare life. *Space and Culture*, 5(3), pp. 290–307.

Dillon, M., 2003. Virtual security: A life science of (dis) order. *Millennium*, 32(3), pp. 531–558.
Dolhnikoff, M., 2003. *Elites regionais e a construção do Estado Nacional. Brasil: formação do estado e da nação*. São Paulo: Hucitec, pp. 431–468.
Doty, R., 1993. The bounds of 'race' in international relations. *Millennium*, 22(3), pp. 443–461.
Doty, R.L., 1998. The bounds of 'race' in international relations, in *Culture in World Politics* London: Palgrave Macmillan, pp. 134–155.
Dussel, E., 1995. *The Invention of the Americas*. New York: Continuum.
Duviols, P., 1971. La represión del paganismo andino y la expulsión de los moriscos. *Anuario de estudios americanos*, 28, pp. 201–207.
Edkins, J., 2007. Whatever politics, in *Giogio Agamben: Sovereignty & Life*. Stanford, CA: Stanford University Press.
Edkins, J., 2011. *Missing Persons and Politics*. Ithaca, NY: Cornell University Press.
Edkins, J., and Pin-Fat, V., 2005. Through the wire: Relations of power and relations of violence. *Millennium*, 34(1), pp. 1–24.
Edkins, J., Pin-Fat, V., and Shapiro, M.J., 2004. Introduction, in Edkins, J., Pin-Fat, V., and Shapiro, M.J. (eds.), *Sovereign Lives: Power in Global Politics*. New York: Routledge.
Eilbaum, L., 2017. Resenha do livro Pessoas desaparecidas. Uma etnografia para muitas ausencias. *Mana*, 23(2), pp. 551–555.
Eilbaum, L., and Medeiros, F., 2016. 'Onde está Juan?': Moralidades e sensos de justiça na administração judicial de conflitos no Rio de Janeiro. *Anuario Antropologico UnB*, 41(1), pp. 9–33.
Elkins, J., 2010. The model of war. *Political Theory*, 38(2), pp. 214–242.
El Pais, 2011, by Francho Baron. *Rio de Janeiro Cierra un ciclo con la ocupacion de la favela Rocinha*. Available at: https://elpais.com/internacional/2011/11/13/actualidad/1321175032_012991.html
Erichsen, C.W., and Olusoga, D., 2010. *The Kaiser's Holocaust. Germany's Forgotten Genocide*. London: Faber and Faber.
Fanon, F., 1952/2008. *Black Skin, White Masks*. New York: Grove Press.
Fanon, F., 1963. *The Wretched of the Earth* (vol. 36; trans. C. Farrington; introduction by J.P. Sartre). New York: Grove Press.
Fanon, F., 2004. *The Wretched of the Earth* (trans. R. Philcox). New York: Grove Press.
Farias, J., 2014. *Governo das Mortes: uma etnografia da gestão de populações de favelas no Rio de Janeiro*. Tese de doutorado defendida no Programa de PósGraduação em Sociologia e Antropologia – IFCS/UFRJ.
Fausto, B., 2006. *Getúlio Vargas*. Companhia das Letras.
Feitosa, G.R.P., and de Pinheiro, J.A.O., 2012. Brazilian shoot-down law (lei do abate), war on drugs and national defense. *Revista brasileira de política internacional*, 55(1), pp. 66–92.
Ferreira, L.C. de M., 2015. *Pessoas Desaparecidas: Uma etnografia para muitas ausências*. Rio de Janeiro: Editora UFRJ.
Fiola, J., 1990. Race relations in Brazil: A reassessment of the 'racial democracy' thesis (No. 24). Latin American Studies Program. The University of Massachusetts at Amherst.
Fischer, R.M., 1985. *O direito da população à segurança: cidadania e violência urbana*. Petrópolis: Vozes/Cedec, São Paulo.
Flexor, M.H.O., 2006. *'Civilização' dos índios e a formação do território do Brasil. Histedbr, Campinas*.

Florindo, M.T., 2011. O DEOSP/SP na Era Vargas. *Aurora*, 7, pp. 124–139.
Florindo, M.T., 2015. O Estado brasileiro e a repressão política na era Vargas: Montagem institucional do aparato de contenção e de controle da. *Revista de Estudios Brasileños*, 2(2), pp. 36–47.
Folha, de São Paulo, 2007. Cabral apoia aborto e diz que favela e fabrica de marginal. Available at: https://www1.folha.uol.com.br/fsp/cotidian/ff2510200701.htm
Folha, de São Paulo, 2009. Editorial. Limites a Chavez. Available at: https://www1.folha.uol.com.br/fsp/opiniao/fz1702200901.htm
Folha, de São Paulo, 2016a. Argentina cria precedente e decide veredito sobre operacao condor. Available at: https://www1.folha.uol.com.br/mundo/2016/05/1775398-argentina-cria-precedente-e-decide-veredito-sobre-operacao-condor.shtml
Folha, de São Paulo, 2016b. Negros e Pardos sao 77% dos mortos pela policia do Rio. Available at: https://m.folha.uol.com.br/cotidiano/2016/02/1742551-negros-e-pardos-sao-77-dos-mortos-pela-policia-do-rio-em-2015.shtml
Fon, A.C., 1979. *Tortura: A historia da repressao politica no Brasil*. São Paulo: Global Editora.
Forte, F.A.D.P., 2007. Racionalidade e legitimidade da política de repressão ao tráfico de drogas: uma provocação necessária. *Estudos Avançados*, 21(61), pp. 193–208.
Fórum Brasileiro de Segurança Pública, 2014. *Anuario Brasileiro de Seguranca Publica 2014*. Available at: https://forumseguranca.org.br/storage/8_anuario_2014_20150309.pdf
Foucault, M., 2007. *Security, Territory, Population: Lectures at the Collège de France, 1977–1978*. New York: Palgrave Macmillan.
Foucault, M., 2008. *The Birth of Biopolitics – Lectures at the College de France, 1977–1978*. New York: Palgrave Macmillan.
Foucault, M., 2009. *Security, Territory, Population – Lectures at the College de France, 1977–1978*. New York: Palgrave Macmillan.
Foucault, M., 2019. *The History of Sexuality, Vol. 1: The Will to Knowledge*. London: Penguin UK.
Freire, C.P., 2013. *Sobre(viver) apos o desaparecimento: as estrategias das mulheres familiares de desaparecidos*. Universidade do Estado do Rio de Janeiro.
Freire, G., 1981. *Casa grande e senzala: formação da familia brasileira sob o regime de economia patriarcal*. Lisboa: Livros do Brasil.
Freyre, G., 1933. *The Masters and the Slaves* (trans. S. Putnam).
FUNAI, 2016. Available at: http://antigo.funai.gov.br/index.php/indios-no-brasil/quem-sao
Furtado, H., 2017. On demons and dreamers: Violence, silence and the politics of impunity in the Brazilian Truth Commission. *Security Dialogue*, 48(4), pp. 316–333.
Gaffney, C., 2012. Conflict and security securing the Olympic city. *Georgetown Journal of International Affairs*, 13(2), pp. 75–82.
Gaspari, E., 2003. *A Ditadura Derrotada*. São Paulo: Companhia das Letras.
Gatti, G., 2010. O detido-desaparecido: Catastrofe civilizacional, desmorobnamento da identidade e linguagem. *Revista Crítica de Ciências Sociais*, 88, pp. 57–78.
Gatti, G., 2014. *Surviving Forced Disappearance in Argentina and Uruguay: Identity and Meaning*. New York: Springer.
Geraldo, E., 2012. A 'lei de cotas' de 1934: controle de estrangeiros no Brasil. *Cadernos AEL*, 15(27).
Gilmore, R.W., 2007. *Golden Gulag*. Berkeley, CA: University of California Press.
Gobineau, A.D., 1967. *Essai sur l'Inégalité des Races Humaines (1853)*. Paris: Éditions Pierre Belfond.

Bibliography   169

Godoi, R., Grillo, C., Tonche, J., Mallart, F., Ramachiotti, B., and Braud, P.P.D., 2020. Letalidade policial e respaldo institucional: perfil e processamento dos casos de "resistência seguida de morte" na cidade de São Paulo. *Revista de Estudios Sociales*, 73, pp. 58–72.

Goes Filho, S.S., 2015. *Navegantes, bandeirantes, diplomatas – um ensaio sobre a formação das fronteiras do Brasil*. Brazil: FUNAG.

Gomes, A.D.C., 1994. *A invenção do trabalhismo*. Rio de Janeiro: Relume Dumará, 2.

Gomes, M.P., 2000. *The Indians and Brazil*. Gainesville, FL: University Press of Florida.

Graham, S., 2006. Cities and the 'war on terror'. *International Journal of Urban and Regional Research*, 30(2), pp. 255–276.

Guerra, M.P., 2016. *Polícia e Ditadura: a aquitetura institucional da segurança pública de 1964 a 1988* Brasilia: MJ.

Gvac in JusBrasil, 2014. Estudo sobre Violencia policial revela 'racism institucional' na PM de SP. Available at: https://lunatenorio.jusbrasil.com.br/artigos/114873464/estudo-sobre-violencia-policial-revela-racismo-institucional-na-pm-de-sp

G1, 2015. Registros de desaparecidos cresce 26% no Rio. Available at: http://g1.globo.com/rio-de-janeiro/noticia/2015/10/registros-de-desaparecidos-crescem-26-no-rio.html

G1, 2016, by Acayaba, Tomaz, Piza, Araújo and Leite. Ha dez anos, Sao Paulo parou durante serie de ataques contra policiais e civis. Available at: http://g1.globo.com/sao-paulo/noticia/2016/05/ha-dez-anos-sao-paulo-parou-durante-serie-de-ataques-contra-policiais-e-civis.html

G1, 2017, by Felipe Gradin and Henrique Coelho. Rio tem 33 mil desaparecidos em 15 anos; Zona Oeste e Bonsucesso concentram casos. Available at: https://g1.globo.com/rio-de-janeiro/noticia/rio-tem-33-mil-desaparecidos-em-15-anos-zona-oeste-e-bonsucesso-concentram-casos.ghtml

Harvey, D., 2007. *A Brief History of Neoliberalism*. New York: Oxford University Press.

Harvey, D., 2015. *Seventeen Contradictions and the End of Capitalism* (Reprint edition). New York: Oxford University Press.

Harvey, L.P. 1990. *Islamic Spain, 1250 to 1500*. Chicago: University of Chicago Press.

Hegel, G.W.F., 1977. *Phenomenology of Spirit*. Durham, NC: Duke University Press.

Heinz, W.S., 1995. Motives for 'disappearances' in Argentina, Chile and Uruguay in the 1970s. *Netherlands Quartely of Human Rights*, 13(1), pp. 51–64.

Herz, M., 2006. Regional security- a critical perspective. (March), pp. 1–23.

Herzog, L., 1990. Border commuter workers and transfrontier metropolitan structure along the United States–Mexico border. *Journal of Borderland Studies*, 5(2), 1–20.

Hickman, C., 1997. The devil and the one drop rule: Racial categories, African Americans, and the U.S. census. *Michigan Law Review*, 95(5), 1161–1265. doi: 10.2307/1290008.

Hobsbawm, E., and Ranger, T. eds., 2012. *The Invention of Tradition*. Cambridge: Cambridge University Press.

Holloway, T.H., 1989. "A healthy terror": Police repression of Capoeiras in nineteenth-century Rio de Janeiro. *Hispanic American Historical Review*, 69(4), pp. 637–676.

Holloway, T.H., 1997. *Polícia no Rio de Janeiro* (Portuguese Brazilian edition). Rio de Janeiro: Fundação Getúlio Vargas.

Htun, M., 2004. From 'racial democracy' to affirmative action: Changing state policy on race in Brazil changing state policy on race in Brazil. *Source: Latin American Research Review*, 39(1), pp. 60–89.

Hülsse, R., and Spencer, A., 2008. The metaphor of terror: Terrorism studies and the constructivist turn. *Security Dialogue*, 39(6), pp. 571–592.

Human Rights Watch, 2009. *Forca Letal: Violencia Policial e Seguranca Publica no Rio de Janeiro e em Sao Paulo*. Available at: https://www.hrw.org/reports/brazil1209ptweb.pdf

Human Rights Watch, 2013. *Mexico's Disappeared: The Enduring Costs of a Crisis Ignored*. New York: Human Rights Watch.

Human Rights Watch, 2016. *'Good Cops are Afraid': The Toll of Unchecked Police Violence in Rio de Janeiro*. New York: Human Rights Watch.

Huskisson, D., 2005. The air bridge denial program and the shootdown of civil aircraft under international law. *Air Force Law Review*, 56, pp. 109–166.

Huysmans, J., 2006. International politics of insecurity: Normativity, inwardness and the exception. *Security Dialogue*, 37(1), pp. 11–29.

Huysmans, J., 2008. The jargon of exception – On Schmitt, Agamben and the absence of political society. *International Political Sociology*, 2(2), pp. 165–183.

Ianni, O., 2004. *Pensamento Social no Brasil*. Bauru: EDUSC.

IBGE (Instituto Brasileiro de Geografia e estatistica), 1999. *Pesquisa Nacional por Amostra de Domicilio* (vol. 21). Rio de Janeiro.

IHRC, 2011. Violência Institucional em Maio de 2006 SÃO PAULO SOB ACHAQUE.

INDEC Censo, 2010. Available at: https://www.indec.gob.ar/indec/web/Nivel4-CensoNacional-3-8-Censo-2010

Instituto de Pesquisa Econômica Aplicada (Ipea), 2013. *Texto para discussão/Instituto de Pesquisa Econômica Aplicada*. Brasília, Rio de Janeiro: Ipea.

Isin, E., and Rygiel, K., 2007a. Of other global cities: Frontiers, zones, camps, in Drieskens, B., Mermier, F., and Wimmen, H. (eds.), *Cities of the South: Citizenship and Exclusion in the 21st Century*. London: Saqi, pp. 170–209.

Isin, E.F., and Rygiel, K., 2007b. Abjects spaces: Frontiers, zones, camps, in Dauphinee, E., and Masters, C. (eds.), *Logics of Biopower and the War on Terror: Living, Dying, Surviving*. New York: Palgrave Macmillan, pp. 182–203.

ISP-RJ (Instituto de Segurança Pública), 2009a, by Renata Fortes and Marianna Carmelini. ISP divulga dados iniciais da pesquisa de desaparecidos no estado do Rio de Janeiro. Available at: http://www.isp.rj.gov.br/Noticias.asp?ident=82

ISP-RJ (Instituto de Segurança Pública), 2009b. Desaparecidos no Estado do Rio de Janeiro no ano de 2007. Report by Instituto de Seguranca Publica do Rio de Janeiro.

Jones, M., Jones, R., Woods, M., Whitehead, M., Dixon, D., and Hannah, M., 2014. *An Introduction to Political Geography: Space, Place and Politics*. London: Routledge.

Jornal do Brasil, 2008. ONG faz protesto em Copacabana contra casos de pessoas desaparecidos. Available at: http://www.jb.com.br/index.php?id=/acervo/materia.php&cd_matia=365920&dinamico=1&preview=1

Kant de Lima, R., 1989. A cultura jurídica e as práticas policiais. *Revista Brasileira de Ciências Sociais*, 4(10).

Kant de Lima, R., 1997. Polícia e exclusão na cultura judiciária. *Tempo Social*, 9(1), pp. 169–183.

Karam, M.L., 2003. Redução de danos, ética e lei, in Sampaio, C., and Campos, M. (org.), *Drogas dgnidade e inclusao social a lei e a prática da redução de danos*. Rio de Janeiro: Aborda.

Khanna, N., 2010. 'If you're half black, you're just black': Reflected appraisals and the persistence of the one-drop rule. *The Sociological Quarterly*, 51:1, pp. 96–121. doi: 10.1111/j.1533-8525.2009.01162.x.

Klein, H.S., and Luna, F.V., 2009. *Slavery in Brazil*. Cambridge: Cambridge University Press.

Klein, N., 2007. *The Shock Doctrine: The Rise of Disaster Capitalism*. London: Penguin.

Kristeva, J., 1982. *Powers of Horror: An Essay on Abjection*. New York: Columbia University Press.
Lage, V.C., 2016. *Interpretations of Brazil, Contemporary (De) Formations Victor Coutinho Lage Interpretations of Brazil, Contemporary (De) Formations*. PUC-Rio.
Lago, M.C., 2015. O trabalho e o trabalhador no estado Novo de Vargas. *Dia-Lagos*, 9, pp. 89–102.
Lahon, D., 2001. *Esclavage et confréries noires au Portugal uerra l'Ancien Régime (1441–1830)*. Doctoral dissertation, Paris, EHESS.
Lauren, P.G., 1996. *Power and Prejudice: The Politics and Diplomacy of Racial Discrimination*. Boulder, CO: Westview Press.
Leandro de Araujo, C., 2011. O Surgimento do inimigo interno: Ditadura Militar no Brasil (1964 a 1985). *Historia Em Reflexao*, 5(9), pp. 1–16.
Leite, M.P., 2012. Da 'metáfora da uerra' ao projeto de 'pacificação': favelas e políticas de segurança pública no Rio de Janeiro. *Revista Brasileira de Segurança Pública*, 6(2).
Lemgruber, J., Cano, I., Musumeci, L., and Lopes, P.V.L., 2017. *Olho por olho? O que pensam os cariocas sobre 'bandido bom é bandido morto'*. Rio de Janeiro: CESeC.
Lemos, N.G., 2012. *Um império nos trópicos: a atuação do Intendente Geral de Polícia, Paulo Fernandes Viana, no Império Luso-Brasileiro (1808–1821)*. Dissertação (Mestrado em História) UFF – Universidade Federal Fluminense – Niterói.
Lissovsky, M., and De Matos, M.V.A.B., 2018. The laws of image-nation: Brazilian racial tropes and the shadows of the slave quarters. *Law and Critique*, 29(2), pp. 173–200.
Lopes, J.R.D.L., 2003. *Iluminismo e jusnaturalismo no ideário dos juristas da primeira metade do século XIX*. Brasil: formação do Estado e da nação; São Paulo: Hucitec, pp. 195–218.
MacCormack, S., 2021. *Religion in the Andes: Vision and Imagination in Early Colonial Peru*. Princeton, NJ: Princeton University Press.
Mandolessi, S., and Perez, M.E., 2014. The disappeared as a transnational figure or how to deal with the vain yesterday. *European Review*, 22(4), pp. 603–612.
Manning, P., 1990. *Slavery and African Life: Occidental, Oriental, and African Slave Trades* (vol. 67). Cambridge: Cambridge University Press.
Manso, B.P., and Dias, C.N., 2017. PCC, sistema prisional e gestão do novo mundo do crime no Brasil. *Revista brasileira de segurança pública*, 11(2).
Marquese, R.D.B., 2006. A dinâmica da escravidão no Brasil: resistência, tráfico negreiro e alforrias, séculos XVII a XIX. *Novos Estudos – CEBRAP*, 74, pp. 107–123.
Martins, J.V.N., 2013. Politicas Publicas de guerras as drogas: o estado de excecao e a transicao do inimigo shmittiano ao homo sacer de Agamben. *Revista Brasileira de Politicas Publicas*, 10, pp. 270–2780.
Mattos, H., 2006. 'Pretos' and 'Pardos' between the cross and the sword: Racial categories in seventeenth century Brazil. *European Review of Latin American and Caribbean Studies*, 80, pp. 43–55.
Maxwell, K., 1999. Por que o Brasil foi diferente? O contexto da independência, in Mota, C.G. (org.), *Viagem Incompleta: A Experiência Brasileira (1500–2000)*. Formação: Histórias; São Paulo: Editora SENAC, pp. 177–196.
Mbembe, A., 2003. Necropolitics. *Public Culture*, 15(1), pp. 11–40.
Mbembe, A., 2019. *Necropolitics*. Durham, NC: Duke University Press.
McMillan, N., 2017. Racialising global relations: The Rwandan genocide and the ethics of representation. *Postcolonial Studies*, 20(4), pp. 431–455.

Meade, T., 1989. 'Living worse and costing more': Resistance and riot in Rio de Janeiro, 1890–1917. *Journal of Latin American Studies*, 21(2), pp. 241–266.

Melo, A.C., 2009. Saudosismo e crítica social em Casa grande & senzala: a articulação de uma política da memória e de uma utopia. *Estudos Avançados*, 23(67), pp. 279–296.

Mello, M.E.A. de S. *Fé e Império: as Juntas das Missões nas conquistas portuguesas.* EDUA, pp. 179–192.

Memoria Globo, 2013. Caso Amarildo (2013) *O Globo*. Available at: http://memoriaglobo.globo.com/programas/jornalismo/coberturas/caso-amarildo.htm; see also, caso Amarildo: http://memoriaglobo.globo.com/programas/jornalismo/coberturas/caso-amarildo/caso-amarildo-a-historia.htm

Mezarobba, G., 2003. *Um acerto de contas com o futuro a anistia e suas conseqüências – um estudo do caso brasileiro.* Universidade de Sao Paulo.

Mezarobba, G., 2007. O preco do esquecimento: as reparacoes pagas as vitimas do regime militar.

Mignolo, W., 2000. *Local Histories/Global Designs: Coloniality, Subaltern Knowledges, and Border Thinking.* United Kingdom: Princeton University Press.

Mignolo, W., 2011. *The Darker Side of Western Modernity: Global Futures, Decolonial Options.* Durham, NC: Duke University Press.

Mignolo, W.D., 2005. *The Idea of Latin America.* Oxford: Oxford Blackwell Publishing.

Mignolo, W.D., 2007. Delinking: The rhetoric of modernity, the logic of coloniality and the grammar of de-coloniality. *Cultural Studies*, 21(2–3), pp. 449–514.

Mignolo, W.D., 2012. *Local Histories/Global Designs: Coloniality, Subaltern Knowledges, and Border Thinking.* With a new preface by the author. Princeton, NJ: Princeton University Press.

Minca, C., 2006. Giorgio Agamben and the new biopolitical nomos. *Geografiska Annaler: Series B, Human Geography*, 88(4), pp. 387–403.

Minca, C., 2007. Agamben's geographies of modernity. *Political Geography*, 26(1), pp. 78–97.

Minca, C., 2015. Counter-camps and other spatialities. *Political Geography*, 49, pp. 90–92.

Misse, M., 2011. *'Autos De Resistência'.* Available at: http://fopir.org.br/wp-content/uploads/2017/04/PesquisaAutoResistencia_Michel-Misse.pdf

Misse, M., 2018. Violence, criminal subjection and political merchandise in Brazil: An overview from Rio. *Journal of Criminology and Sociology*, 7, pp. 135–148.

Misse, M., Grillo, C.C., Teixeira, C.P., and Neri, N.E., 2013. *Quando a polícia mata: homicídios por 'autos de resistência' no Rio de Janeiro (2001–2011).* Necvu.

Montag, W., (2005) Necro-economics: Adam Smith and death in the life of the universal. *Radical Philosophy*, 134(7).

Monteiro, L.A., 2007. "Matar Bandido não é Serviço Social"? Cultura Política e Justiçamentos em uma Periferia Fluminense. *Politeia-História e Sociedade*, 7(1).

Moraes, A.C.R., 2001. Bases Da Formaçnao Territorial Do Brasil. *Geografares*, 2 (Vitória).

More, A., 2019. Necroeconomics, originary accumulation, and racial capitalism in the early Iberian slave trade. *Journal for Early Modern Cultural Studies*, 19(2), pp. 75–100.

Motta, D., and Misse, M., 1979. Crime: o social pela culatra. Ed. Achiamé.

Munster, R. van, 2004. The war on terrorism: When the exception becomes the rule. *International Journal for the Semiotics of Law*, 17(2), pp. 141–153.

National Truth Commission, 2014. *Final Report.* Brasília: Comissao Nacional da Verdade.

Neal, A.W., 2006. Foucault in Guantánamo: Towards an archaeology of the exception. *Security Dialogue*, 37(1), pp. 31–46.
Netanyahu, B., 1995. *The Origins of the Inquisition in Fifteenth Century Spain*. New York: Ramdom House.
New York Times, 2011, by Simon Romero. Rio Slum is 'Pacified' in advance of games. Available at: https://www.nytimes.com/2011/11/14/world/americas/authorities-take-control-of-rios-largest-slum.html
Nobre, C., 2010. *O negro na polícia militar: cor, crime e carreira no Rio de Janeiro*. Luminária Academia, Editora Multifoco.
NSD-18, 1989. *International Counternarcotics Strategy*. Washington: The White House, 21 ago. Disponível em: http://www.fas.org/irp/offdocs/nsd/nsd18.pdf. Acesso em: 16 abr. 2012.
NSDD-221, 1986. *Narcotics and National Security*. Washington: The White House, 8 abr. Disponível em: http://www.fas.org/irp/offdocs/nsdd/nsdd-221.htm. Acesso em: 14 abr. 2012.
O Estadão, 2015, by Felipe Resk, Bruno Ribeiro, Alexandre Hisayasu and Clayton Souza. Morte Suspeita. Available at: http://infograficos.estadao.com.br/cidades/morte-suspeita-assassinatos-que-a-policia-nao-conta/a-epidemia-continua
O Estado de São Paulo, 2008, by Pedro Dantas. Rio fabricou queda de homicidios, diz ex-diretota do ISP. Available at: https://www.estadao.com.br/noticias/geral,rio-fabricou-queda-de-homicidios-diz-ex-diretora-do-isp,244267
O Globo, 2017. A guerra do Brasil. Available at: https://infograficos.oglobo.globo.com/brasil/a-guerra-do-brasil.html
Oliveira, D.D. de, 2007. Desaparecidos civis: conflitos familiares, institucionais e segurança pública. *Sociedade e Estado*, 22(3).
Oliveira, D.D. de, 2014. *O desaparecimento de pessoas no Brasil*. Cânone Editoração Ltda.
Oliveira, J., and Kimberly, F., 2003. The politics of culture or the culture of politics: Afro-Brazilian mobilization, 1920–1968. *Journal of Third World Studies*, 20(1), pp. 103–120.
Oliveira, L.L., 2001. *O Brasil dos imigrantes*. Rio de Janeiro: Jorge Zahar Editor.
Oosterbaan, S., and van Wijk, J., 2015. Pacifying and integrating the favelas of Rio de Janeiro An evaluation of the impact of the UPP program on favela residents. *International Journal of Comparative and Applied Criminal Justice*, 39(3), pp. 179–198.
Paixão, C., 2006. A Constituição subtraída. *Constituição e Democracia*, pp. 4–5.
Pandolfi, D.C., 2006. Os anos 1930: As incertezas do regime. *O Brasil Republicano*, pp. 15–35.
Passetti, E., 2013. O carcereiro que há em nós. Entre Garantia de Direitos e Práticas Libertárias. Available at: http://www.crprs.org.br/upload/edicao/arquivo60.pdf#page=148
Patto, M.H., 1999. Estado, ciência e política na Primeira República: a desqualificação dos pobres. *Estudos Avançados*, 13(35), pp. 167–198.
Peceny, M., and Durnan, M., 2006. The FARC's best friend: U.S. antidrug policies and the deepening of Colombia's civil war in the 1990s. *Latin American Politics & Society*, 48(2), pp. 95–116.
Picker, G., and Pasquetti, S., 2015. Durable camps: The state, the urban, the everyday: Introduction. *City*, 19(5), pp. 681–688.
Pinheiro, P.S., 1979. *O Estado autoritário e movimentos populares*. Rio de Janeiro.
Pinheiro, P.S., 1982. Polícia e crise política: o caso das polícias militares. *A violência brasileira*, pp. 57–92.

Bibliography

Pinheiro, P.S., 1991. Autoritarismo e transição. *Revista Usp*, 9, pp. 45–56.
Pita, M.V., 2010. *Formas de morir y formas de vivir: el activismo contra la violencia policial*. Buenos Aires: Editores del Puerto.
Quijano, A., 2000. Coloniality of power, ethnocentrism, and Latin America. *Nepantla*, 1(3), pp. 533–580.
Rae, H., 2002. *State Identities and the Homogenisation of Peoples* (vol. 84). Cambridge: Cambridge University Press.
Rajaram, P.K., and Grundy-Warr, C., 2004. The irregular migrant as homo sacer: Migration and detention in Australia, Malaysia, and Thailand. *International Migration*, 42(1), pp. 33–64.
Raminelli, R., 2012. Impedimentos da cor mulatos no Brasil e em Portugal c. 1640–1750. *Varia História*, 28(48), pp. 699–723.
Raymundo, F.A.O.R.O., 1958. *Os donos do poder: formação do patronato político brasileiro*. Editora Globo.
Redclift, V., 2013a. Abjects or agents? Camps, contests and the creation of 'political space'. *Citizenship Studies*, 17(3–4), pp. 308–321.
Redclift, V., 2013b. *Statelessness and Citizenship: Camps and the Creation of Political Space*. London: Routledge.
Regional Secretariat of Public Security of São Paulo, 2016. Historico: Origem da Polícia no Brasil. Available at: http://www.ssp.sp.gov.br/Institucional/Historico/Historico.aspx
Reiter, B., and Mitchell, G.L., 2010. *The New Politics of Race in Brazil*. Brazil's New Racial Politics.
Reis, J.J., 1988. Slave Resistance in Brazil: Bahia, 1807–1835. *Luso-Brazilian Review*, 25(1), pp. 111–144.
Resumo de Estado do Rio de Janeiro – Dezembro de 2008. 2008. Estatísticas Trimestrais.
Ribeiro, P.J., and Oliveira, R., 2010. O impacto da ação das milícias em relação às políticas públicas de segurança no Rio de Janeiro. Transnational Institute. Amsterdan, pp. 1–8.
Ricupero, R., 2011. O Brasil no Mundo, in Schwarcz, L.M. (dir.), *História do Brasil Nação: 1808–2010. Volume 1: Crise Colonial e Independência, 1808–1830*. Coordenação: Alberto da Costa e Silva. Rio de Janeiro: Objetiva; Madrid: Fundación MAPFRE, Parte 3, pp. 115–160.
Rio de Janeiro, 2015. *Comissão Estadual da Verdade*. Rio de Janeiro.
Rio de Janeiro (Estado), 2015. *Comissão da Verdade do Rio*. Relatório / Comissão da Verdade do Rio. – Rio de Janeiro: CEV-Rio.
Robben, A.C.G.M., 2005. *Political Violence and Trauma in Argentina*. Philadelphia: University of Pennsylvania Press.
Robinson, C.J., 1983. *Black Marxism: The Making of the Black Radical Tradition*. London: Zed.
Robinson, C.J., 2020. *Black Marxism: The Making of the Black Radical Tradition* (Revised and updated 3rd edition). Chapel Hill: University of North Carolina Press.
Rocha, L. de O., 2012. Black mothers' experiences of violence in Rio de Janeiro. *Cultural Dynamics*, 24(1), pp. 59–73.
Rocha, L. de O., 2014. Outraged mothering: Black women, racial violence, and the power of emotions in Rio de Janeiro's African Diaspora. PhD dissertation, University of Texas at Austin.
Rodrigues, T., 2012. Narcotráfico e Militarização nas Américas: Vício de Guerra *. *Contexto Internacional*, 34(1), pp. 9–41.

Romani, C., 2011. Antecipando a era Vargas: A Revolução Paulista de 1924 e a efetivação das práticas de controle político e social. *Topoi (Rio de Janeiro)*, 12(23), pp. 161–178.
Rygiel, K., 2012. Politicizing camps: Forging transgressive citizenships in and through transit. *Citizenship Studies*, 16(5–6), pp. 807–825.
Rygiel, K., 2016. Dying to live: Migrant deaths and citizenship politics along European borders: Transgressions, disruptions, and mobilizations. *Citizenship Studies*, 20(5), pp. 545–560.
R7, 2014. MP investiga denuncia de trafico de orgaos na USP. Available at: https://noticias.r7.com/sao-paulo/salasocial-mp-investiga-denuncia-de-trafico-de-orgaos-na-usp-06062014
Said, E., 1978. *Orientalism: Western Representations of the Orient*. New York: Pantheon.
Salter, M.B., 2008. When the exception becomes the rule: Borders, sovereignty, and citizenship. *Citizenship Studies*, 12(4), pp. 365–380.
Samara, T.R., 2011. *Cape Town after Apartheid: Crime and Governance in the Divided City*. Minneapolis: University of Minnesota Press.
Santos, B. de S., 2003. Entre Próspero e Caliban: Colonialismo, PósColonialismo e Interidentidade. *Novos Estudos*, 66, pp. 23–51.
Schallenberger, E., and Schneider, I.E., 2010. Fronteiras agrícolas e desenvolvimento territorial: Ações de governo e dinâmica do capital. *Sociologias*, 12(25), 202–222.
Schultz, K., 2005. The Crisis of Empire and the Problem of Slavery: Portugal and Brazil, c. 1700–c. 1820. *Common Knowledge*, 11(2), pp. 264–282.
Schwarcz, L.M., and Starling, H.M., 2015. *Brasil: uma biografia: Com novo pós-escrito*. Editora Companhia das Letras.
Schwartzman, S., 1980. Da violência de nossos dias. *Revista de Ciências Sociais*, 23(3), pp. 365–369.
Schwartzman, S., 2013. A igreja e o Estado Novo: o Estatuto da Família. *Cadernos de Pesquisa*, 37, pp. 71–77.
Seyferth, G., 1990. *Imigração e cultura no Brasil*. Brasília: Editora da Universidade de Brasília.
Shapiro, M.J., 1999. The ethics of encounter: Unreading, unmapping the Imperium, in Campbell, D., and Shapiro, M.J. (eds.), *Moral Spaces: Rethinking Ethics and World Politics*. Minneapolis: University of Minnesota Press.
Shapiro, M.J., 2004. *Methods and Nations: Cultural Governance and the Indigenous Subject*. London: Routledge.
Shapiro, M.J., 2008. *Cinematic Geopolitics*. London: Routledge.
Shapiro, M.J., 2012. *Studies in Trans-Disciplinary Method: After the Aesthetic Turn*. London: Routledge.
Shilliam, R., 2018. *Race and the Undeserving Poor*. Newcastle, UK: Agenda Publishing.
Sicroff, A.A., 1960. *Les controverses des statuts de 'pureté de sang' en Espagne du 15e au 17e siècle*. Paris: Didier.
Silva, M.B.N. da, 1986. A Intendência-Geral da Polícia: 1808–1821. *Acervo: Revista do Arquivo Nacional, Rio de Janeiro*, 1(2), pp. 187–204 (jul./dez.).
Silva, T.V.Z. da, 2014. Machado de Assis and the mulatto with a 'Greek soul'. *Machado de Assis em Linha*, 7(14), pp. 229–239.
Silva Pessoa, A.E. da, 2006. Familia, propriedade e poder no nordeste colonial: a Casa da Torre de Garcia d'Avila. *Portuguese Studies Review*, 14(1), pp. 1–35.
Skidmore, T.E., 1976. *Preto no branco: raça e nacionalidade no pensamento brasileiro*. Rio de Janeiro: Editora Paz e Terra.

Bibliography

Smith, A., 1863. *An Inquiry into the Nature and Causes of the Wealth of Nations*. New edition, revised, corrected and improved. Edinburgh: A. and C. Black.

Smith, A., 2010. *The Theory of Moral Sentiments*. Penguin.

Souza, T.L.S., 2010. *Constituição, segurança pública e estado de exceção permanente: A biopolítica dos autos de resistência*. Doctoral dissertation, Dissertação (mestrado)– Pontifícia Universidade Católica do Rio de Janeiro, Departamento de Direito.

Spivak, G.C., 1983. Can the subaltern speak? in Morris, R.C. (ed.), *Can the Subaltern Speak? Reflections on the History of an Idea*. New York: Columbia University Press, 2010, pp. 21–78.

Squire, V., and Darling, J., 2013. The 'minor' politics of rightful presence: Justice and relationality in city of Sanctuary. *International Political Sociology*, 7(1), pp. 59–74. doi: 10.1111/ips.12009.

State of Rio de Janeiro Press, 2016. Unidade soluciona 88% dos casos de desaparecimento. Available at: http://www.rj.gov.br/web/seseg/exibeconteudo?article-id=2717227

Sylvester, C., 2017. Post-colonialism, in Baylis, J., Smith, S., and Owens, P. (eds.), *The Globalization of World Politics: An Introduction to International Relations*. Oxford: Oxford University Press, pp. 184–197.

Talavera Baby, N.E., 2015. Soberanía, crueldad y biopolítica. Apuntes sobre el caso Ayotzinapa. *Las Torres de Lucca: revista internacional de filosofía política*, 4(7), pp. 23–48.

Telesur, 2018. 'We are all descendants from Europe': Argentine President. Available at: https://www.telesurtv.net/english/news/We-Are-All-Descendants-from-Europe-Argentine-President-20180125-0013.html

The Guardian, 2013a, by Jonathan Watts. Brazil erupts in protests: More than a million on the streets. Available at: https://www.theguardian.com/world/2013/jun/21/brazil-police-crowds-rio-protest

The Guardian, 2013b, by Dom Phillips. Violence at Rio de Janeiro protest. Available at: https://www.theguardian.com/world/2013/oct/16/violence-rio-de-janeiro-protests

The Guardian, 2013c, by Jonathan Watts. Brazil protests erupt over public services and World Cup costs. Available at: https://www.theguardian.com/world/2013/jun/18/brazil-protests-erupt-huge-scale

The Guardian, 2015, by Spencer Ackerman. Homan Square revealed: How Chicago police 'disappeared' 7,000 people. Available at: https://www.theguardian.com/us-news/2015/oct/19/homan-square-chicago-police-disappeared-thousands

The Guardian, 2016. Philippine president Rodrigo Duterte to extend drug war as 'cannot kill them all'. Available at: https://www.theguardian.com/world/2016/sep/19/philippine-president-rodrigo-duterte-extend-drug-war-kill-them-all

The Intercept, 2017. Rio de Janeiro toma conhecimento da Guerra na Cidade Alta apos cinco meses de confront, by Juliana Gonçalves. Available at: https://theintercept.com/2017/05/02/rio-de-janeiro-toma-conhecimento-de-guerra-na-cidade-alta-apos-cinco-meses-de-confronto/

Tzvetan, T., 2003. *A conquista da América*. El Problema del Otro. Ed. Siglo XXI.

UNICEF, 2017. Report 'A familiar face: Violence in the lives of children and adolescents'. Available at: https://data.unicef.org/resources/a-familiar-face/

UNWGEID, 2017. UNDOC/GEN/G14/176/73/. Available at: http://daccess-dds-ny.un.org/doc/UNDOC/GEN/G14/176/73/PDF/G1417673.pdf?OpenElement

UOL, 2014. Policia faz busca por desaparecido dentro de presidio em Pedrinhas. Available at: https://noticias.uol.com.br/cotidiano/ultimas-noticias/2014/08/08/preso-desaparece-de-pedrinhas-e-policia-faz-buscas-em-presidio-no-ma.htm

UPP, 2014. *UPP, o que e?* Available at: http://www.upprj.com/index.php/o_que_e_upp
Valladares, L. do P., 1976. Favela, política e conjunto residencial. *Dados*, 12, pp. 74–85.
Valladares, L. do P., 1978. *Passa-se uma casa: Análise do programa de remoção de favelas do Rio de Janeiro*. Rio de Janeiro: Zahar Editores.
Valladares, L. do P., 2005. *A Invencao da Favela*. FGV.
Vaughan-Williams, N., 2009. The generalised bio-political border? Re-conceptualising the limits of sovereign power. *Review of International Studies*, 35(4), pp. 729–749.
Vaughan-Williams, N., 2010. The UK border security continuum: Virtual biopolitics and the simulation of the sovereign ban. *Environment and Planning D: Society and Space*, 28(6), pp. 1071–1083.
Veja, 2016. *A ocupação da Rocinha pelas forças de segurança*. Available at: https://veja.abril.com.br/galeria-fotos/a-ocupacao-da-rocinha-pelas-forcas-de-seguranca/
Velho, G., and Alvito, M. orgs., 1996. *Cidadania e violência*. Rio de Janeiro: Editoras UFRJ/FGV.
Ventura, Z., 1994. *Cidade partida*. Companhia das Letras.
Vianna, H., 1965. *História do Brasil* 2 vols. São Paulo: Melhoramentos.
Vitale, A.S., 2017. *The End of Policing*. Verso Books.
Waiselfisz, J.J., 2013. *MAPA DA VIOLÊNCIA 2013 Homicídios e Juventude no Brasil*. p. 96. Available at: http://flacso.org.br/files/2020/03/mapa2013_homicidios_juventude.pdf
Walker, M.U., 2006. The cycle of violence. *Journal of Human Rights*, 5(1), pp. 81–105.
Walker, R.B., 2010. *After the Globe, before the World*. London: Routledge.
Wallerstein, I.M., 2007. Universalismo Europeo/European Universalism: El Discurso Del Poder/the Discourse of Power. Siglo XXI.
Weeks, G., 2006. Fighting terrorism while promoting democracy: Competing priorities in U.S. Defense policy toward Latin America. *Journal of Third World Studies*, 23(2), pp. 59–77.
Weffort, F.C., 2006. *Formação do Pensamento Político Brasileiro: Idéias e Personagens*. São Paulo: Ática.
Western, J., 1996. *Outcast Cape Town* (2nd edition). Berkeley, CA, and London: University of California Press. (Originally published 1981, Minneapolis: University of Minnesota Press).
Wilding, P., 2010. 'New violence': Silencing women's experiences in the favelas of Brazil. *Journal of Latin American Studies*, 42(4), pp. 719–747.
Williams, D., 2001. *Culture Wars in Brazil: The First Vargas Regime, 1930–1945*. Durham, NC: Duke University Press.
Willis, G.D., 2015. *The Killing Consensus: Police, Organized Crime, and the Regulation of Life and Death in Urban Brazil*. Berkeley, CA: University of California Press.
Wojtalewicz, P.D., 1993. *The "Junta de Missões": The Missions in the Portuguese Amazon*. Tese de mestrado, Universidade de Minnesota, pp. 158–159.
World Bank, 2011. *World development report 2011: Conflict, security, and development – overview (English)*. World development report. Washington, DC: World Bank Group. Available at: http://documents.worldbank.org/curated/en/806531468161369474/World-development-report-2011-conflict-security-and-development-overview
World Bank Group, 2015. *Indigenous Latin America in the Twenty-First Century: The First Decade*, p. 118. Available at: https://openknowledge.worldbank.org/handle/10986/23751
WP Costa, 2003. *Do domínio à nação: os impasses da fiscalidade no processo de Independência. Brasil: formação do Estado e da nação*. São Paulo: Hucitec, pp. 143–193.

Zaluar, A., 1999. Um debate disperso: violência e crime no Brasil da redemocratização. *São Paulo em Perspectiva*, 13(3), pp. 3–17.

Zaluar, A., and Conceição, I.S., 2007. Favelas sob o controle das milícias no Rio de Janeiro: Que Paz? *São Paulo em Perspectiva*, 21(2), pp. 89–101.

Zevnik, A., 2009. Sovereign-less subject and the possibility of resistance. *Millennium – Journal of International Studies*, 38(1), pp. 83–106.

Zevnik, A., 2011. Becoming-animal, becoming-detainee: Encountering human rights discourse in Guantanamo. *Law and Critique*, 22(2), pp. 155–169.

Index

Note: Page numbers followed by 'n' refer to chapter notes.

Acari Massacre 16, 35, 100, 102
Acari Mothers 100
Agamben, G. 24, 46; ambivalence 47–48; bare life 9, 18, 22–23, 47–48, 54, 133–134, 137, 149–150, 157; biopolitics 134; camps (concentration camps) 9, 22, 47–48, 54, 130–135, 138, 150, 153, 154n2, 157; Greek political thought 9; Holocaust 47–48, 72; lacuna in law 67, 98–99; 'law' (language and norms) 60; logic of exception 59–60, 68, 134, 159; logic of the field 132, 135; Nazi state parallels 60; notion of 'ban' 137, 142; postcolonial critique of 10–11; sovereignty and life 8–9, 19, 52, 54, 67, 76, 80; unworthy lives 20, 48, 72; 'zone of indistinction' 150
agrarian disputes 100
Alckmin, Geraldo 149
Algranti, L.M. 114, 116–117
Allende, Salvador 27–28
Al-Qaeda 60–61
Alves, J.A. 4, 20, 75, 91
Alves, Mario 36, 51n9
Amarildo case 1; attempts to link to drug dealers 35; CCTV images 1; Copacabana Beach demonstrations 40; newspaper articles 15; not a political dissident 5, 25; Pacifying Police Unit (UPP) 3; public concern 16, 18, 34, 45, 156; suspicion of the increase in disappearances 4
Amar, P. 2
Amazon Surveillance System (SIVAM) 64
Amerindians: Church's duty to 57; different categories 111; enslaved populations 113; protection from Jesuits 109–111; 'rights of the people' 109–110; Royal Charter (1680) 111; as a *tabula rasa* 56, 108, 110; Vieira's Sermon for Epiphany (against slavery) 110–111
Amnesty International 3, 15, 31, 45
Amnesty Law 25, 36, 50n1
Andean Strategy policy 63
Anderson, B. 56
Andrews, G.R. 120
Anievas, A., Manchanda, N. and Shilliam, R. 10, 108
Aradau, C. 39–40
Araguaia Guerrilla, Navy Forces 36, 51n10
Araujo, F.A. 6, 14, 39–41, 43
Arbex, D. 85
Archivos del Terror, Condor Operation 27, 50n3
Arendt, H. 133, 137
Argentina: as archetypical case 26–29; Condor Operation 27; de-politicisation of police killings 18; *'desaparecido'* 31; dictatorship 93; disappearance as primary tool of state repression 27; General Vilas 29; indigenous nationalities 58; motivations for disappearances 28–29; number of victims 26, 50n2; Tucuman 29
armed forces, political disappearances 25, 36
Auchter, J. 130
Auschwitz 9
authoritarian regimes, and enforced disappearance 59
autos de resistência (resistance killings): abandonment of term 98; distorted

Index

crime scenes 97; extrajudicial killings 3, 23, 24n2; fake evidence 97–98, 102; Juan case 151–152, 154; killings in favelas 130–131, 154n1; lacuna in law 98–99; lawful homicide in Criminal Code 3, 96; Mateus case 104–105; National Secretariat of Human Rights 98; Patricia case 154; peak 45, 99; protection of police officers 79; re-democratisation period 96–99; register filled by police officer 44, 97; São Paulo use of 'suspicious death' 45
A Voz da Raça (The Voice of Race) 120
Ayotzinapa case 31, 49
Ayotzinapa Rural Teacher Training College 31

Bandeirantes expeditions 139–140
Bandeirantes Operation (Oban) 92
Barbacena Mental Health Hospital 85
bare life, Agamben 9, 18, 22–23, 47–48, 54, 133–134, 137, 149–150, 157
Baron of Rio Branco 140, 155n5
Bauer, C.S. 27, 39
Benario, Olga 87
Benjamin, W. 60
Bhabha, H. 7
Bignall, S. 9
Bigo, D. 61, 66, 132, 135, 150, 157
'big skull' (armoured vehicles), war on drugs 61, 78n4
biopolitics: Agamben 8–9; Foucault 8–9; and necroeconomics 72–74; and necropolitics 80; racialisation of subjugated population 73–74
bios politikos 46
Björnehed, E. 63
black bodies 104–129; contextualizing slavery in Latin America 112–119; 'cosmic race' 119, 122; criminalisation 48, 54; dictatorship/violence against indigenous communities 124–127; former slaves 120; freed population (Rio de Janeiro) 116–117; making difference invisible 127–128; overview 104–106; police arrest records (1810-1821) 116–117; police control over slave surveillance 115; public floggings 118; racial democracy and nation-building 119–124; racial hierarchy 106–119; rendering race invisible by whitening the population 121–124; 'social control' after slavery 114, 117–118
Black Capitalism 20

black communities: displaced to the favelas 5, 144; firearm deaths 128, 129n6; housing policy 53; low reproduction rate 121; majority of victims from 19–20; prison population 65; prison population (US) 69, 78n5; state violence towards 6; violence perpetrated against 20; war on drugs 21; war of drugs threat to 5–6
border thinking 7, 135
Bosi, A. 110
Brassett, J., and Vaughan-William, N. 48, 133
Brazilian Black Front 120
Brazilian Institute of Geography and Statistics (IBGE) 106–107, 147
Brazilian National Guard 82
Bretas, M.L., and Rosemberg, A. 83, 86, 90
Britain, working class 123–124
Brito Freire, Francisco de 110
Brito, L.D.C. 111
Brown, A. 117–118
Bueno, A.M. 122
burial, under different names 94
Bush, George, war on drugs 63

Cabral, Sergio 1, 44, 132
Caldeira, T.P. 145–146
Calderón, Felipe 31
Campbell, D. 62, 64, 134
camps (concentration camps): Agamben 9, 22, 47–48, 54, 130–135, 138, 153; ambivalences between *zoe* and *bios* 132–133; biopolitics and territory 134, 154n2; border thinking 135; colonial logic 137–138; favelas and peripheries 158; Shark Island (Namibia) 9; spatial arrangement 134; state of exception 134; undistinguished zone 135; 'zone of indistinction' 150
Cano, I. 97–98, 147
Cao, B. 10
capitalism, origins before Industrial Revolution 70–71
Captain General 81
Cardoso, Fernando Henrique 100
Caririis Resistance 81
Carlos Eboli Institute 152
Carneiro, M.L.T. 87
Casa Grande e Senzala (Master's House and the Slave Quarters, Freyre) 122
Catholic University of Rio de Janeiro 144

Cavalos Corredores (Running Horses) 100
Cerqueira, Daniel 43–44, 46
Chicago Police Department 31, 49
chief of police 84
children's disappearances, media attention 16–17
Chile: dictatorship period 27–28; imprisoned population 27
Christianity, framing those outside Europe as 'pagans' 140
Church: notions of skin colour 108, 110; racial hierarchy 106, 128; as sovereign actor 69; Treaty of Tordesillas 138–139
Cidade Alta, different drug cartels fighting for control 161
Cidade Partida (Ventura) 142
citizenship, people incapable/unworthy of 131
City of God (movie) 138
City of Sanctuary 136
Civil Code (1916) 125
'civil-disappeared' 34
Civil Police 83, 92, 103n3
Clarim d' Alvorada (Clarion of Dawn) 120
coffee market, Vargas control measures 88
coffee plantations 57, 77; European migrants 121, 128; and favelas 24; local elites 8; Paraiba Valley 116; plantation system 158; slave trade 146
colonial capitalism, and racial capitalism 70–72
'coloniality, logic of' 54–55, 58–59
colonial logic of governmentality 140
colonial space as 'empty space' 139–140
colour-line 108
Commission of Dead and Political Disappeared 37
communist groups 5, 23, 36, 38
Communist Revolt (1935) 88
communist revolution, feared 144
communist-subversive (term) 91
community policing 4
Conceição, I.S., and Zaluar, A. 40
conceptual framework 7–11; de-colonial thinking 7–8; logic of coloniality 8–9; necropolitics 9–10; postcolonial thought 7; sovereignty and life 8–9
conceptual vocabulary, war on drugs 22
concluding thoughts 156–161
Condor Operation: *Archivos del Terror* 27, 50n3; Argentina 27; deaths 27

Constitution (1824) 86, 125; treatment of slaves 113–114, 116
Constitution (1934) 125
contemporary cases: democracies/authoritarian regimes 31; invisible (challenges dealing with) 13–17; political contexts 31–32
Copacabana Beach demonstrations 40
Corumbiara 100
'cosmic race' 119, 122
Costa Vargas, J.H. 130, 147, 153
coup d'état 'The 1930s Revolution' 86–87
Creole elites 58
Creole identity, historical foundation 57–58
Criminal Code, *autos de resistência* (resistance killings) 3
critical security studies, Foucaultian accounts 53
Cuba, Spanish colonial power 9
cultural community 56
Cunha, M.C.P. 84–85

Da Costa, E.V. 83–84
Dalby, S. 61
dangerous populations, idea of 53
data (messy): 'death by undetermined cause' 44; misclassification 44; missing person reports 41–46, 50, 98; Public Security Institute of Rio de Janeiro (ISP-RJ) 44
death squads: criminalisation of those killed by 160; emergence 95–96; National Truth Commission 38; Philippines 31–32; police officers 146; 'slaughters' 99–100; training and weapons from the state 39
Declaration of the Protection of all Persons from Enforced Disappearance (UN General Assembly) 33
de-colonial thinking 7–8
De Matos, M.V.A.B., and Lissovsky, M. 122
Department of Information Operations and Centre for Internal Defence Operations (DOI-CODI) 92, 103n7
Department of Political and Social Order 146
Department of Public Security of São Paulo 45, 83
Department of Social and Political Order (DOPS) 79, 92
Department of Social and Political Order of São Paulo (DOPS/SP) 93

182   Index

de Paula, F.R. 75
'desaparecido,' Latin America 30–31
de Souza, Amarildo Dias *see* Amarildo case
detention centres 136
Dias, C.N., and Manso, B.P. 145
dictatorship period: black-power activism prosecution 123; communist groups 5, 23, 36, 38; leftist guerrillas 25, 39, 127, 146, 156; police violence 79; political disappearances 5–6, 11–13, 18, 21, 33, 50, 156; Spain 26, 30, 32, 49; tortured numbers 93–94; Truth Commission Working Group of Rio de Janeiro 38–39; violence against indigenous communities 124–127
Diken, B. 138; and Laustsen, C.B. 135
Dillon, M. 60
Directory of the Indians 140, 155n4
disappearance (term in Brazil) 11, 32–33
ditabranda 50, 51n14
DNA recognition in Brazil 160, 161n1
Dossier on Political Deaths and Disappearances 13
Du Bois, W.E.B. 48, 108
Dussel, E. 81
Duterte, Rodrigo 31

Edkins, J. 32, 134; and Pin-Fat, V. 47; Pin-Fat, V. and Shapiro, M.J. 52
Eilbaum, L. 41; and Medeiros, F. 152
Eldorado do Carajás 100
Elkins, J. 64
enforced disappearance: and authoritarian regimes 59; and dictatorships 59; elusive practice 32–35; expanding the conceptualisation 49–50; increase of child/teenager victims 43–44; indigenous populations 95; motivations for 28–29; National Truth Commission 12–13, 38; National Truth Commission Report 93; no body no crime 42; no specific legislation (Brazil) 33, 41, 157; pedagogical reasons 28–29; police officer participation 33; re-democratisation period 6–7, 11, 50, 156; and sovereign power 46–49
epistemicide 18
Erichsen, C.W., and Olusoga, D. 9
European migrants, coffee plantations 121, 128

'exceptionality, logic of' 55, 59–60; context of war on drugs 62–66, 68; context of war on terror 60–62
External Commission to Find Political Disappearances 36
Extra: Facebook page 160; war section (Rio de Janeiro) 160–161
extrajudicial executions, democracies/authoritarian regimes 31

Facebook, fake profile entrapment by police officer 148
Faoro, R. 81
Farias, J. 98
Fausto, Boris 86
favela dwellers: problematisation of violence towards 52–53; violence perpetrated against 19
favelas: as abject space 141–145; 'big skull' (armoured vehicles) 61, 78n4; black communities displaced to 5, 53, 144; and coffee plantations 24; criminalised space 132; drugs operations in 61; home to 'marginal people' 138; killings that occur 130–131, 154n1; liminal spatiality 131–135; military incursion 21, 38, 91; as places of criminality 81; reputation 130; stray bullets near schools 161; Truth Commission Working Group of Rio de Janeiro 38–39
Federal Police Agency 98
Feitosa, G.R.P., and Pinheiro, J.A.O. 64
Felizburo 100
Ferreira, L.C. de M. 6, 14, 16, 41–43
fieldwork (this book) 12, 24n3, 79, 159; semi-structured questionnaires 14–15; *see also* interviews
15th District Police Unit 1
First Brazilian Conference of Immigration and Colonization (1949) 125
First Command of the Capital (PCC) 100–101
First Republic: police apparatus 83–85; positivism 87, 103n6; racialised notions in the police 23
First World War, imperial determinants 108
Fleury, Sergio Paranhos 93, 146
Flexor, M.H.O. 124
Florindo, M.T. 87–89
Forte, F.A.D.P. 65
Foucault, M. 10; biopolitics 8–9, 19, 46, 80; 'biopower' 48; disciplinary power

framework 84; power and knowledge 141; sovereignty 48, 67, 72, 76
4th Political Police Station 83–84, 87
Franco, Marielle, killing 17
Freyre, G. 122
Furtado, H. 25
further research, 159–161, 159

Garotinho, Rosinha 44
Gatti, G. 8, 11, 18, 26, 32, 41, 59
gendered racial violence 20
Genoa, trade relation in European Middle Ages 70–71
Gilmore, R. 75
Goes Filho, S.S. 139
Golden Law 112, 114, 121
Gomes, A.D.C. 123
Gomes, Anderson, killing 17
Gomes, Luiz Flavio 34
Goncalves Martins, Francisco 115
Greek political thought, Agamben 9
Grupo Globo 1
Guanabara state 143–144
Guantanamo Bay 133, 136
Guarani ethic group 126–127

Harvey, D. 53
Hegel, G.W.F. 73
Heinz, W.S. 27–29
Hobbes, T. 68
Hobsbawm, E. 56
Holloway, T. 81–82, 84, 115, 117
Holocaust 47–48, 72
homicide numbers: not in official figures 46; Rio de Janeiro 44
Homicide Unit, Amarildo case 1
homo sacer 9, 47, 134, 150
Hülsse, R., and Spencer, A. 60–61
human rights: concept of enforced disappearance 37; indigenous populations violation 95; liberal notions 62
Human Rights Bureau Special Committee 101
Human Rights Commission 148
Human Rights Watch 15, 31, 45

Ianni, O. 122
identity politics, studies 10
ideological border (idea) 27
'imagined communities' 56
Imperial Penal Code 82
indigenous lands, 'March to the West' 125
indigenous populations 21; ancestral lands 125; 'conversion' to Christianity 124; enforced disappearance 95; food poisoning 125; Guarani ethic group 126–127; immunisation 126; kidnapping of children 127; killed by diseases (un/intentionally) 125–126; Law for Indigenous People (1755) 124; military officers violent acts 126–127; 'Negative Evidence of the Existence of Indigenous Communities' 127; relocation from original community 126; violence against 124–127
Indigenous Rural Guard 126
Industrial Revolution 68–69, 74; capitalism origins before 70–71, 74; and Marxist theory 70
Institute for Applied Economic Research (Ipea) 43; 'Map of the Hidden Homicides in Brazil' 46
Institutional Act (AI-1) 90–91
Institutional Act (AI-2) 90
Institutional Act (AI-4) 90
Institutional Act (AI-5) 94, 126
Institutional Acts, above all other laws 90
Inter-American Convention on Enforced Disappearance of Persons 33–34
Inter-American Court, slavery and human trafficking in Brazil 114
internal enemy idea 90–91, 93, 95
interracial marriage 124
interviews 12, 24n3, 160; cases in Recife 159; 'If we can kill them why to disappear them?' 14, 79; impeachment of Rousseff 17–18; local /national truth commissions members 13; mothers whose children were killed by police 19; operation designed to kill gang members 46; respondents' safety 16; semi-structured questionnaires 14–15
Investigative Body for Public Security 83
invisible (challenges dealing with) 11–21; contemporary cases 13–17; what was possible to investigate 17–21; 'wrong' victim 35–36
Isin, E., and Rygiel, K. 133, 135–137
Itaipu hydroelectric dam 126–127
Italy, control of Bedouin population (Libyan colony) 141

Jesuit priests 124; Amerindians 109–111; notions of skin colour 110
Jewish citizens, prohibition 87, 89

Jewish communities, persecution 87
Joao III, of Brazil 81
Juan case 98, 131, 150, 154, 158; *'a normal boy'* 152, 154; attempts to frame for drugs 152; *autos de resistência* (resistance killings) 151–152; body found (stopped fake 'evidence') 152; compensation 155n9
Juan, media attention 16
Juquery Psychiatric Hospital 84

kidnappings, babies from revolutionary mothers 29
Kimberly, F., and Oliveira, J. 121
Kingdom of Congo, Portuguese trade 112
Klein, H.S., and Luna, F.V. 113
Kristeva, J, 136

labour force, commodification 71
Lacerda, Carlos 38, 143
Lage, V.C. 57
Lagoa Rodrigo de Freitas 147
Lago, M.C. 123
Latin America: colonial roots 8; colonisation 56, 69; contextualizing slavery 112–119; coup d'états 90; *'desaparecido'* 30–31; dictatorships 22, 26, 49; 'discovery' and Christianity 56; local elites 157; military aid from US 63; nation-building process 54; political disappearances 26; Southern Cone 27
Laustsen, C.B., and Diken, B. 135
Law for Indigenous People (1755) 124
Law for the Disappeared 36
Law on Drugs (Law number 11343) 65, 67, 98
leftist guerrillas 38; dictatorship period 12, 21, 25, 39, 124, 127, 146, 156; and drug cartels 63
Leite, M.P. 61
Lemos, N.G. 83
LGBT communities 159
liminal spatiality 130–155; abjection and the logic of coloniality 153–154; bare life 133–134, 137, 149–150; boundaries of belonging 152; camps (concentration camps) 131–135, 150, 153; colonial logic of death in favelas and peripheries 148–153; colonial space as 'empty space' 139–140; logic of the field 132, 135; modern camps, abject spaces 135–138; notion of territory and population 138–147; overview 130–131; 'right type of population' 139–140, 146; Rio de Janeiro' favelas as abject space 141–145; São Paulo's peripheries as abject space 145–147; threshold 141, 150–153; urban peripheries as abject space 140–141
Lissovsky, M., and De Matos, M.V.A.B. 122
logging camps 112
'logic of coloniality' 54–55, 58–59
'logic of exceptionality' 55, 59–60; context of war on drugs 62–66, 68; context of war on terror 60–62
Lopes, Tim 35
Luiz, Washington 88
Lula (Luiz Inacio da Silva) 18
Luna, F.V., and Klein, H.S. 113

Machado de Assis 107
Macri, Mauricio 58
Malhães, Paulo, National Truth Commission testimony 12
Manchanda, N., Anievas, A. and Shilliam, R. 10, 108
Mandolessi, S., and Perez, M.E. 26, 30
Mangueira 147
Manso, B.P., and Dias, C.N. 145
Marxist theory, and Industrial Revolution 70
Marx, K. 74
Massacre of Saltpetre River (1676) 81
Mateus case, *autos de resistência* (resistance killings) 104–105
Mattos, H. 111
May Crimes 16, 35, 100–102, 148–150, 160, 161n1
Mbembe, A. 24; critique of Agamben's work 55; liminal spatiality 130; 'logic of coloniality' 59; necropolitics 9–10, 14, 22, 48–49, 54, 72–73, 80, 130, 141, 154, 158–159; reducing a human person to a thing 75; sovereignty and death 19–20, 52, 76–77, 153, 158–159
McCann, B. 116
Meade, T. 142–143
Medeiros, F., and Eilbaum, L. 152
media attention: cases that can't be linked to drug activities 17; children's disappearances 16–17
Mediterranean, expulsion of the Moors 56
mental health issues, senior adults 42
Mexico, Ayotzinapa case 31, 49
Mexico-US border 141

Mezarobba, G. 36
'Micro-wave Demonstration' 40
Mignolo, W. 8, 24, 57, 70, 77, 108, 139–140, 144, 153, 157, 159; Creole identity 58; 'discovery' of Latin America 56; 'logic of coloniality' 54–55, 58; 'purity of blood' 109–110; 'rights of the people' 109–110
migration policy, Arian doctrine and social Darwinism 122
migration studies, camps 133
Military Police 148, 157
militia: killing local drug lords 99; off-duty or retired police officers 99
Minca, C. 134
Ministry of Justice 37, 82, 84
Ministry of Work 123
Miranda, Ana Paula 44
Misse, M. 3, 43–45, 82, 96–97, 131
missing person cases, specialising police station Rio de Janeiro 14–15
missing person (English term) 11, 32–33
missing person, formal notification 14
missing person reports: data (messy) 41–46; increase of child/teenagers 43–44
Mitchell, G.L., and Reiter, B. 119
Montag, W. 69, 72–73
Monument to the Flags 139, 154n3
More, A. 74
Mortality Information System (SIM) 44
Munster, R. van 61

Namibia, Shark Island concentration camp 9
narcoterrorism, war on drugs 63
National Army 87
National Conference of Brazilian Bishops of Brazil 144
National Council of Civil Chiefs of Police 98
National Criminal Code, *autos de resistência* (resistance killings) 3, 96
National Defence Policy 91
National Indian Foundation (FUNAI) 126–127, 141
National Institute on Drug Abuse, report (1990) 64
National Intelligence Directorate (DINA) 28
National Intelligence Service (SNI) 91, 93
National Park of Xingu 125

National Secretariat for Drug Policy (SENAD) 64
National Secretariat of Human Rights, *autos de resistência* (resistance killings) 98
National Security Council 90
National Security Directive Administration 221 (NSDD 221) 63
National Security Police 91
National Service of Indigenous Protection 125
National Truth Commission 25, 33, 35, 37, 49–50, 51n8, 86, 156; enforced disappearance 12–13, 37–38; grounds to exclude victims 38; indigenous populations 124–126; interviews with members 13; leftist guerrillas and militaries 39; Malhães testimony 12; rural workers exclusion 38; victims' historical-social context 37
National Truth Commission Report 25; enforced disappearance 93; indigenous communities human rights 95; killings and disappearances by year 94; official number of political disappearances 91–92
nation-building and modernity 52–78; anti-black violence 75–76; biopolitics to necroeconomics 72–74; Creoles of Spanish and Portuguese descent 57; declaration of independence (Brazil) 57; former colonies 57, 78n3; governing death and racial capitalism 68–70; ideas of belonging 55; life as excess 74–76; logic of exception and metaphors of war 59–66; nation-state 55–59; overview 52–55; police as apparatus 66–68; Portuguese Crown 57, 82, 90, 102; racial and colonial capitalism 70–72; racial democracy 119–124; racial hierarchy 106–119; religiously motivated 56, 77n1; territorial entities 56
nation-state, and religion 56, 77n1
Navy Forces, Araguaia Guerrilla 36, 51n10
Nazi state parallels 60
Neal, A.W. 62
necroeconomics: and biopolitics 72–74; regulate excess life 72; slave trade 74
necropolitics 69, 154; and biopolitics 80; black life as surplus 75; market mechanism (number of labours) 73; Mbembe 9–10, 14, 22, 48–49, 54, 80,

186 Index

130, 158–159; racial capitalism 53; settlements 141
neoliberal capitalism 4
newspaper articles: Amarildo case 15; homicide numbers 45
New State 88, 120
New World, divided between Portugal and Spain 138–139
New World market 71
Nixon, Richard, election campaign (anti-drugs) 62–63
non-governmental groups (NGOs) 15

O Estadão 45
O Globo 1; 'The Brazilian War' 161; pacifying operations 130
Oliveira, J., and Kimberly, F. 121
Olusoga, D., and Erichsen, C.W. 9
Olympic Games (2016) 2, 4, 18
Organisation of American States 33

'pacification' programme 2–3, 24n1
Pacifying Police Unit (UPP) 18, 44–45, 66; Amarildo case 3; collapse after Olympic Games 160; regarded as important to public security 3–4; Rocinha 1, 3; World Bank approval 4
Palestinian conflict with Israel 73
Paraguay War 139
Parnassianism 107
Pasquetti, S., and Picker, G. 137–138
Patricia case 131, 150–151, 154, 158; attempts to frame her for drugs/alcohol 152, 155n8; compensation 155n7
Patto, M.H. 84–85, 121
Pedro I of Brazil 57
Pedro II of Brazil 117
Penal Code, reformulated (1890) 84
Penitentiary Tiradentes 146
Perez, M.E., and Mandolessi, S. 26, 30
Perus Cemetery, unidentified people buried 159
Philippines: death squads 31–32; war on drugs exceptionalities 31, 49
Picker, G., and Pasquetti, S. 137–138
Pimentel, Rodrigo 1
Pin-Fat, V.: and Edkins, J. 47; Edkins, J. and Shapiro, M.J. 52
Pinheiro, J.A.O., and Feitosa, G.R.P. 64
Pinochet, Augusto 27
Pita, M.V. 18–19
plantation system 158; *see also* coffee plantations

police action, against 'dangerous' groups 22–23
police apparatus: *autos de resistência* (resistance killings) 96–99; colony to empire (1500-1888) 81–83; control enslaved populations 82; First Republic (1889-1936) 83–85; governing death 101–103; institutionalised police roots 81–85; leftist groups investigation/control 92–95; military dictatorship (1964-1985) 90–95; militia groups and death squads 99–102; noticeable killings/unnoticed disappearances 79–103; overview 79–81; psychiatric institutions 84–85; racialised communities (victims) 103; racialised embodiment 23; re-democratisation period 95–101; risk to social order 85; social regulation 89; Vargas Era and 'The New State' 86–90, 102
police forces: 'Bravery Bonus' 98; de-militarisation 106; as *dispositif* 66–67, 79, 96; and drug dealers militarised relationship 105; and drug dealers partnership acts 40; financial resources 89; militarisation 34–35, 54; missing persons report errors 43–44, 98; mistreatment of people registering a missing person 42
Police Inquest Department 82
police killings: racialised communities (victims) 157; racialised terms 19–20; São Paulo numbers 98; United States 3
police officers, death squads 146
Police Ombudsman Service 101
Police School 84
police violence: CCTV images 1, 104–105; flagrant incidents 45; number of victims 105; United States 69, 97; and urban growth (1990s) 99; videos on social media 17, 45
police violence figures, Brazil figures against Britain and US 4
political disappearances: armed forces 25; crystallisation 26; dictatorship period 5–6, 11–13, 18, 21, 33, 50, 156; Latin America 26; Law (9140) 33; narrow connotation 36, 156–157; trans-nationalisation 30; 'travelling' concept 29–31
Political Police 83
Portuguese Crown, nation-building and modernity 57, 90, 102

Portuguese Royal Court, Rio de Janeiro 82
positivism, First Republic 87, 103n6
poverty, criminalisation 121
'prisoner' exchanges 39
prison population: black people 65; disappearances from custody 159; United States 75
Pronasci 18
psychiatric institutions, police apparatus 84–85
public morgues, unidentified corpses 159
Public Prosecution Agency of Rio de Janeiro 1
Public Prosecutor's Office 104
Public Security and Investigation Inspection 83
public security, federal state funds 2, 18
Public Security Forum, annual survey of police killings 12
Public Security Institute of Rio de Janeiro (ISP-RJ): figures on missing persons 40–41; manipulating data released 44; missing person survey (2009) 42–44, 51n12; resistance killings 44
Public Security Secretary 100
public transport fares 2
public universities, urban violence studies 15–16

Quijano, A. 8, 58, 68–71, 74–75, 109

racial capitalism: and colonial capitalism 70–72; governing death 68–70, 77; lives deemed as excess 75; necropolitics 53, 74
racial democracy: Brazil's claim 5; myth 6, 10, 21, 48, 119, 122, 146, 158
racial hierarchy 106–119, 128; *black* 107; colour-line 108; contextualizing slavery in Latin America 112–119; expulsion of Jews and Moors from Spain 109; mixed-race persons 110; 'mulatto' 111; Native Peoples right to traditional territory 111; one-drop rule 107; 'pardo' 111; 'purity of blood' 56, 108–111; race 'invented' as a concept 108; 'rights of the people' 56; segregation policies (US) 111; skin colour as climatic consequence 110; Vieira's Sermon for Epiphany (against slavery) 110–111; *white* 106–107
racialisation, and unworthiness 8
Rae, H. 56, 90, 108–109

Ranger, T. 56
Reagan, Ronald, war on drugs 63
Real Military Police Guard 82
Recife, peasants killed during dictatorship 159
Recife Truth Commission Report 95
Redclift, V. 135
Rede Globo 1, 35
refugee camps 136
Regional Secretariat of Public Security of São Paulo 81
Reiter, B., and Mitchell, G.L. 119
religion: Church as sovereign actor 69; and the nation-state 56, 77n1
Research Centre for Citizenship Conflict and Urban Violence (Necvu-UFRJ) 43
resistance killings *see autos de resistência* (resistance killings)
resistance movements, women as protagonists 20–21
Rio Branco Law (free-womb law) 114
Rio da Paz 40
Rio de Janeiro: East Zone neighbourhoods 15; favelas as abject space 141–145; favelas and wealthy neighbourhoods proximity 142; freed population 116; homicide numbers 44; housemaids and cleaners live in favelas 143; Mangueira 147; missing person cases specialising police station 14–15; Municipal Theatre 143; narrative of war 160–161; Old City destruction of unsanitary tenements 142–143; Olympic Games (2016) 2, 4, 18; Pacifying Police Unit (UPP) 160; police pre-emptive operation 142; Portuguese Royal Court 82; urban development 5, 77, 143; Vila Aliança 143; Vila Kennedy 143; World Cup (2014) 2, 4, 18
road checks, young black males targeted 142
Robben, C.G.M. 28–29, 93
Robinson, C. 68–69, 70, 72
Rocha, L de O. 21
Rocinha, Pacifying Police Unit (UPP) 1, 3
Rodrigues, T. 65
Roman Catholic Church, Treaty of Tordesillas 138–139
Rome Statute 34
Rosemberg, A., and Bretas, M.L. 83, 86, 90
Rousseff, Dilma, impeachment 17

188 Index

rural workers, National Truth Commission 38
Rygiel, K. 131, 133; and Isin, E. 133, 135–137

Sabino, Rodrigo Lopes 148–149
Said, E. 7
Salter, M.B. 61, 65
Samara, T. 75
samba 123
São Paulo: black police victims 149; development of urban areas 77; flats bought (middle and upper classes) 146; geography of 145; irregular land development 146; peripheries as abject space 145–147; police killings (number) 98; social segregation 145; use of 'suspicious death' not *autos de resistência* 45
Schallenberger, E., and Schneider, I.E. 125
Schmitt, Carl 60
Schneider, I.E., and Schallenberger, E. 125
securitisation: as excess regulation 74–76; neoliberal dimension 75–76
Security Public Bureau 148
Security Secretary 148
senior adults, mental health issues 42
September 11 terrorist attack 59, 61, 72
Sexagenarian Law 114
Shapiro, M. 14
Shapiro, M.J. 56–57; Edkins, J. and Pin-Fat, V. 52
Shilliam, R. 123; Anievas, A. and Manchanda, N. 10, 108
Silva, T.V.Z. da 107
Single Convention on Narcotic Drugs (UN) 64–65
skin colour survey: Brazilian Institute of Geography and Statistics (IBGE) 106–107; surveys and censuses 119
'skulls,' revenge for guards murder 148–150
slaughter or massacres 15–17, 19, 35, 41, 99–100, 156
slave patrol members 47
slave plantation model (Brazilian) 113; overseers 116
slave trade 20–21; Africanness and Blackness 57; African peoples in Brazil 112; arrival port in Brazil 112; attempts to end in Brazil 114; coffee plantations 146; curfews 115; death penalty abolition (1889) 118; end 83, 112, 114, 121; enslaved persons higher value than overseers 116; fear of a revolution 114; freed population 116, 121; Golden Law 112, 114, 121; Haiti rebellion 114; justification towards enslavement of certain populations 70; Malê Revolt 114–115; necroeconomics 74; overseers at plantations 116; police control over slave surveillance 115–116; police punishing enslavers and enslaved 115; Portuguese system 113; post-abolitionist policies 121; Rio Branco Law (free-womb law) 114; Sexagenarian Law 114; 'social control' after slavery 114, 117–118; socio-economic survival 118–119; unworthy lives 21, 23
Smith, A. 73
social classes, bourgeoisie 58
social network, absence 30
social relations, militarisation 19
South Africa: apartheid 73, 141; Group Areas Act 141
Souza, T.L.S. 97–98
sovereign power: postcolonial thinkers 153; and subjects 52; territorial aspect 52
sovereignty: and ambivalence 47–48; and death 19–20, 46–49, 69; killable lives 19; and life 8–9, 69; and modernity 58; race-related decisions 47–48; right to kill 10, 49, 77, 158–159; sacredness-sovereignty-life 47; and spatiality 23–24, 48, 54, 56; ways of dying 48–49
space of abjection 24
Spain: expulsion of Jews and Moors 109; Franco's dictatorship 26, 30, 32, 49; Paraguay War 139
Spanish Civil War 30
spatiality: idea of 'empty space' 24; and sovereignty 23–24; *see also* liminal spatiality
Special Bureau on Human Rights of the President of the Republic of Brazil (1995) 13
Special Commission for 'May Crimes' 101
Special Commission for the Dead and Political Disappeared 33
Special Commission of Relatives of Political Deaths and Disappearances 13
Special Commission on Political Deaths and Disappearances 13

Special Police Operations Battalion (BOPE) 2, 4
Special Unit for Social and Political Security (DEOPS) 88–89
Spencer, A., and Hülsse, R. 60–61
Spivak, G.C. 7
State Department of Social and Political Order (DEOPS/SP) 93
Subaltern Studies 7
suicides, fake 94
Superintendence for Amazonia Development 126
Superior School of War, internal enemy idea 90–91
Svirsky, M. 9

Third World cities, development and securitisation 75–76
Todorov, T. 81, 109
Torture Never Again 13, 37
Trans-Amazonian Highway 126
transitional justice 25
Treaty of Tordesillas 138–139
Truth Commission of Rio de Janeiro 140–141
Truth Commission of São Paulo 140–141
Truth Commission Report in Rio de Janeiro 38, 95–96, 144
Truth Commission Research Group 19
truth commissions (local), interviews with members 13
Truth Commission Working Group of Rio de Janeiro 38–39
2013 Protests/World Cup Riots 2

UN General Assembly, Declaration of the Protection of all Persons from Enforced Disappearance 33
Unified Black Movement (MNU) 120
United Nations: Single Convention on Narcotic Drugs 64–65; Working Group on Enforced or Involuntary Disappearances of the United Nations (UNWGEID) 38
United States: black prison population 69, 78n5; Chicago Police Department 31, 49; killings by police officers 3, 97; military aid 63; police violence 69; prison population 75; 'purity of blood' 111; Richard Nixon election campaign (anti-drugs) 62–63; segregation policies 111; war on drugs 62–63, 66; war on terror security discourse 61

University of São Carlos 149
UN Working Group on Enforced or Involuntary Disappearances, report 29–30, 51n4, 51n5
unworthiness, and racialisation 8
unworthy lives: Agamben 20, 48; slave trade 21, 23
Uruguayan citizens, disappearances 27

Valladares, L. do P. 144
Vargas, Getúlio 86–87; appreciation of fascist government of Italy and Gestapo police 89; coup d'état 'The 1930s Revolution' 86–87; labour related reforms 88; national identity 123; New State 120; *pax republican* 88; protection against communist threat 88; public propaganda 123; racial democracy myth 122
Vargas government 80; police apparatus 86–90
Vasconcelos, Simão 110
Vaughan-William, N. 47, 132–135, 150; and Brassett, J. 48, 133
Ventura, Z. 142
Vianna, H. 139
Vieira, Antonio 110–111
violence research centres, public universities 15–16
Vitale, A.S. 85
vocabulary limitations 35

Wallerstein, I. 109
war on drugs: annihilation of black communities 5–6; 'big skull' (armoured vehicles) 61, 78n4; conceptual vocabulary 22; consumer/traffickers no set possession amount 65, 67, 98; exceptionalities attached to war narrative 31–32, 49, 53, 55, 64, 76, 80, 128, 134, 161; as excuse to kill favela dwellers 21; killing of certain populations 153; killing of drug dealers 54; lacuna in law 67; 'logic of exceptionality' 62–66; narcoterrorism 63; Rio de Janeiro as a city under war 61; United States 62–63, 66; and war on terror 54, 59, 76, 157
war on terror: 'logic of exceptionality' 60–66; security discourse in US 61; and war on drugs 54, 59, 76, 157
whitening the population 23, 121–124, 128, 157; Creole elites 58; migration of from Europe 5
Williams, D. 85, 87

Willis, G.D. 40
Witness Protection Program 152
workfare-warfare state 75
working class: Britain 123–124; deserving/undeserving poor 123–124; former slaves 120
Working Group on Enforced or Involuntary Disappearances of the United Nations (UNWGEID) 38
World Cup (2014) 2, 4, 18
World Economic Forum (Davos 2018) 58
'wrong' perpetrator 39–41
'wrong' victim 35–39

Xingu area 125

Zaluar, A. 96; and Conceição, I.S. 40
Zevnik, A. 52, 62
Zurara, G.E. de 74